ACTING BLACK

ACTING BLACK

COLLEGE, IDENTITY, AND THE PERFORMANCE OF RACE

SARAH SUSANNAH WILLIE

ROUTLEDGE
New York & London

Published in 2003 by
Routledge
29 West 35th Street
New York, NY 10001
www.routledge-ny.com

Published in Great Britain by
Routledge
11 New Fetter Lane
London EC4P 4EE
www.routledge.co.uk

Copyright © 2003 by Taylor & Francis Books, Inc.

Routledge is an imprint of the Taylor & Francis Group.
Printed in the United States of America on acid-free paper.

10   9   8   7   6   5   4   3   2   1

Library of Congress Cataloging-in-Publication Data
Willie, Sarah Susannah, 1963–
    Acting Black : college, identity, and the performance of race
Sarah Susannah Willie.
        p. cm.
Includes bibliographical references and index.
    ISBN 0-415-94409-0 (hardcover) — ISBN 0-415-94410-4 (pbk.)
    1. African American college students—Social conditions.   2. African American college students—Attitudes.   3. African Americans—Education (Higher)   4. African Americans—Race identity.   5. Educational surveys—United States.   I. Title.
    LC2781.7 .W57   2003
    378.1'9829'96073—dc21

2002012974

to Mom, Dad, Martin, and James

CONTENTS

ACKNOWLEDGMENTS

Murray Kenney was the rector of Christ Church, the Episcopalian congregation to which my family belonged, in Cambridge, Massachusetts. Willing to share the pulpit with a junior in college, he invited me to preach in January 1985. In that unusual opportunity, I first articulated some of the questions and observations about race, college, and identity that I have continued to pursue in my scholarship. Though Murray Kenney has passed away, I will always be glad for his humility, encouragement, and challenge to think out loud in community.

I am grateful to many people for their roles in helping me to complete this project, but above all to the men and women who participated in the study. They gave generously of their time and candidly of their memories. I had hoped to stay in touch with many of them and regret my inability to have done so.

Although I have changed the names of the persons I interviewed for this study, I have chosen to let the names of the colleges they attended and my own alma maters stand without pseudonym. No college is above or immune to the systems of stratification outside its walls. Neither the historically black nor the traditionally white schools I discuss were immune from the replication of systems of oppression behind their campus gates. Because the focus of this exploration, however, is the black student experience in a country still wrestling with white supremacy, the challenges of the historically white institutions are highlighted. Although my experience at Haverford College in the mid-1980s was a difficult one, I remain deeply fond of Haverford, pleased with the changes it has undergone, and grateful for the good friends it has given me.

Many people from grade school through graduate school deserve thanks: my parents, who modeled a passion for social justice through intellectual and artistic pursuit, public school teachers in Syracuse, New York, and Concord, Massachusetts, professors and deans at Haverford College, especially Mark Gould, Freddye Hill, and Bill Hohenstein, and faculty and staff at Northwestern University, including Charles Payne, Arlene Kaplan Daniels, Aldon Morris, Howard Becker, Andrew Gordon, Leila Edwards, and Penny Warren.

I'm grateful to all those people who read everything from parts of chapters to the entire manuscript and offered critique: Jonathan LeBreton, Betty Sasaki, Lyn Mikel Brown, Darrell Moore, Becky Thompson, Gladys Topkis, Amy Cheng, Gloria Chun, Minnie Singh, John Feffer, Lise Funderburg, Sande Smith, Theresa Tensuan-Eli, Lisa Hajjar, Bruce Grant, Miguel Diaz-Barriga, Michelle Hermann Raheja, Mari Shullaw, Jayne Fargnoli, Robert Bogdan, Joe Feagin, Kristi Lowery, and the anonymous reviewer. Others offered me invaluable conversations (in person or over e-mail) with which I wrestled: Christine Bowditch, Eric Lott, Amy Ansell, Leah Gilliam, Becky Thompson, Howard Winant, and the members of the Black Graduate Student Roundtable while I was at Northwestern during the late 1980s. My colleagues in the Department of Sociology and Anthropology and the Program in Black Studies at Swarthmore have offered me suppport, comaraderie, and wonderful models of serious teaching and engaged scholarship.

For financial support, transcription, library and research assistance, and thoughtful counsel, I thank Elaine van der Stok, Grace von Tobel, the Bueschel family—Betsy, David, Andrea, Lydia, Cynthia, and Barney—Susan Bouchard, Deborah Anna Luepnitz, Anna McLellan, Karen Fried, Matthew Kidd, Sarah Anderson, at Howard University Dr. Florence B. Bonner and Ms. Kenya M. Huckaby, a Howard alumnus who asked to remain anonymous, various librarians at Northwestern and Howard Universities, the financial support of the Lilly Foundation and its Committee on Institutional Cooperation, Northwestern University, the Spencer Foundation, Colby College as a member of the Consortium of Liberal Arts Colleges for a Strong Minority Presence, Bard College, Swarthmore College, the Chuck and Mary Sue Willie Fund for Their Adult Children, and my editor at Routledge, Ilene Kalish, who expertly shepherded the book to completion. Finally, for his keen editorial eye, useful marginalia, Epicurean wizardry, and willingness to travel the journey with me, I thank my favorite librarian and my life partner, Jonathan LeBreton. The shortcomings of the project remain my own responsibility.

S.S.W.
Swarthmore, Pennsylvania

NOTE FOR THE READER

I have used *black, African American, white,* and *European American* to refer to the racial identities and categories of people. *Black* and *white* are capitalized when an author or interviewee I quote does so or implies such.

I regularly use *America* as an abbreviation for the United States of America and *Americans* as an abbreviation for people who live in the United States of America. It is with frustration for lack of a pithier phrase that I acknowledge the limitations of such substitutions, since, despite the vast geography "America" actually covers, the word has come to be used synonymously with citizens of the United States, denying or ignoring the presence of people from other countries and cultures in the Americas.

For the sake of brevity, I regularly subsume *alumnae* within *alumni*.

I occasionally refer to Northwestern alumni and alumnae by the name of their university mascot, the Wildcat, and to Howard alumni and alumnae by their mascot, the Bison.

HBCU is an acronym for historically black college or university. Although used less frequently, HWCU is an acronym for historically white college or university. The racial homogeneity of most white colleges was not accidental. Like historically black colleges, they had a historical mission, if usually informal, to educate white people. Unlike HBCUs, theirs was often exclusive. Therefore I use *traditionally*, *historically*, and *predominantly* as modifiers for both mostly black and mostly white colleges.

$\boxed{1}$

INTRODUCTION

*[T]he project of history is . . . to understand [the] production [of
identity] as an ongoing process of differentiation, relentless in its
repetition, but also . . . subject to redefinition, resistance and
change.*

> —Joan Scott, "Multiculturalism
> and the Politics of Identity"

This book is one take on college and race. It is based on interviews with fifty-five college-educated African Americans in the Chicago area during 1990 and 1991. The
people I interviewed were undergraduate students between 1967 and 1989 at either
historically black Howard University in Washington, D.C., or predominantly white
Northwestern University in Evanston, Illinois.[1] Desiring to understand my own experience at a predominantly white college with one semester spent at a historically
black one, I decided to speak with African-American alumni and alumnae of two institutions of higher education, comparable (as I show in chapter 4) but for the racial
composition of their student bodies. I wondered why some African Americans chose
mostly white colleges and others chose historically black ones. I wondered if the
racial sense African Americans had of themselves was influenced by the college they
attended. I was especially interested in the ways that *formal equality* coexisted with
informal inequality—that is to say, the contradiction that everyone is equal on paper
because discrimination has been made illegal and the reality that most people of color
still experience racial discrimination.

With each question I asked, respondents answered twice—first addressing my
question and then addressing the salient question of their lives. With the first answer
came portraits of college life—from socializing with friends and sense of community
to enduring the rigors of academics and, for many, a sense of alienation and isolation.
Alumni focused on the trade-offs made to pursue a degree with unequivocal prestige
to those made with the hope of enjoying four years undistracted by explicit racism.

With the latter answer came extensive commentary on what it means to be black in the late-twentieth-century United States. The men and women with whom I spoke taught me about college in particular and how it feels to be a college-educated African American more generally. They taught me about the flexibility of race as a social identity, and the ways that all Americans, not just African Americans or other racial minorities, play or inhabit race roles at this moment in history.

In college and graduate school—and now as a college professor—I have seen most people of color in these settings forced to participate in a metaphorical racial trial. We are presumed to be guilty; in this case, guilt is synonymous with not being a "good fit" with the college, unless we prove ourselves otherwise. This phenomenon is not limited to the college campus. At times the trial is explicit, but these days, it is usually implicit. Sometimes the players in this metaphorical race trial refuse to play their roles, other times they have no choice. But the limited roles of prosecutor and defendant, judge and juror remain Durkheimian social facts, coercing even the most stubbornly anti-racist individuals into them as we interpret, ignore, or take a stand on anything having to do with race.

Why, well after the gains of the Civil Rights movement, were black college students still experiencing these racial trials? The answer, I believe, can be found in the powerful history of white supremacy in the United States. The ways in which the ideology of white supremacy persists are often difficult to see. Nonetheless, racism persists, woven into the fabric of the culture with even more subtlety, and, to many, less visibility after the dramatic changes wrought by the Black Freedom Movement.

When I began this project, I felt as if I were the defendant in one of these "Does she or doesn't she fit?" trials, and I saw conducting interviews with other African Americans as a way to begin gathering evidence. But evidence to prove what? That white colleges are racist? That African Americans are exhausted by racism? That black colleges are the answer? The more evidence I gathered, the more the paradigm of defense and prosecution seemed inadequate to the task of examining race and college. Scholarship, though often adversarial, offered another way of approaching the situation of black students in college. My professors encouraged me to listen carefully, to investigate, to describe, and to examine previous scholarship. The scientific method paid off, and my interviews with black college alumni brought me beyond the quadrangle of the college campus and revealed ways to understand race better.

Institutions of higher education are diverse, as are the students who attend them. My observations apply to many students of color, but students of color, too, are a varied group. They come from groups with different practical and experiential histories and with different relationships to the ideology of white supremacy. So while this book is about college and race, it is not about all racial groups and it is not a large quantitative comparison. It does not include interviews with European Americans,

Asian Americans, Native Americans, multiracial Americans, and Latinos and Latinas, and it does not look at colleges and universities where other racial minority groups are in the majority.

Indeed, "a more complex racial climate is emerging within the historically White colleges and universities in the United States" (Bowman and Smith 2002: 103). This racial climate change is not limited to white campuses, for on historically black campuses, especially at the graduate school level, more white, Asian, and Latino students are also present.

> This new racial climate is tempered by three contemporary trends: (1) the growing opposition to civil rights-era policies to provide access and support services for African American college students who still remain underrepresented; (2) the increasing demands for more multiethnic institutional changes from both Latina/o and Asian American students who make up an expanding portion of the college student population; and (3) the changing racial ideologies that college students [bring] from distinct ethnic backgrounds. (Bowman and Smith 2002: 103)

Qualitative scholarship on the specificity of these experiences, in addition to that on African Americans, must be supported and encouraged so that we have more comparative data and can further appreciate the differences and similarities among groups.

In the rest of this chapter I describe the study, the sample, and the methodology I used, and I briefly outline the book.

FROM STUDENT TO RESEARCHER: SAMPLE AND METHOD

My dissertation project proposed an investigation of the experiences of blacks in college between the late 1960s, when Martin Luther King, Jr., was assassinated, through the late 1980s, when the toll of mounting resistance to civil rights initiatives was becoming obvious. As late as 1954, over 90 percent of black students were educated at historically black colleges. In contrast, by 1995 these same schools were educating only 20 percent of the African Americans in college as a result of the dramatic changes wrought by the gains of the Civil Rights Movement. I assumed that speaking to alumni from both a predominantly white and a predominantly black college would yield insights I had not even considered about the relationship between race and higher education.

Using the snowball method of sampling,[2] I sought African-American alumni who had been undergraduates at either Howard University in Washington, D.C., or Northwestern University in Evanston, Illinois, both of which had large bodies of alumni in the Chicago area where the study was conducted. As midsized urban universities, Howard and Northwestern are similar in many ways, though the racial composition of each is almost the photographic negative of the other. About 80 percent of the Northwestern student body was European American when I did the study, and about 80 percent of Howard's student body was African American. Their similarities and differences are described at greater length in chapter 4.

I set out in search of Howard and Northwestern alumni with a list of questions about college expectations, student-faculty relations, student social life, economic background, and career aspirations. The conclusions of this study are based on fifty-five interviews with black college alumni—fifteen men and fifteen women who attended Northwestern and fourteen men and eleven women who attended Howard—that I conducted in 1990 and 1991. Two-thirds of the interviews took place in person and the rest over the phone. Respondents had begun college as early as 1967, and everyone had graduated or left school by 1988. Each respondent spent at least two years as an undergraduate at either Howard or Northwestern.[3] The interviews were a combination of closed and open-ended questions and they lasted from twenty-five minutes to three hours.[4]

FROM RESEARCHER TO TEACHER: THE DIALOGUE OF INTERPRETATION

As I expected, college alumni told me about friends and roommates, social and academic obstacles, personal triumphs and tragedies, classes, advisors, professors, and parties. They remembered painful experiences of individual and institutional racism,[5] all narrated against the backdrop of and sometimes intimately connected to the tumultuous events unfolding in the United States.

I soon learned that social research rarely brings us the insights we expect to find. When the formal interview stopped, many of my respondents continued to talk. They described what it meant for them to be black, how they participated in the expansion and contraction of that meaning, how their understanding of what it meant to be black had changed over time, and how they negotiated racially polarized settings. Some alumni gave long answers to the question of why they chose the school they attended, and I began to interpret their soliloquies as racial justifications. Indeed they often told me what they thought their decision conveyed about their commitment to other black people. Others spoke at length, with nuance and poignancy, about their continued struggle to understand race and the implications this aspect of their identity had for their personal and professional lives. Their ideas encouraged me to focus on racism and racial identity as much as on the college experience.

By the time I began to analyze the transcripts of the interviews, I was well beyond my own college experience. I had finished three years of graduate study, one year as a teaching assistant, and two more years teaching my own courses, first at Northwestern University and then at Colby College. At both places, I taught on race and ethnicity in the United States. As I prepared for my third year of teaching, the voices from the interview transcripts took on the role of a Greek chorus. They urged me to investigate whether the definitions of race I was encountering in textbooks and scholarship were explaining *their* experiences.

As my role had changed from student to teacher, I was seeing others struggle with issues I had confronted. If I had ever believed that race and racial identity were salient issues only for me or even only for the respondents in my study, these beliefs were refuted during class times and office hours. Not only were the classes I taught on race fully enrolled, the discussions were weighty and charged. The students who came to my office hours documented race as a central issue by their numbers and the substance of their concerns. In addition, the journal entries of those who did not drop by my office revealed little knowledge about the country's racial history and few spaces in which to wrestle with its implications.

As I moved between the interview transcripts, the classroom, and the library, I discovered that many sociologists' definitions of race were accurate, but that most were incomplete. Influenced by the scholarship of postmodernists who were questioning whether individuals exist as unified subjects and whether representation—racial and otherwise—was enough of a political goal (Butler 1991, Young 1990), I began to appreciate arguments about the complexity of identity. In particular, the idea that individual identity is a uniquely modern phenomenon and always in flux was an "Aha!" moment for me.

At the same time, I found it difficult to reconcile this with the seeming coherence and realness of identity for myself, my respondents, and my students. In the transcripts of the interviews, respondents talked with greater clarity and distance than I have heard most people talk about their identities, and for them racial identity held both constraint and liberation. They were unlike those postmodernist scholars who question the relevance of racial representation, since they understood representation in politics, on television, and in textbooks to be a crucial aspect of achieving a positive sense of self as well as a more accurate understanding of the world. They were like the postmodernists, however, in the multiple ways they talked about race. In their memories of college and their present lives, black alumni described the ways they consciously *acted white* in certain settings and *acted black* in others. Although they saw themselves as black, that did not mean they understood blackness as something simple or simplistic. *The people with whom I spoke treated race as sets of behaviors that they could choose to act out*, as expectations they had of themselves and others, as physical difference, and as ethnicity and subculture. Consciously negotiating their identities, even when there was sometimes very little room to do so, the men and women in this study described *performing*.

The observations that I heard during people's interviews were distinct from what I had seen in the sociological literature on race. As Michael Omi and Howard Winant argue in *Racial Formation in the United States* (1994), theories about race and race relations in twentieth-century America are characterized by three approaches. These approaches focus on ethnicity, class, and nation. The racial theory dominant in each historical period "is shaped by actually existing race relations," and whatever theory is dominant provides the members of society "with 'common sense' about race, and with categories for the identification of individuals and groups in racial terms" (Omi and Winant 1994:11). Omi and Winant criticize these approaches, arguing that race scholars have done everyone a disservice by not pushing the intellectual envelope when it comes to race. Race theories are often as

> political and ideological as . . . theoretical. They neglect both the institutional and ideological nature of race in America, and the systemic presence of racial dynamics in [a wide range of] social spheres. . . . Instead they focus attention on racial dynamics as the irrational products of individual pathologies. (Omi and Winant 1994:10)

While scholars have had limitations, they have both reflected and contributed to the difficulty that regular people have had wrapping their minds around race. Throughout this study, I heard individuals conceive of and describe race in the ethnic, economic, and nationalistic terms that Omi and Winant note have characterized twentieth-century American thinking. But I also observed black alumni speaking about race in terms going well beyond these three approaches.

Omi and Winant are correct that much is missing in the sociological literature on race. My respondents' discussions revealed an acknowledgment that race is relational, situational, and interpersonally dynamic. When understood with these added dimensions, race cannot be defined only as a characteristic of identity that limits and circumscribes life chances, or only as a stigma for nonwhites, or, in the case of whites, only as an "invisible knapsack" that opens doors and provides privilege.[6] Understood with greater dimensionality, race and racial identity become another site of human agency, a characteristic or fact that individuals can and often do manipulate, despite its extraordinary power to proscribe social life.

Sociologists have long used dramaturgical metaphors to describe human life (Everett C. Hughes and Erving Goffman stand out as two). When it comes to race, however, such metaphors are often absent. Race expert Winant calls for new ways of thinking about race in *Racial Condition*:

> we may have to give up our familiar ways of thinking about race once more. If so, there may also be some occasion for delight. For it may be possible to glimpse yet another view of race, in which the concept operates neither as a signifier of comprehensive identity nor of fundamental difference, both of which are patently absurd, but rather as a marker of the infinity of variations we humans hold. (1994:21)

While Winant's work is broad in focus and examines how race has been treated historically and differently between nation-states, this study is narrower in focus and examines how race is understood by and between individuals. That said, what initially seem to be individual perspectives and interactions reveal broader sociological patterns. Winant appreciates the need for examination at the level of the individual when he argues that previous approaches to the study of race offer "an insufficient appreciation of the *performative* aspect of race" (1994: 18, emphasis in the original). His understanding of race as flexible and contingent confirms the argument I make in this volume about its malleability and its performability, and how it is defined by both subject and situation.

Race, like class, has often been treated like sex—biological, inherited, and (until very recently) immutable. To the contrary, race did not just *happen to* the men and women with whom I spoke (even if they happened to be born into racial categories); these people pushed its envelope and denied the expectations that accompanied their racial designations, showing me, among many things, that college was not just about race and race was not just about feeling trapped.

SUMMARY

Just as my own college experience was the springboard for this investigation, so my teaching experience over the last decade at four predominantly white, selective liberal arts institutions has offered a landing ground. I have observed that predominantly white colleges—especially those that are elite—need to examine the ways in which their admissions policies, assumptions held by faculty and administrative staff, and campus cultures retain vestiges of exclusive social clubs and continue to perpetuate institutional racism. As most of these institutions have become more diverse in terms of the race and class backgrounds of their students, they have already begun to change for the better. Though a diverse learning community is sometimes painful and often exhausting, the challenge is never gratuitous and social heterogeneity makes for a more vibrant and genuine intellectual environment.

In contrast, black colleges are crucial sites in which African-American students are assumed to be capable, and all students who attend them can observe governance by faculty and staff that are among the most multiracial in the country. Historically black colleges and universities, too, face the challenge of teaching black students how to build coalitions with those unlike themselves and how to handle majority status responsibly when such a situation arises. They are charged with the complex task—which they do not always accomplish—of teaching their students to be critical of *all* systems of oppression, not just racial ones. Finally, HBCUs are some of the few places in the country, besides neighborhoods, schools, and religious congregations, where people of color are the majority, which can provide a space in which white students can learn the skills of handling minority status.

The ideas presented about race parallel those that are emerging across disciplines with regard to rethinking other primary characteristics associated with identity. My findings buttress those of psychologists Patricia Gurin and Edgar Epps, who argued in the 1970s that blackness is not merely a negative marker but a complex and often positive characteristic around which individuals and groups bolster identity, nurture dignity, induce political action, and mobilize for change (1975: 4). By treating race as acquired, like a skill or a behavior, we can begin to see it as something over which individuals have differing degrees of control and varying options for agency, as an aspect of identity that is at least partly performed, continuous, and contingent. The experiences of blacks in college reveal that each person has differing but definitive degrees of power over their social identities. Their experiences challenge us to think about race and racial identity in new ways for all Americans, regardless of racial identity or level of education achieved.

One way to subvert white supremacy is to reveal the fiction of purity and superiority that whiteness claims. One corollary to this endeavor is to reveal the reality of a place where persons who do not identify as white are successfully, if hazardously, negotiating the environment. That place is the contemporary university. Taking a bit of issue with Fordham and Ogbu's concept of oppositional culture (1986), I argue that the act of going to school, in this case, college, is both conformative *and* oppositional to the dominant culture. For millions of men and women of African descent, going to college is *acting black*. Although my work and my hope is for a transformation of racial designation into a meaning away from social hierarchy and injustice that I cannot yet imagine (Ware and Back 2002), for today, I hope this study contributes to the growing body of evidence that race is contingent, contested, and negotiated even as it protects inequality.

OUTLINE OF THIS BOOK

Chapter 2 provides an overview of the history of higher education for blacks in the United States while alluding to the literature on blacks in predominantly black and predominantly white colleges. Studies germane to the experiences of respondents are fleshed out in chapters 5 and 6.

In chapter 3, I look back over my own experience as a student in college during the 1980s through the lens of race. My college experience provided the original impetus for this study, and my subsequent experience as an educator has provided evidence for the necessity of continuing to wrestle with the importance and challenges of multiculturalism.

Chapter 4 provides a brief introduction to the institutions where the men and women I interviewed attended college.

Chapters 5 and 6 are devoted to the college memories of black Northwestern University and Howard University alumni.

Chapter 7 looks at the ways and reasons that black communities on college campuses are sites of idealization, disappointment, and nostalgia for their participants.

In chapter 8 I allude to some of the ways that race has been treated in the sociological literature and turn to the scholarship of other disciplines as well, in order to theorize the multidimensionality of race.

Chapter 9 returns to the interviews to reveal empirical examples of race as a characteristic that is simultaneously ascribed, symbolically mediated as status or stigma, socially constructed, and consciously manipulated or performed.

In chapter 10, I offer recommendations for colleges and universities based on the observations and experiences of Howard and Northwestern alumni and I review the implications for sociology of treating race as a performed characteristic.[7]

BLACKS IN COLLEGE: PAST AND PRESENT

Today, discussions about race and college center on issues of diversity, the presence or absence of affirmative action, and multiculturalism in the curriculum. All of these are interrelated, and while they are not only about race they are almost always about who is included and who is excluded. These debates represent passionately held views on serious questions: What defines merit? Should education be conceived of as a privilege? Who gets to say what's fair? Are difference and equality mutually exclusive? Should education serve democracy, and, if so, what would that look like? What experts and lay people all agree on is that educational attainment is highly correlated with the ability to choose one's occupation and by extension the income and prestige associated with occupation. Perhaps it should not surprise us, then, that since higher education is a gateway to opportunity, access to it and what happens on campus have become contentious issues.

The history that follows contains within it a review of the literature, revealing that the contemporary debates about justice and fairness with regard to blacks and college are as old as this country. It also reveals that African Americans have been central as both subjects and objects in the struggle among people in the United States over the impulse toward education as a right versus education as a privilege. As Ruth Sidel observes in *Battling Bias: The Struggle for Identity and Community on College Campuses* (1994), higher education "mirrors, just as it did in earlier eras, the values, the divisions, and the debates within the larger society, and, in fact, college campuses are often the arenas in which the schisms and conflicting values of the larger society are played out" (9).

ILLEGAL TO READ: BEFORE THE CIVIL WAR

The majority of African-descended people living in the United States before the Civil War were slaves.[1] Legal codes maintained the legitimacy of slavery, recognized slaves as property, and guaranteed the rights of property owners. The Black Codes, as these statutory rights for whites and restrictions on blacks were called, were especially enforced in Southern states where slavery was the backbone of regional life.[2] Although blacks were treated as if they were not human, the extensive legislation white Americans enacted to restrict the behavior of both slaves and free persons of color demonstrates white people's knowledge, or at least their fear, that blacks were indeed human and had to be schooled in ignorance in order to be kept subservient.

Alan Pifer interprets the Black Codes as an acknowledgment on the part of whites that blacks living in slavery both resented and resisted their situation:

> The Black Codes . . . contained provisions aimed at safeguarding the white population against black uprisings. Fears of such uprisings were not baseless. Blacks could and did engineer minor and major uprisings against the white community which kept them in bondage. . . . In every Southern state these codes had statutes which forbade the schooling of black slaves. Education was thought to give the slave too high an opinion of himself and access to such pernicious ideas as those expressed in our Declaration of Independence, namely that all men are created equal and have certain inalienable rights. (1973: 8)

The legal circumscription of black peoples' behavior—including forbidding the teaching or learning of reading—discouraged any explicit show of revolutionary spirit. More insidiously, however, the constant threat of violence upheld the fragile social dynamic of the antebellum South and coerced from blacks the active display of ignorance, even if such display were not genuine.

Outlawing literacy, Cheryl Townsend Gilkes has argued,[3] was a dam for a revolutionary river already flooding, and a goal of many slaves was to learn to read the Bible. While some slave owners had allowed the Bible to be *taught* selectively, literate slaves (and abolitionist whites) secretly read passages aloud that contradicted the hierarchy of slavery. Many slaves understood the central tenet of the New Testament to be equality among God's people. Others identified with the biblical Hebrews of Egypt, seeing themselves as God's chosen people, and believed that the afterlife or freedom—whichever came first—would be a time when justice would prevail, making the last first and the first last.[4]

Not all blacks who lived in the antebellum United States, however, were slaves. "By 1790, when the United States had its first census, there were some 628,000 black slaves in the country. In addition, there were some 60,000 free blacks, making a total of 688,000 or nearly one black to four whites in the total population of just under four million" (Pifer 1973: 7). By the start of the Civil War, the number of slaves had risen to 4 million, but the number of free blacks had risen to almost 500,000. This latter group, who lived almost exclusively in the North, were descended from free people, or had been manumitted by their owners through purchase of their freedom or upon their owner's death, or were runaways, many of whom had used the Underground Railroad to escape bondage.[5]

With few exceptions, the colleges founded to educate America's white citizenry before the Civil War did not admit these free or freed African Americans. Three colleges, however, were established before the Civil War for the specific purpose of educating blacks: in Pennsylvania, Cheyney State College and Lincoln University, established in 1830 and 1854, respectively, and Wilberforce University of Ohio, established in 1856. Still, "[u]p to the Civil War . . . only 28 Negroes had graduated from college" (Pifer 1973: 29).

THE SECOND HALF OF THE NINETEENTH CENTURY: FREE BUT SEPARATE

As Harold F. Williamson and Payson S. Wild report, the mid-nineteenth century saw the emergence of hundreds of colleges in the country.

> [The] federal . . . attitude toward education empowered the individual states to grant colleges charters at will. As a result, America became a land of many small colleges. . . . By 1860, over 800 colleges had been founded, although only about 180 of these had succeeded in gaining a permanent foothold. . . . That one's children—especially males—should be educated was part of the democratic creed; there was nothing particularly exclusive about these numerous small colleges. (1976: 1–2)

At the close of the Civil War, most blacks, even free men and women in the North, had no formal education. The land grant for public colleges that had been established with the Morrill Act of 1862,[6] for the most part, did not admit or court blacks who were born free or who had been freed.

After the Civil War, a few historically white colleges opened their doors to a handful of blacks. The view that blacks were inherently inferior, however, was widespread, and greatly affected the attitude of their benefactors. "This 'inherent' inferiority view was so widely held in the North that it excluded most Negroes from the burgeoning public schools. Most private schools for white students were also segregated" (Logan 1969: 8). Records indicate that over the thirty-year span from 1865 to 1895, about two hundred blacks graduated from Northern white schools. Most noteworthy among these colleges is Oberlin, in Ohio, for it graduated seventy-five of the two hundred. The rest were scattered sparsely among the North's other historically white colleges.

Although the doors of most Northern white colleges were closed, the hearts of many Northern white missionaries were open, and it was these people, because of their connections to people with money and their own educational experiences, who made the greatest effort to provide education for blacks. Many saw it as their Christian duty to offer freed men and women the benefit of their knowledge. Still, the white founders of such schools often treated their black students as inferiors, and saw shaping the behavior and morals of former slaves as one of their primary responsibilities. Most of the educational facilities that missionaries established for freed men and women were colleges in name rather than in curriculum. Baptists, Methodists, Presbyterians, and Congregationalists—with help from Northern philanthropists—were among the most responsible for establishing institutions of higher education for blacks.

White religious philanthropists, however, were not alone in this cause. Contrary to the notion that African Americans do not have a history of helping their own, blacks, through their churches, contributed large portions of their meager earnings to found "a significant number of Black colleges and universities" (Anderson 2002: 6). According to James Anderson, these include the American Methodist Episcopal Church, which founded Allen University, Morris Brown College, Wilberforce College, Paul Quinn College, Edward Waters College, Kittrell College, and Shorter College. The American Methodist Episcopal Zion Church founded Livingston College. The Colored Methodist Episcopal Church founded Lane, Texas, Paine, and Miles colleges. And the black Baptists founded Arkansas Baptist College, Selma University, and Virginia College and Seminary (Anderson 2002: 6). Although most of the schools were seminaries and colleges for teachers and home economists (the former called normal schools), a handful offered a postsecondary level of study. It looked as if the black South was on the move.

The white South, however, fought back. It may have lost the war, but Southern lawmakers continued to win numerous legal battles for decades, slowing and subverting Negro education. As the twelve years of postwar Reconstruction came to an end (1865–77), the notion of separate but equal became more popular as a way for the power brokers of the South to circumvent both integration and equality for blacks. In an election-year deal, President Rutherford Hayes agreed to allow Southern legislators to police their own treatment of freed blacks, and promised that the Northern-dominated federal government would no longer interfere in Southern political life. "There was the feeling," the eminent historian John Hope Franklin concludes,

> on the part of most white persons that the success or failure of Negroes . . . depended on the type of education to which they were exposed. There were those who felt that the amount of education that blacks could or should receive was limited. . . . Still others contended that Negroes . . . could best serve themselves and their country with a type of education that could most rapidly help them find an indispensable place in the American social order. (Franklin and Moss 1988: 244)

At the close of the Civil War, then, there were those who interpreted *any* education for Negroes as preferential treatment.

Into this debate over what kind of education would best serve free and freed blacks stepped two educated men of African descent from very different backgrounds, Booker T. Washington and William Edward Burghardt DuBois. Washington was a former slave and a graduate of Hampton Institute, in Virginia, a college that began as a vocational school for blacks. He became the spokesman for the Industrial Education Movement, popular among Southern whites, Northern philanthropists, and even some Southern blacks. Believing that patience, hard work, and thrift were the route by which blacks would eventually gain their constitutional rights, Washington offered a charismatic example of the benefits of this kind of education. He successfully opened the purse strings of wealthy white philanthropists not only for Tuskegee Institute, which he founded in Alabama in 1881, but also for other vocational colleges by speaking to the ideological leanings of those in power. "[D]isproportionate amounts of public funds were [therefore] channeled into vocational institutions" (Fleming 1984: 6), while many liberal arts colleges and professional schools were forced to shut down (Pifer 1973: 18). Clandestinely, Washington supported lawyers who were challenging Southern Jim Crow laws, but publicly he espoused a stance of accommodation and remained opposed to groups that strove for equality of civil rights (Mullane 1993: 355).

DuBois, on the other hand, was educated both at Fisk, a historically black university in Tennessee, and at Harvard, the nation's preeminent (and a traditionally white) university, in Massachusetts. A Massachusetts native, DuBois argued that classical and liberal arts training helped Negroes to understand their potential and fight for civil rights and political power. Although he believed in the rights of all Americans and "rejected the policy of accommodation" (Mullane 1993: 369), DuBois believed in the education of a black intelligentsia, who, he argued in his essay "The Talented Tenth," had a special mission to lead the masses of African Americans.

In 1890, Congress passed the Morrill-McComas Act (also known as the Second Morrill Act), which made a feeble effort to require all states to admit blacks to existing institutions or to provide separate and equally funded schools for them (Fleming 1984: 5). In response, most Southern and border states ignored the act altogether, and only four—Virginia, Alabama, North Carolina, and Maryland—made any effort "to establish tax-supported institutions for African Americans" (Anderson 2002: 7).

In 1896, the Supreme Court, in the truest form of flattery, ratified Congress's interpretation of the principle of equality (as contained in the Second Morrill Act) and reaffirmed the legality of the separate but equal doctrine. The landmark case of *Plessy v. Ferguson* followed later that year, and segregation of public facilities was protected by a Court that saw its duty as the protection of political rather than social equality. The Court's stamp of legitimacy on *Plessy* essentially repeated Congress's 1890 decision to allow the South a wide berth in self-governance. Southern states interpreted the decision in *Plessy* broadly, well beyond the scope of public transportation and public facilities that the case had covered, and began to pass laws affecting every sphere of public and private life to keep blacks separate from whites.

Plessy's implications for private higher education became clear as a result of a ruling in the 1908 case of *Berea College v. Commonwealth of Kentucky*. In 1904, the state of Kentucky had passed a law requiring segregation in all state schools, both public and private. Berea, a small private institution in eastern Kentucky that had admitted both Blacks and Whites since its founding in 1859, challenged the constitutionality of a law (obviously aimed solely at the school, as there were no other unsegregated educational institutions in the state). For the hearing before the state Supreme Court, Kentucky provided an openly racist brief, suggesting that "if the progress, advancement and civilization of the twentieth century is to go forward, then it must be left not only to the unadulterated blood of the Anglo–Saxon-Caucasian race, but to the highest types and geniuses of that race." Seven of the sitting Justices in the *Berea* case had participated in *Plessy*, six of them concurring with Justice Brown's decision. Thus the decision not to overturn the Kentucky Supreme Court's ruling was not surprising; nevertheless, it broke new ground by permitting states to outlaw voluntary as well as obligatory contact between the races. (Drewry and Doermann 2001: 21)

These laws became known as Jim Crow laws (*Jim Crow* was a slang term in the South for any black man [Pifer 1973: 14]). The Kentucky statute, once upheld by the Supreme Court, had serious implications in the realm of education, where it was used to justify separate funding at every level of public educational institutions.

While the "separate" was carried out, the "equal" was not, and public schools for Negroes in the South were severely underfunded. By rhetorical contortion and with the support of Booker T. Washington, the doctrine of separate but equal in educational settings was interpreted to emphasize industrial rather than liberal arts training for blacks. At the turn of the century, then, when many local government leaders used extralegal means, especially lynching, to keep blacks subservient and to discourage them from leaving the South in search of better jobs, DuBois' support of classical education for blacks was far less popular among Southern whites than Washington's limited formula.

Whether they followed in the tradition of Washington or the spirit of DuBois, the majority of HBCUs that are still running today were established by 1890—forty private colleges and seventeen public colleges.[7] "[B]y 1895 there had been more than eleven hundred graduates of the Negro colleges, most of whom entered teaching, the ministry, or other professions to serve their own people" (Pifer 1973: 12). The number of blacks with college degrees was beginning to reach a critical mass and, with self-help organizations, they began to articulate the political aspirations of their group. Two of the more important self-help organizations with an emphasis on education were the Afro–American League of the United States, founded in 1890, and the American Negro Academy, founded in 1897. They each encouraged black youth to continue their education beyond high school.

BEYOND EMANCIPATION: THE FIRST HALF OF THE TWENTIETH CENTURY

By the turn of the century, it is estimated that 2,500 Negroes had graduated from both black and white colleges. This growing number of college-educated blacks highlighted the cultural disjunction between rising educational and professional status and continued low social status. Depending on one's point of view, of course, there was no contradiction: racial status trumped all others and either privileged or disadvantaged a person. How were blacks and fellow civil rights advocates to fight this legally? As long as defenders of segregation assured the courts that they could and would provide equal but separate protection under the law, civil rights advocates were stymied in their goals for justice. By attacking the very legality of separateness, however, there was the chance to undermine the continuation of segregation. To this end, two more organizations were founded: the National Association for the Advancement of Colored People (NAACP) in 1910 and the National Urban League in 1911.[8] During the first half of the twentieth century, lawyers working on behalf of black plaintiffs changed their strategy from focusing on the right of Negroes to equal protection under the law (as provided under the Fourteenth Amendment to the Constitution) to attacking the legality of racial separation.

Success was finally achieved with the NAACP's triumph in the decision of *Brown v. Board of Education of Topeka, Kansas,* in 1954. Several other cases had preceded what became the most famous one, challenging states to provide plaintiffs with equal professional school training. One of those cases, *Sweatt v. Painter* (1950), came before the Supreme Court. Sweatt, a black applicant, had been denied admission to the University of Texas Law School solely on the basis of color. The Court ruled that although there was a standing black law school, it was unequal and the State of Texas had to admit the applicant to the white law school.

The decision in *Sweatt* and several like it filed and won during the 1930s and 1940s encouraged the NAACP and other organizations to attack segregation in public elementary and secondary schools. In 1952, the NAACP filed appeals in cases from Kansas, South Carolina, Virginia, Delaware, and the District of Columbia. It was the NAACP's case against the School Board of Topeka, Kansas, however, that convinced the Court in 1954 that separate educational facilities were inherently unequal.[9]

Despite this legal victory, the road to implementation would be long and would sometimes double back upon itself. The South refused to cooperate. "Although the Border States showed a disposition to comply with the Supreme Court's mandate, states in the deep South began a campaign of active and passive resistance" (Mason and Stephenson 1987: 542). Almost a hundred years after the Civil War had ended, state's rights, as interpreted by white Southern lawmakers, were again in contention with the federal government's right to make and enforce the law of the land.

While the federal government was struggling with state governments over control and autonomy, the numbers of black colleges, black students, black alumni, and black college administrators were slowly increasing. And although African Americans were forced to enroll in private colleges (Anderson 2002: 9),[10] they were beginning to organize themselves for the betterment of the community as well.

THE SECOND HALF OF THE TWENTIETH CENTURY: NEGOTIATING FAIRNESS

Although Southern lawmakers obstructed and therefore retarded change, the desire of blacks for a better life catalyzed it. From World War I through the Korean War, blacks moved from rural to urban areas within the South and from southern to northern cities in search of jobs and better treatment, an event now characterized by historians as the Great Migration. Beginning in the South, the Civil Rights Movement followed suit. After several successful anti-segregation protests throughout the South in the 1950s and the success of the March on Washington in 1963, civil disobedience by blacks continued, including in the North, where racism was also entrenched but manifested differently.

> [U]nlike the legally mandated barriers that characterized state systems of higher education in the South, the racial barriers in northern systems of public higher education were achieved through a complex process of institutionalized discrimination. . . . This process was based on an elaborate rationale that fused racism and meritocracy. Since institutionalized racism was a matter of social practice and not a matter of law, its defense and rationale became deeply entrenched in the cultural values and social norms of northern society. While southern institutions of public higher education barred African Americans as a matter of law, northern institutions barred them as a matter of educationally and socially rationalized practices. (Anderson 2002: 6)

As African Americans had political successes and yet material and educational gains failed to follow for most, rioting became an inevitable expression of frustration in most major northern and southern cities throughout the 1960s. It was at this point that "the nation as a whole had to face squarely the question of prejudice and discrimination" (Pifer 1973: 21).

With regard to education, "[t]he pace of integration quickened after 1965." In part, this more immediate response was a reaction to the race riots that were plaguing so many American cities. Social protests threatened to disrupt educational institutions as well. Many schools acquiesced to the protests of their students and concerns of surrounding neighborhoods at least in part to continue receiving federal funds, now made "conditional on integrated education" with passage of the 1964 Civil Rights Act (Mason and Stephenson 1987: 543).

The growing momentum of the Civil Rights Movement catalyzed an anxious reexamination of the federal funding that historically black colleges and universities received: Were they getting their fair share? Were they receiving enough to survive? After several studies that demonstrated the continued importance and need for funding, Congress reaffirmed its support of HBCUs in a more substantial way than it ever had, with the 1965 Higher Education Act. Also called Title III, the act legislated aid to historically black colleges, defined as "colleges founded prior to 1964" and

> whose founding purpose was the education of black students. . . . [T]here are about a hundred two- and four-year historically black colleges, about half of which are public. Their student bodies are predominantly but usually not exclusively black. A few, mostly public schools, started as completely black but now have white student majorities: Kentucky State University, Lincoln University (Missouri), Bluefield State College (West Virginia), West Virginia College, Alabama A & M, Albany State College (Georgia), and the University of Arkansas (Pine Bluff).[11] (Drewry and Doermann 2001: 257)

The commitment of the federal government to support historically black colleges and universities came from two unlikely bedfellows. First, there were those politicians who were convinced by black college presidents and Civil Rights Movement leaders that supporting greater funding for historically black colleges was simply the right thing to do. And second, there were those legislators whose support of black colleges was based on the desire to minimize black student attendance at historically white campuses (Nabrit 1969: viii).

Although up to 1968, "80 percent of all African Americans who were awarded undergraduate degrees [still] graduated from HBCUs" (Anderson 2002: 10), the population of the higher education pipeline was changing. True, elementary and secondary schools were still far from achieving court-ordered desegregation, but the presence of blacks in institutions of higher learning, especially in the North, had begun to increase dramatically. This was a result of several factors that came together over a twenty-year period. First, black World War II and Korean War veterans were beginning to go to college on the GI Bill. Second, several Supreme Court rulings during the late 1940s and early 1950s ruled in favor of admitting blacks to institutions that received federal monies. Third, the Civil Rights Act of 1964 forbade discrimination based on race, color, sex, or national origin among federal government agencies and all organizations that received funding from the federal government. And finally, the Higher Education Act of 1965 made monies available to traditionally white colleges that were considered "developing" as well.

Those campuses that had begun to enroll black students were not immune to the climate of frustration and sense of empowerment among African Americans and young people of all colors that was emerging in the country at large. Black student frustration and desire for change were being channeled into groups like the Student Nonviolent Coordinating Committee (SNCC) and the Black Panther Party. Indeed, anecdotal evidence suggests that almost every predominantly white college or university with a population of more than twenty black students experienced a dramatic racial confrontation between blacks and whites between 1968 and 1971.

One of those dramatic confrontations occurred on Cornell University's campus in Ithaca, New York, in 1969 when African-American students took over a building and defended themselves with guns. Professors at a nearby university, Charles Willie and Arline Sakuma McCord, decided to examine the experiences of black students on other New York state campuses. *Black Students at White Colleges* (1972) is a study of black students at four predominantly white colleges in upstate New York during the 1969–70 school year. Willie and McCord interviewed black students and discovered that adaptation to an often hostile environment was the chief challenge for students. Willie and McCord observed three types of adaptation: black students cooperated or complied with white students and faculty; black students withdrew from white students and faculty; or black students were aggressive and protesting toward white students and faculty. Willie and McCord found that "the social life of most blacks on white college campuses is limited to interaction with other blacks" (1972: 15). And while many of the students they surveyed had not expected to spend a great deal of time with white students when they arrived at college, "the actual experience of racial exclusivity" both exceeded and disappointed their expectations (1972: 15).

Like Willie and McCord, William Exum also searched for explanations in this passionate era a bit further downstate. In his study *Paradoxes of Protest: Black Student Activism in a White University* (1985), Exum examined the black student movement of the late 1960s and early 1970s at New York University. Studying it as an empirical example of social movement theory, Exum distinguished between value-oriented movements—those that seek to change fundamental values in an organization—and norm-oriented movements—those that adhere to organizational values. He argued that although NYU's black student movement was reform or norm-oriented, it was misconstrued as radical and dangerous because of its apparent spontaneity, the level of anger and bitterness that was sometimes expressed, and because of students' refusal to use traditional avenues of dissent. Finally, Exum demonstrated the inherent contradictions that undermined the full success of the movement: its members had a necessarily short tenure, all relationships were defined by formally unequal roles, and members were more financially dependent upon the organization than the reverse.

By the early 1970s, most public universities in states with large black populations were admitting significant numbers of black students, and many private universities and colleges were admitting blacks regularly, even if they remained underrepresented as compared with their proportion in the national population. Many places added black faculty, black cultural houses, and black deans or residential staff to anticipate, massage, and if possible avoid the racial crises of the previous decade. "The proportion of twenty-five to twenty-nine-year-old Blacks who had completed four or more years of college increased by more than 150 percent between 1960 and 1975." (Astin et al. 1982: 87).

In their massive study *Black Consciousness, Identity, and Achievement* (1975), Gurin and Epps argued that black colleges have been oases of acceptance, allowing otherwise excluded or disappointed black students the opportunity to learn while achieving positive self-concepts in nonracist settings. This study defended HBCUs, which began to suffer during the initial opening up of the white academy. Title III was now proving "to be a mixed blessing" for historically black schools, for, in addition to providing federal funds that "together amounted to almost half of an average private black college's annual budget," it also

> helped northern and western predominantly white colleges to seek greater variety among their students, and thus stimulated an unprecedented recruitment and competition for the best-prepared black high school graduates. . . . Any black college president who took the long view was unlikely to complain, since the new competition meant that for the first time, able black high school graduate enjoyed something like the same national range of college choice that had been reserved for Whites only a few years earlier. But the effects of the new competition on many black colleges were severe. . . . Of all the changes of the 1970s, this probably provided the greatest challenge to the leadership of private black colleges. (Drewry and Doermann 2001: 8–9)

HBCUs were not alone, however, in facing challenges. The mood of the country was beginning to shift to the right, and increasing complaints of "reverse discrimination" revealed growing resentment on the part of whites, who were now expected (in the post–Civil Rights Movement era) to forfeit the unearned privilege of their racial status.

In 1978, the Supreme Court ruled in *The Regents of the University of California v. Bakke* that race *could* "be used as a criterion for admission to undergraduate or graduate and professional schools, or for job recruitment." Stipulations included the following: it had to be for the purpose of improving racial diversity (Drewry and Doermann 2001: 280); the race of an applicant had to be "combined with other criteria"; and "rigid racial quotas" could not be used (Andersen and Taylor 1999: 306). Thus, the outcome of that case continued to protect the right of university and college admissions offices (and other organizations that received federal funding) to consider race in attempting to achieve diverse student bodies or workplaces. This was yet another mixed blessing for those who were interested in racial equity in education, for the challenge to the law itself proved to be a warning of increasing conservatism and retrenchment both among the general public and on college campuses.

Despite this Supreme Court ruling, which appreciated the importance of diversity and fairness, the executive branch of the federal government began to chip away at results civil rights advocates thought had already been won. Philip G. Altbach, Kofi Lomotey, and Shariba Rivers observe that "By the 1980s . . . the growth rate for most [underrepresented] groups had slowed significantly" (2002: 26). Donald Deskins agrees:

> Since 1976, with changes in the political climate . . . support for "remedial action"—which once was dominant—lost ground to "no preferential treatment," evolved into "undeserving advantage," and finally culminated in the doctrine of "reverse discrimination." Throughout this progression the plight of Blacks in higher education has worsened. . . . In essence, academia began to follow the color-blind doctrine of the Reagan administration and, in the process, dismantled equal-opportunity and affirmative-action programs. . . . During this period of increasing college tuitions, federal funding of education—particularly student aid—has declined, significantly so under the leadership of William Bennett, the former Secretary of Education (1991: 36–37).

During the 1980s, then, black students lost ground, especially at traditionally white schools, suffering from massive cutbacks in financial aid funding and the anti–affirmative action/anti-minority tone set by the executive branch.

In this moment of seeming crisis, psychologist Jacqueline Fleming attempted to find out about the experiences of blacks on both kinds of campuses for herself. Her study *Blacks in College* (1984) provided an updated and more comparative examination of Gurin and Epps's work of a decade earlier. Adding interviews with black students on predominantly white campuses to her study and offering a policy-oriented discussion, Fleming found that black women who went to black colleges showed "strong improvement in academic functioning . . . [and] subjective gains in intellectual self-confidence [while also showing] consistent losses in social assertiveness and more submission to external authority" (Fleming 1984: 168). On the other hand, African-American women who went to white colleges suffered from "painful frustration in every domain of experience." These same women, however, also showed gains in their ability to develop "coping skills, working under pressure, role modeling, assertiveness, and career orientation" (Fleming 1984: 169). The African American men who attended black schools in Fleming's study exhibited "the happiest adjustment to college life," becoming more assertive, gaining confidence in dealing with others, and feeling that they could master any situation. Black men who went to predominantly white schools, however, had the "most grim" experiences. "[G]ains in educational aspirations . . . occur in the context of falling grades in the . . . major subject, diminishing feelings of intellectual ability, declining social adjustment, and losses in perceived energy level" (168–69). In short, Fleming's work showed that coeducational HBCUs were doing for black men what coed white colleges were doing for white men. On these campuses, Fleming observed, "it turns out to be a man's world" (138).

Although the numbers of black students fell at white colleges during the 1980s, the numbers rose at HBCUs. As *The Chronicle of Higher Education* reported in 1990,

> The freshmen classes at many [predominantly white] colleges and universities shrank this year, with some institutions enrolling up to 35 percent fewer first year students than they did a year ago. . . . Many historically black colleges, however, experienced a surge in freshman enrollment. Several have had increases of 10 and 15 percent over their totals for academic 1989–90, and in many cases this is the second or third year of increases. (Wilson 1990: A1)

The *Wall Street Journal* confirmed *The Chronicle*'s report above: while college enrollments are down across the board, applications and enrollments for black colleges are up.

> [T]he increase in class size has been accompanied by an improvement in applicants' grades and test scores. . . . [I]n the past five years, the number of blacks attending black institutions has increased 10 percent to 294,427, according to the National Association for Equal Opportunity in Higher Education. And that increase has come, the U.S. Education Department says, as the percentage of black 18- to 24-year-olds enrolled in colleges has declined. Educators attribute the renaissance at black institutions in part to racial conflicts in many cities and on many predominantly white campuses. . . . But other factors in the trend include high-profile alumni; awareness created by the television show "A Different World";[12] . . . low tuition; and a renewed desire among many blacks to study in an environment that is more sensitive to their history, culture and needs. (Alexander 1990: B1)

For the first time since the turbulent 1960s, white colleges were getting negative publicity for what it was like to be a black student there. "[R]acial incidents ranging from name-calling to beatings [were] reported on more than 250 campuses" in the three years period between 1987 and 1990 (Camper 1990: 1). It is unknown whether reports of harassment reflected rising numbers of incidents or the fact that violence against black students finally began to warrant media coverage. The results of *Acting Black* suggest the latter.

In addition, the 1980s also saw increasing political activism over the U.S. relationship with apartheid South Africa. Black students took leadership roles at historically black and traditionally white colleges in campaigns urging boards of directors to divest invested funds from companies that conducted business with the overtly racist government of South Africa.

Although there were moments of declining enrollment, as the articles quoted above indicate, overall, between 1976 and 1994, there was a dramatic increase (of 30 percent) in enrollment at all higher education institutions across the country. Enrollment at HBCUs in particular rose by 26 percent, only slightly behind that of HWCUs.[13] By the early 1990s, then, black colleges were holding their own in the competition for students; they were in the news as legitimate subjects for television fiction; white students were in the news for their bad behavior vis-à-vis blacks on predominantly white campuses; and black students were in the news for their political activism.

TURN OF ANOTHER CENTURY: THE 1990S TO THE PRESENT

The men and women interviewed for *Acting Black* were all enrolled in college in the first two decades after the heyday of the Civil Rights Movement, between 1968 and 1988. What is striking in their words are the similarities to the experiences of current black students. While there have been some dramatic changes on college campuses, those changes have not just happened; they are hard won with the sweat and tears of many students, faculty, and staff who have been willing to confront others and themselves in helping their campuses, and the people on them, to become more welcoming, inclusive, educated about difference, and conscious about living with it.

The situation of blacks in college from the late 1980s to the present is best described as mercurial, if not ambivalent. On the one hand, the percentage of black students attending college has begun to increase again (as have the percentages of Asian and Latino and Latina students, which have increased dramatically[14]), and most public and private selective, traditionally white colleges and universities embrace multiculturalism. This has meant an increase in the number of people of color at all levels of the campus, including representation in the curriculum.

On the other hand, the numbers of black students remain skewed—with men even more underrepresented than women—on both traditionally white and predominantly black campuses, and black students remain vulnerable to federal cutbacks, recession, and the sustained attack on affirmative action.[15] Furthermore, multiculturalism has been most enthusiastically embraced as an idea rather than in practice, in some cases creating "a break with the past [and a] basis for the neoconservative claim that present inequities cannot be the result of discriminatory practices because this society no longer discriminates against blacks" (Crenshaw 1995: 107).

When racism is overtly expressed in a putatively anti-racist atmosphere, its presence is difficult for many students and faculty to make sense of as anything other than an "isolated incident" perpetrated by an "off-campus element." The lack of dialogue on many campuses about racism and the inability or unwillingness of scholars to delineate for their colleagues and students the history and sociology of white supremacy has left many people, even in the academy, without the tools to analyze individual, institutional, and structural racism.

Today, there are roughly one hundred historically black colleges and universities in the United States that were established prior to 1964 with the principal mission to educate Americans of African descent (U.S. Department of Education 1991: vii). And, while HBCUs enroll only 15 to 20 percent of the nation's black students, they produce 37 percent of black college graduates.[16] Although about 75 percent of all African Americans begin at predominantly white institutions, only 57 percent of them receive baccalaureate degrees from white institutions (Allen et al. 1991: 4). "At a time when they constitute only 3 percent of US colleges and universities, HBCUs educate almost 20 percent of the country's African American youth, and enrollment continues to grow each year" (Manuel 1994b: B6). Even more striking, about 46 percent of African Americans who graduate from any college have attended a black college at some point during their college career (Rowland 1990: 2). One might argue, then, that HBCUs allow many black students to get through college, whether by providing a start, a bridge, or a place to finish.

Turning to HWCUs, it is important to recognize that most colleges in the United States "accept all qualified applicants and thus do not give preference to any group defined by ethnicity or any other criterion" (Anderson, 2002: 15). Indeed, neither college nor graduate school is a universal experience for Americans. Thirty-five years ago, the majority of adults in the United States—black and white—had not completed high school. Today, the overwhelming majority of adults do so, yet the absolute numbers of people who have completed college or more remain small.[17] In 1965, one in ten white adults and one in twenty black adults had completed at least four years of college. By 2000, the numbers had jumped dramatically to one in four whites (26 percent) and one in six blacks (17 percent) who had completed college.[18]

Of those who do attend college, most do not attend colleges where admission is competitive, so why is there such passionate talk about affirmative action? In addition to the backlash against the challenges to race privilege mounted by the Civil Rights Movement, James Anderson argues that competition among privileged white parents who want privileges for their children drives the resistance:

> [Twenty to thirty] percent of U.S. colleges receive enough qualified applicants to select on a competitive basis. These institutions have become the focal point for the current debate over the admission and support of stu-

dents of color. This is so primarily because [privileged] Whites compete strongly to get their children into the most highly selective colleges. . . . [T]hey feel that affirmative action programs to recruit and retain students of color deprive their children of privileges and opportunities. They favor a system based on "strict merit," meaning essentially that selective institutions should give preference to individuals with the highest grade point averages and standardized test scores[,] standards [that] favor the children of the dominant class since income is highly correlated to performance on standardized tests scores. (Anderson 2002: 15–16)

Many whites still expect race and class privilege to translate into educational and occupational privilege. Vaguely aware for the first time in American history of the inappropriateness of their privilege, they are uncomfortable with the racist implications of their desires. The seemingly objective and neutral idea of merit, and merit measured in a particular fashion, allows many to cling to the idea that they are really endorsing fairness rather than self-interest.[19] Moreover, former president Bill Clinton's discomfort with affirmative action[20] and most Republicans' outright dismissal of it, have led many fence sitters to feel that it is, in fact, a bad thing.

With *Bakke* in 1978, the Supreme Court implicitly acknowledged the importance of diversity in the health of organizations, especially a public, educational organizations. However, the University of California Board of Regents' 1995 decision to stop using ethnicity, race, or gender in their consideration of students for admission reveals a rejection of that principle. On the heels of UCal's decision came the Fifth Circuit Court of Appeal's 1996 ruling in *Cheryl J. Hopwood v. the University of Texas* that the policy of attending to race in consideration for admission to the University of Texas at Austin Law School was unconstitutional. Margaret Andersen and Howard Taylor observe, "Legal opinion on affirmative action is inconclusive" (1999: 306), but Henry N. Drewry and Humphrey Doermann offer a more cynical warning. The *Hopwood* decision has overturned a precedent set twenty years ago with *Bakke,* at least within the states of the Fifth Circuit Court's jurisdiction, Texas, Louisiana, and Mississippi. "The inconsistency . . . has yet to be dealt with at the Supreme Court level," but many schools are preemptively greatly diminishing race as one of their admissions considerations, revealing fear of lawsuits as well as "deeper currents of racial resentment that continue to flow through the American social landscape" (Drewry and Doermann 2001: 280–81).

It should be no surprise, then, that in a 1996 poll of college freshmen, the majority favored eliminating affirmative action. Yet with campuses more racially diverse than ever in U.S. history, an even larger majority favored prohibiting hate speech and most agreed that racial discrimination is still a problem in the United States (Altbach et al. 2002: 24). These statistics represent the tension within many white college students: although the protection of race privilege remains a powerfully motivating force, civility becomes a priority in face-to-face contact with fellow students of color.

Face-to-face encounters increase the likelihood of friendships, and, since the end of the 1980s, campus racial tensions have become less severe. "The numbers of [racial] incidents have declined, and race is a *somewhat* less divisive issue on most campuses" (Altbach, et al. 2002: xvi). Does this actually mean greater civility? Not necessarily, for racial incidents have not disappeared. Joe R. Feagin, Hernàn Vera, and Nikitah Imani's research in *The Agony of Education: Black Students at White Colleges and Universities* (1996) revealed scores of reports from colleges and universities across the country during the 1990s where black students were the targets of racist expressions ranging from faculty insensitivity to racial condescension to explicit harassment and violence.[21] Indeed, Feagin and his colleagues noted that the withdrawal and confrontational modes of behavior Willie and McCord observed back in the early 1970s were adaptive responses that black students still used in the 1990s. To the charge of reverse discrimination, Feagin, Vera, and Imani reply:

> The creation of distinct social support groups by the black students is *not* in any sense the counterpart of the old Jim Crow segregation. . . . On white-centered college campuses, most black student groups are defensive and protective, a response to what whites have done to exclude African Americans from white privileges and places. They are typically an attempt at self-determination and cultural maintenance in a sea of whiteness. (1996: 72)

Altbach, Lomotey, and Smith also note that "the location of racism has moved. E-mail and the Internet now seem to be a major source of racist messages and sentiments" (2002: xvi). While tensions may have eased, for those students still hanging on to racist ideas, the spaces in which to express them have become more private and anonymous, making confrontation especially challenging. Adding evidentiary fuel to the legitimacy of explicitly expressed racism is the lack of nonwhite students on some campuses. "[W]ithout affirmative action programs, public institutions in California and Texas have seen their admissions of students of color plummet" (Tierney and Chung 2002: 276).

In *The Shape of the River: Long-Term Consequences of Considering Race in College and University Admissions* (1998), William G. Bowen and Derek Bok examine the College and Beyond survey of more than eighty thousand students over almost forty years. Their focus is on the highly selective schools that expressed high expectations of their students. Black students graduated at a rate of 79 percent over five years from these schools, compared to the national graduation rate for African Americans in 1996 of 38 percent (Anderson 2002: 14).[22] Anderson buttresses Bowen and Bok's positive findings with the observations that "the affirmative action policies of the

1960s did not fail; indeed, they worked all too well and the thirty-year success of students of color has created a strong backlash against such programs" (2002: 15).

HBCUs, perhaps unwitting winners in this battle over affirmative action at the most selective colleges and universities, have continued to hold their own:

> According to American Council on Education (ACE) data for 1983–84 through 1996–97 . . . , "the percentage of bachelor's degrees awarded to African Americans by HBCUs remained consistently between 27 percent and 29 percent of the total awarded by all institutions." Thus, HBCUs have kept pace with the general increases in African American undergraduate enrollment and graduation rates over this time period. (Teddlie and Freeman 2002: 90)

Despite the good news for the continued relevance of historically black colleges, anti-racist activists at traditionally white schools are still struggling.

For more than sixty years, the separate but equal clause of *Plessy* confounded activists who pursued equality. Today's anti-racist activists find themselves similarly hamstrung by the language of nondiscrimination and rhetorical equality used by their adversaries. Most civil rights activists of the 1960s interpreted the Civil Rights Act to mean that racial designation would no longer be held against people of color or used to exclude them. Today, racial conservatives, and even some liberals, interpret the Civil Rights Act as proof that the nation had successfully made the transition from being a racist country to being a nonracist one. For such people, the 1965 act of legislation was a final goal rather than a first step. Those who disagree are seen as oversensitive, race-obsessed, or asking for preferential treatment. As Feagin, Vera, and Imani argue (1996), the reverse is as often true; it is sometimes whites who are race-obsessed and oversensitive.

CONCLUSION

Becoming familiar with the history of blacks in college and the work of scholars who have studied it prepared me for what I would hear when I began to interview black college alumni. I found scholarly conclusions repeated and affirmed. Indeed, in research completed even more recently than the college experiences of the men and women with whom I spoke, the trends remain intact. Where it is useful to show the continuation of such trends, I cite the work of these scholars throughout the chapters on experiences of Northwestern and Howard alumni. The experiences of those who were in college in the late 1960s through the late 1990s reveal that black students continue to face dramatic challenges, despite the increasing diversity of the American college campus. Indeed, while technology has provided a new venue for all kinds of expression, racist and anti-racist alike, black students continue to wrestle with many of the same problems that faced them in the years immediately following the heyday of the Civil Rights Movement.

On predominantly white campuses, they continue to be underrepresented compared to their proportion of the national population; they continue to suffer racial misunderstanding, ignorance, and in some cases explicit racism. Now a more diverse group themselves, they wrestle their own heterogeneity, the frustrating lack of curricula addressing black experiences, and the continued lack of black faculty. Indeed, as Robin Wilson reported in *The Chronicle of Higher Education* in summer 2002, the "proportion of black faculty members at predominantly white universities—2.3 percent—is virtually the same as it was 20 years ago" (2002: A11).

At HBCUs, black students continue to struggle with facilities underfunded relative to comparable white institutions; they wrestle, now more than in the past, with class, sexual orientation, and religious differences; and they are still trying to convince a skeptical public that their schools are vitally necessary on the landscape of American higher education.

ONE BLACK IN COLLEGE: QUAKER FRIENDS AND BAPTIST SISTERS

The intervener, who intends to lead others into the jungle of racial conflict, will first have to take the journey herself or himself.
—*Janet Helms*, Black and White Racial Identity

When Congress passed the Civil Rights Act of 1964, it ushered in unprecedented opportunities for African Americans in the United States. The implications of this legal liberation continue to be debated. Its implications for my own educational career were profound. In this chapter, I share my own experience as a black student at a predominantly white college, and a semester spent at an HBCU. My experience was not only about race, nor is race the only lens through which I might have interpreted my college years. But, as Tatum observes, "The parts of our identity that *do* capture our attention are those that other people notice, and that reflect back to us. The aspect of identity that is the target of others' attention, and subsequently of our own, often is that which sets us apart as exception or 'other' in their eyes" (1997: 21). It was the racial aspect of my identity that captured my attention and that, to use Erik Erikson's words, aggravated in painful and elated ways my racial identity-consciousness (1968: 22).

I was born in 1963 to interracially married persons who worked as a college professor and a church musician.[1] Like other middle-class African Americans of my generation, I had the opportunity to live in predominantly white neighborhoods; our family belonged to predominantly white churches; and my brothers and I attended predominantly white public schools. After attending a predominantly white, highly selective private college, I went on to earn my doctorate from an elite, predominantly white research university. I have taught sociology at four predominantly white institutions of higher learning. Such a trajectory would have been highly unlikely for any African American, regardless of aptitude, personality, or pedigree prior to the gains of the Civil Rights Movement.[2]

The townspeople where I grew up were unequivocally devoted to public education. The town was also a participant in METCO—a program in which black students from Boston were bussed to the more generously funded public schools of Boston-area suburbs.[3] And yet, many of the townspeople were similar to people in many mostly white towns and villages across the United States: they seemed to believe in their racial innocence despite the town's homogeneity and collective ignorance of any history other than that of Massachusetts's colonial days. At the same time, Concord was also home to many thoughtful and generous residents who, in the tradition of Emerson, Thoreau, and Alcott, wrestled with democracy and diversity. Although I remember perhaps a dozen families of color who lived in our town of about eighteen thousand people during the 1970s, I had no close friends who were black, Latino or Latina, Native American, or Asian American.[4]

By my senior year of high school, I was hoping that college would offer an environment where I could embrace my racial identity in an atmosphere where everyone was beyond it. Although experiences during which I came face-to-face with racist insults were infrequent, they startled me and depleted my emotional reserves. My fantasies for a world beyond race were no doubt conflated with the desire to have a different relationship to myself, to be "grown" and less dependent on my parents and my community. Part of my desire to be beyond race was the desire for relief from racism.

Immediately attracted to the lush suburban campus of Haverford College, I decided it was my first-choice school because it seemed both radically different and soothingly familiar. I believed that Haverford had a multiracial student body and that the village of Haverford surrounding it closely resembled my hometown. I anticipated that I would find both social comfort and intellectual challenge there. I found the latter but not the former.

Haverford is a small, private, liberal arts college on the Main Line, an exclusive row of suburban enclaves west of Philadelphia. It is regularly listed among the nation's fifteen most rigorous, selective, and expensive undergraduate colleges. From the first half of the nineteenth century, when the college was founded by the Society of Friends, through the late 1960s, its student body grew to roughly four hundred young men, most of whom were from middle-class and affluent, white, Protestant families. As the demand for all-male colleges waned and its applicant pool decreased, Haverford tried to convince its wealthier and better-known sister college, Bryn Mawr, to join in a coeducational endeavor. When that proposal was rejected, the college began admitting women in the 1970s and was fully coeducational with a student body that had more than doubled, to one thousand, by the early 1980s. Even after these changes, Haverford continued to enroll a relatively narrow student population that was largely affluent and—for a school eager to attract a national student body—disproportionately European American and from the Northeast.

Though the official affiliation with the Society of Friends does not go beyond its governing board, Haverford has continued to take seriously its Quaker origins. The Quaker belief that "there is that of God in every man" buttressed the tenets of the college's social and academic honor code, legislated and enforced by students themselves. Moreover, most faculty, staff, and student meetings were run by consensus, two features that have continued to distinguish the college from most of its peer institutions.

Although I had been the object of racial slurs by a handful of kids in the hallways of the public schools in my hometown, white students had been my best friends and my reference group. At Haverford, however, in both subtle and explicit ways I found myself warned against identifying too closely with whites. I was reminded of my difference by those white students who spoke to me in black English, coaxed me into black handshakes, or made fun of my kilts and penny loafers. One white classmate, having no idea about my vocal ability, asked me to sing with his jazz band, explaining, "Everyone knows all black women sing."

Despite my frustrations in high school, there were few places where I did not feel entitled or welcome; I was ultimately elected president of the student government. In college, I did not feel a similar campus ownership. As Feagin, Vera, and Imani observe, "The failure of many whites to recognize the great diversity of interests and inclinations among black students may seem an innocent misunderstanding, yet it nonetheless conveys an eloquent message about white assumptions about social positions on campus" (1996: 67).

The pronouncements and assumptions of other white students were more aggressive than the comment about singing. I was lectured that if I were not from an all-black urban neighborhood, I was an example of how affirmative action had been misused. Convinced that they had nothing to learn about race or racism from me, these few classmates commented, "You're not like other blacks." This is one of the most frequently recited insults-passing-for-compliments that white Americans bestow upon colleagues, acquaintances, and friends of color whom they have deemed worthy of friendship or association. Being biracial was evidence for a few other white students that I was admitted to the college because I was neither too crude nor too confrontational. I appreciated the irony that these same classmates seemed to be secretly grateful for the characteristics that made me seem more like them. On other occasions, I was invited to collude against fellow black classmates who did not come from backgrounds like mine—white, suburban, and affluent. When I refused, I became the object of their frustration and confusion.

Several of the black friends I have made since college who also attended predominantly white colleges have told me that they remember feeling "too black" in some circles and "not black enough" in others. This is an especially common experience for black students who themselves feel marginal vis-à-vis other blacks on campus. Although I don't remember expressing this feeling in the same way, I must have expected rejection from both camps, for I do remember being anxious to resist the expectations of whites that I would spend time only with other blacks. I remember being more uncomfortable sitting at the dining center table where many of the black and Latino students customarily sat than if I sat elsewhere. I remember being equally anxious how that choice was interpreted by fellow students of color. In hindsight, the speed with which I learned black and brown students' names and my attendance at Black Student League and Minority Coalition meetings was probably compensatory.

After overcoming that initial anxiety of what fellow students of color thought about me, I relaxed enough to realize that *most* of us did not assume about each other the same things that some of our white classmates assumed about us. Perhaps because we were such a small contingent,[5] most of us learned not to jump to conclusions about each other. We all came from "unique" situations—educated at private, magnet, or suburban schools, sometimes from the West Indies or Europe, our parents were often very rich or very poor, and we were valedictorians, school presidents, or athletes who had taken Advanced Placement classes. Because of our few numbers, there was rarely anything typical about us.

My professors offered different, if related, challenges than did my classmates. They were both demanding and parsimonious with praise, qualities that moved the more privileged students at the college beyond self-absorption and convinced most of us, of all colors, that the life of the mind was important. Although I had left public high school with a sense of myself as a thinker and a writer, I had not honed the ability to concentrate or to devote long hours to study; I lacked confidence in math, and my reading comprehension was weak. I yearned to understand the underlying structure of things that I hoped would clarify so many of life's mysteries.

That first year in college was a mighty struggle. Receiving barely satisfactory grades in every course but English, I feared I was disappointing everyone except those who expected African Americans and women to be academic failures. Yet I was so ashamed of my academic difficulties that I rarely sought help outside of class. Academic anxiety and the demands of deflecting what seemed to be regular though not easily decipherable racial jabs exhausted me. My white classmates were spending their energy on other things. I was unable to burn the candle at both ends; I could neither work twice as hard nor be twice as good; and I was often despairing and depressed.

I have learned since that my experience is not uncommon for black students. Psychologist Claude Steele has shown that black students often spiral downward in college in response to negative stereotypes. The awful conundrum is that black students' efforts at successfully meeting challenges are undermined by the fear not of success but of fulfilling the low expectations of others: "When a black student sits down to take a test, he or she can sense that their intellectual abilities are under suspicion. That apprehension is a very underestimated factor in test performance. Stereotype vulnerability creates a loaded situation in which students often perform poorly and thus confirm low expectations or choose to not achieve anything at all in that do-main" (quoted in Jackson 1994: 23).[6] These negative racial experiences I've described happened with only a handful of people, but they were delivered with such certitude and I was so much less confident than I had been in high school that I was completely preoccupied by them. With mounting anxiety, I wondered if my closer friends were simply keeping their prejudices to themselves.

William E. Cross, Jr., (1991) observes five stages of racial identity development for black Americans who, because of their relationship to a society still wrestling with white supremacy, experience racial identity differently from white Americans.[7] He describes what I was going through as the second stage which he calls *encounter*: "Transition to the encounter stage is typically precipitated by an event or series of events that force the young person to acknowledge the personal impact of racism. As the result of a new and heightened awareness of the significance of race, the individual begins to grapple with what it means to be a member of a group targeted by racism" (as paraphrased in Tatum 1997: 55). Despite the fact that I had made friends and my grades had gone from Cs to Bs by sophomore year, I remained preoccupied over the question of whether the culture of the college tacitly endorsed the bigotry and ignorance of a few. While Haverford clearly valued diversity (indeed, the director of multicultural affairs, a black woman, was promoted to dean of the college during my time there), the value sometimes seemed rhetorical. From my perspective, the college's ambivalence was reflected in what seemed like small numbers of students, faculty, and staff of color enrolled and employed there.[8] I was not just unhappy, I felt dislocated. I was both angry over the racism I was experiencing and deeply frustrated because I did not know how to respond constructively to it.

Janet Helms offers hindsight psychological explanation of the crisis that was ensuing:

[O]ne's quality of adjustment has been hypothesized to result from a combi-nation of "personal identity," "reference group orientation," and "ascribed identity." . . . Personal identity concerns one's feelings and attitudes about oneself, in other words, generic personality characteristics such as anxiety, self-esteem, and so on. Reference-group orientation refers to the extent to which one uses particular racial groups; for example, Blacks or Whites in this country, to guide one's feelings, thoughts, and behaviors. One's reference-group orientation is reflected in such things as value systems, organizational memberships, ideologies, and so on. Ascribed identity pertains to the indi-vidual's deliberate affiliation or commitment to a particular racial group. Typically one can choose to commit to one of four categories if one is Black or White: Blacks primarily, Whites primarily, neither, or both. Hence, a per-son who considers one race or the other to be the important definer of Self

> has a mono-racial ascribed identity; a person who feels a connectedness to both racial groups has a bi-racial ascribed identity; and the person who commits to neither group has a marginal ascribed identity. (1993: 5)[9]

Although I felt a connectedness to persons of both racial groups, I found more comfort with whites while my political commitment was to blacks. My personal identity, however, was fragile.

In addition to feeling uncomfortable with my racial place on campus, I was insecure about my sexual desirability having dated neither in high school nor in college. Without romantic affirmation, my sense of racial dislocation was exacerbated. Tatum again confirms that my experience was not unusual: "Black girls, especially in predominantly White communities, may gradually become aware that something has changed. When their White friends start to date, they do not. The issues of emerging sexuality and the societal messages about who is sexually desirable leave young Black women in a very devalued position" (1997: 57). Haverford and Bryn Mawr colleges made up a genuinely bi-college community where, when I was there from 1982 to 1986, women outnumbered men by three to one. I was not alone in my disappointing romantic life, and I do not attribute my situation solely to race. At the same time, not feeling desirable had consequences for my racial identity, and the two were clearly connected for other black female students as well.

By the end of sophomore year, I had not taken classes with the few African-American faculty members on campus. Although most of their courses on race or blackness were restricted by introductory prerequisites, I had been advised to take other courses, and I was a student who responded to advice.[10] I remember observing these black professors on campus and wishing I could know them. I did take courses on the history of colonial Africa, and Francophone literature in Africa, with visiting African professors. I felt myself overwhelmed with names and dates, and I found the cultures I was studying exotic and remote. I did not see connections between these places and times and my own. I remember avoiding the few opportunities I had to study American race issues with white professors, either not trusting them or my own ability to sustain the emotional energy I suspected would be required of me.

Though I was ideologically committed to and intellectually convinced of black equality—indeed, proud to claim my African-American heritage—I did not have everyday experience with African Americans or other people of color. This lack of experience had retarded my comfort with myself and hampered my ability to move among different groups with ease. The gaze of a few white classmates felt like a spotlight, and I was paralyzed, feeling much of the time as though I were on stage without a script. In the comfort of my dorm room, however, I entertained friends, played George Benson's hit "Masquerade" until the tape deteriorated, and was desperately lonely.

When one is faced with what Chester Pierce calls the "mundane extreme environmental stress" of racism, in adolescence or in adulthood, the ability to see oneself as part of a larger group from which one can draw support is an important coping strategy. Individuals who do not have such a strategy available to them because they do not experience a shared identity with at least some subset of their racial group are at risk for considerable social isolation. (Tatum 1997: 70)

Whether it was, as Tatum says, the lack of a "coping strategy" or the lack of a group I could trust on racial matters, I knew I needed change. When friends began to apply for junior-year study abroad programs, I decided to pursue the black experience I had not had growing up.[11] In part, I think I was looking for racial validation, and I did not trust my white friends—sympathetic as many of them would have been had I even been able to articulate my feelings—to be able to offer it. Again, Tatum's work provides context for my experience:

Not only are Black adolescents encountering racism and reflecting on their identity, but their White peers, even when they are not the perpetrators (and sometimes they are), are unprepared to respond in supportive ways. The Black students turn to each other for the much needed support they are not likely to find anywhere else . . . The developmental need to explore the meaning of one's identity with others . . . engaged in a similar process manifests itself informally in school corridors and cafeterias across the country. (1997: 60, 71)

Choosing to sit at the black table in the dining center at Haverford was a less comfortable option for me than transplanting myself to a place where no one knew me. I applied to several HBCUs as an exchange student for the fall semester of my junior year, was accepted at Spelman College, and arrived in Atlanta in August 1984 for orientation.

Fifty years younger than Haverford, Spelman was founded with Rockefeller money in 1881 as a Baptist seminary to train black women freed from slavery. It was on this Southern campus of fourteen hundred women students where I won back some of the intellectual energy and sense of personal efficacy I had lost at Haverford. Kenneth W. Jackson and L. Alex Swan observe, "All in all, what we find for females is that the means by which high academic performance is generated differs according to institutional environment" (1991: 139). I took jazz dance, studied African-American literature and black religion in America, received acclaim from my professors, and made the dean's list for academic achievement. I spent time at the neighboring HBCUs, Morehouse and Clark, took a road trip to Fisk University, finally dated, saw fraternity and sorority step dances, and came into contact with dozens of famous black leaders, including Coretta Scott King, Andrew Young, Julian Bond, and Jesse Jackson. In many ways, Spelman was a lifesaving ring thrown to me in a drowning moment.

Once pulled from the water, however, I caught my breath long enough to find the conditions I had accepted to come aboard troubling. Again, with an ample reserve of naiveté, I expected to walk onto a campus where the shared history of having experienced sexism and racism would lead Spelman's students, faculty, and staff to exist in a utopian atmosphere of noncompetition, an embrace of feminism, and the regular questioning of rote tradition. Spelman was an extraordinary place while I was there—it admitted students from a range of educational, geographic, and financial backgrounds, many of whom would have been accepted at the nation's most selective colleges and others who, though passionate about learning, were underprepared for college-level work. Spelman at that time sent almost two-thirds of its graduates on to graduate and professional school. An atmosphere of both high academic expectation and encouragement permeated the campus.

I soon learned, though, that it was hardly a utopia. It seemed contradictory to me that many traditions—from the tolerance of sorority hazing, deference to very traditional gender norms, and bigoted attitudes about lesbians—went largely unchallenged and unquestioned at a woman's college. Similar to my experience at Haverford, I began to see disjuncture between how Spelman described its mission and what actually occurred on campus.

Nonetheless, Spelman gave me a security with myself as a black person: I saw such a wide range of African Americans that I began to conceive of blackness as inclusive of a variety of experiences, including my own. As I made friends and heard about their experiences, I began to appreciate that many of my black classmates back at Haverford, who had come from mostly black environments, must have felt extreme dislocation. This combination of becoming sure of myself and at ease with other African Americans gave me confidence and compassion. I stopped doubting my own authenticity as an African American. I'd been identified by others as different in my hometown and at college, and no matter how much I valued or took pride in that difference I had longed to feel normal. Feeling this for the first time was grounding. In fact, there were many things that set me apart from my fellow students at Spelman, but my racial uniqueness was not one of them. I began to feel racially integrated both with others and then with myself.

Returning to Haverford, more comfortable with myself, I registered for courses that seemed more relevant to me, I began to speak up more in all of my classes, and I became more politically active. However, the confidence I had gained remained out of synch with my social and emotional life. I felt as if my experience at Spelman had given me new eyes with which to see the world. And, like any convert who has "seen the light," I was deeply frustrated by the continued parochialism of those classmates whose ignorance about the importance of racial issues now seemed willful.

Still, that first semester back had its good moments. One of those good moments was winning the prize for best actress in the Annual Class Night Variety Show. The award was given for my portrayal of one of the few other black female students on campus who stood out as a character. For years afterwards, that evening remained a tangled knot of emotions in my heart—the pride at having so thoroughly portrayed another that I was publicly recognized and the guilt for having imitated a fellow black woman. I don't remember how I justified the moment to myself. But I do remember coming across Judith Butler's observation with a jolt of recognition: while some forms of imitation have been challenges to the dominant group, other forms of parody "are not subversive" (1995: 134). The year before, I had played the part of the library fountain and been part of the group that won the best skit award. Sophomore year I remember refusing to play the dean of the college, also a black woman, in another skit. When I look back on the whole, perhaps I've made too much of a moment of bad taste and good humor. But I continue to ask myself: Whose humor? Why was it funny? What was my investment?

Senior year, I was active in the Black Student League, the Feminist Group, the student campaign urging the college to divest from businesses in apartheid South Africa, and I finally had a boyfriend, another black student. Eager to begin understanding my college experience before it had even ended, the decision to major in sociology proved to be an asset. For my senior thesis, I interviewed twenty fellow black students, listened to them talk about their college experiences, and compared what I learned to four published studies on black students in college.[12] My black classmates confirmed the sense I had that life was particularly difficult as a black student.

METHODIST NORTHWESTERN AND CONGREGATIONALIST HOWARD: BRIEFLY INTRODUCED

In response to Fleming's (1984) observation that "[t]here is little comparative research that demonstrates how black students develop in black versus white educational environments" (3), I decided to compare the experiences of people who had attended a historically white college to those who had attended a predominantly black college. Alumni of Howard and Northwestern fit the bill.

As well-known and well-respected, midsized, private colleges within university settings, Howard (HU) and Northwestern (NU) share much in common, making a comparative analysis of the experiences of the black students who attended them fruitful. Below, I offer a very brief discussion of their beginnings. Because this book is not about Northwestern and Howard *as particular institutions*, the following facts are meant only to provide background to the stories that alumni and alumnae tell.[1]

Howard and Northwestern were both founded in the mid-1800s. Although Howard is a privately governed institution, it is funded largely by the U.S. government,[2] and has been able to keep its tuition to just less than half of Northwestern's. Still, in the late 1980s, 80 percent of Howard students were receiving some financial aid, compared to 60 percent of Northwestern students (Peterson 1989).

Howard spreads itself over more than two hundred acres of the capital city, while Northwestern is situated on two hundred acres of Lake Michigan beachfront in Evanston, Illinois, a few miles north of Chicago. In the early 1990s, Howard had 9,000 undergraduates, 39 percent of whom were male and 61 percent of whom were female. (Because there are so many graduate programs with more men than women in them at Howard, the undergraduate gender disparity is not as apparent as one might expect.) Northwestern's undergraduate student body in the early 1990s consisted of 7,300, half men and half women (*U.S. News and World Report*, "America's Best Colleges," September 1991). While Northwestern is slightly more selective in its admissions policies (in terms of admitted students' SAT scores and high school grade point averages), both schools are prestigious within the circles to which they compare themselves. Howard is often described as "the Mecca for black thought in this country" or "the Black Harvard,"[3] while Northwestern compares itself to Harvard in citing the presence of its alumni as Fortune 500 officers and *Who's Who in America* entrants (Birnbach, 1984: 100). Both schools work to deemphasize the country-club and party-school reputations that have occasionally accompanied their descriptions by students and alumni. While Greek-letter organizations are present at both universities, participation levels are much higher at Northwestern than at Howard.

Especially in the Midwest, Northwestern enjoys a heralded reputation as a site of intellectual rigor and academic seriousness. The only private university among the Big Ten, (before Penn State joined the conference in the 1990s) also a private university and the eleventh member, Northwestern is also known for having maintained its consistently higher than average black student population (between 7 and 10 percent) since the early 1970s.[4]

Northwestern was like hundreds of colleges founded during the mid-nineteenth century in owing its existence to funding by churches, or what Williamson and Wild call the "denominational enterprise" (1976: 1). Its benefactor was the Methodist General Conference, which sought "both to raise the quality of ministerial training and to discourage its young people from attending schools controlled by rival denominations." In fact, "[b]etween 1830 and 1860, the Methodist Church and associated lay groups founded thirty-four permanent schools of higher learning" (Williamson and Wild 1976: 2).

Northwestern was opened, to male students, in 1855. The college raised its initial monies with the sale of "perpetual scholarships"; for one hundred dollars, a man, his son, and his grandson could attend the college (Williamson and Wild 1976: 6). Fewer than fifteen years later, however, and apparently under pressure from the wives of board members, Northwestern became a coeducational college.

Like the two world wars that followed it, the exigencies of the American Civil War "propelled women into new roles and showed that they were capable of work previously reserved for men" (Williamson and Wild 1976: 23). Besides the catalyst of war, the wives of Northwestern trustees also played a role in the change of college policy. These women persuaded the village of Evanston to set aside land for a women's college—the Evanston College for Ladies—next to the plot that their husbands had secured, and the women acquired a state charter for their school (Williamson and Wild 1976: 24). It remains a mystery whether intimate threats or entreaties, or the conviction of these women, encouraged their husbands to act. But act they did, and just before the Evanston College for Ladies was to begin receiving applications, "[i]n June 1869 the trustees [of Northwestern] voted to admit young women to university classes 'upon the same terms and conditions as young men'" (Williamson and Wild 1976: 23). Northwestern, then, began as a school to educate young Methodist men but soon found itself coeducational and nonsectarian.

Howard, too, is indebted to the "denominational enterprise," having been founded by religious men of European descent: specifically, members of the Congregational Church (Logan 1969: 13). The first proposals for "The Howard Normal and Theological Institute for the Education of Teachers and Preachers" were put forth in the autumn of 1866 "with a view to service among the freedmen" (quoted in Logan 1969: 3). The final proposal was for "a liberal arts college and a university," and the charter for Howard was granted in "a bill enacted by Congress on March 2, 1867" (Logan 1969: 14, 20). Named for one of its founders, General Oliver O. Howard, a Union general and Civil War hero, the university was governed by its namesake from 1869 until 1873 (Logan 1969: 18–19).

Although "the founders expected a sizable number of the students to be Negroes," they also expected to educate "white men and women" (Logan 1969: 25). The school opened in spring 1867, and "the first students were white girls," daughters of the founders who were committed to showing the country the possibilities of integrated education (Logan 1969: 34). With the end of Reconstruction, anti-Negro sentiment gained momentum in the South and was tolerated in the North. The pressure on Howard to represent the separate but equal ideal conveyed in *Plessy v. Ferguson* (1896) resulted in Howard's eventual association—solidified by the turn of the century—as a school for colored people.[5] The continued and formalized receipt of money from the federal government also ensured the withering of any vestigial ties to Congregational sectarianism. Like Northwestern, then, Howard began with religious roots that faded. Unlike Northwestern, which became more diverse in terms of gender, Howard began as a multiracial university and became a black college.

Frederick Douglass served on the HU board of trustees, as did Booker T. Washington. Later "Carter G. Woodson, who had founded the Association for the study of Negro Life and History and published the first issue of the *Journal of Negro History*," served as the dean of the School of Liberal Arts. Alain Locke was both an alumnus and member of the faculty (Logan 1969: 61, 208, 209). The luminaries that Howard either gave jobs to or sent forth are too numerous to list but include E. Franklin Frazier, who headed the Department of Sociology from 1934 to 1959. Other alumni include doctors Kenneth B. and Mamie Clark, and Patricia Harris, Thurgood Marshall, Andrew Young, and Toni Morrison (see Logan 1969, Birnbach 1984). Because of its reputation as an educator of the world's black elite, it has been one of the HBCUs that has continued to draw large numbers of applications, including students who are able to choose to attend any college in the country.

THE IVORY TOWER: LIFE AT NORTHWESTERN

*If you're an outsider, all you see is the magic. . . . There are [so]
many [people] who are just in awe of [Northwestern]. It's the
school that they wish they could have gotten into. . . . You auto-
matically get respect.*

—*Lynn, Northwestern '83*

With the passing of the 1964 Civil Rights Act following the Supreme Court's ruling
in *Brown v. Board of Education* a decade earlier, black Americans had the opportunity
to attend historically white as well as historically black colleges and universities. For
African Americans attending college after the heyday of the Civil Rights Movement,
the explicit quotas meant to keep them out were gone, and affirmative action and financial aid programs had been implemented to usher them in.[1] Despite the presence
of these formal policies, the historically white college campus was often a difficult
place for black students to be.

Northwestern was more successful at recruiting black students than most private
universities of its size. With fewer than ten thousand undergraduate students, NU is
smaller than the other, public universities that are also members of the Big Ten football conference. So while its absolute numbers of minority students have never been
as high as those of other Midwestern state schools, after the mid-1960s NU recruited
between 7 and 10 percent of its student body from the African-American community.[2] That meant that black students who went to Northwestern after 1970 were
never alone.[3]

The story that black Wildcats tell of the college experience is, therefore, a complicated one. While racism and racial polarization were nearly universal aspects of the
experience for the NU alumni I interviewed, a majority of them noted the prestige
that having gone to Northwestern has garnered for their careers. These dichotomies
presented themselves repeatedly. True friendships were gained, many said, at the expense of achieving self-confidence during college; there were a handful of wonderful
mentors, along with disinterested advisors; the separate world of black students is

nostalgically recalled, but painful experiences of bigotry, racial discomfort, and most often disinterest from white students are recalled just as frequently. When black alumni describe their entire college experience, *ambivalence* is the common denominator. Most would repeat their decision to attend if they could do it again, and most recall strong friendships that have lasted well into adulthood.

TWO WORLDS: SEPARATE BUT EQUAL?

We had this joke on campus about how when you saw white people out of context you wouldn't recognize them, you know, [even] someone you sat next to in class. It was terrible. I mean, I would see my [white] roommates on the street sometimes and I'd have to do a double take or I'd pass right by [without acknowledging] them.

—Robert, Northwestern '80

The experiences of Northwestern alumni concur with other studies that suggest that predominantly white colleges fall short of facilitating a positive multiracial environment for all students and, further, that this failure has particularly negative ramifications for black students. In many ways, Northwestern serves as an unlikely proxy for other predominantly white colleges and universities, for it appears to have done everything right over the twenty years that my respondents were enrolled. In the late 1960s, Northwestern recruited and admitted several hundred black students. In response to black student activism,[4] it instituted an African American Studies Program, designated a Black Cultural Center, and welcomed the presence of black fraternities and sororities. No doubt its location, just north of Chicago, a city with a large black population, in a suburb that itself has a black population of 40 percent, allowed the university to market itself as welcoming.[5] One might expect, therefore, that Northwestern was similar to the University of California at Berkeley—with students from many different backgrounds engaging in intercultural exchange, political dialogue, and cross-racial coalition against the multiracial backdrop, in this case, of Evanston Township. My data, however, do not suggest such cross-cultural exchange. To the contrary, black alumni describe the campus as socially polarized along racial lines. This situation of black students operating in separate spheres, not always by choice, has been noted in several studies, including those of Harry Edwards (1970), Willie and McCord (1972), Exum (1985), and Chalsa M. Loo and Gary Rolison (1986).

The problems that black students faced on predominantly white college campuses in the post–Civil Rights Movement era were usually not experiences of explicit racism. Rather, they faced racial insensitivity and racial ignorance on a daily basis. While such treatment signals a climate tolerant of bigotry, the validity of their interpretations, alumni recall, was regularly questioned by white advisors and administrators. It was exhausting just to digest such experiences. What exacerbated their frustrations was that many alumni recall not having the tools to respond to these complicated and shape-shifting insults, some of which were unconsciously perpetrated by their assailants. The racist expressions of which they were targets were less explicit than that their parents' generation had experienced a couple of decades earlier both on and off campus, but were nonetheless draining.

According to alumni, the Northwestern campus community felt peculiarly biracial rather than multiracial. Asian students are remembered only in descriptions of the Technological Institute, although a few Asian-American students are remembered as peripheral to the black campus community. In general, however, Asians and Asian Americans are relatively absent from the picture black alumni paint of Northwestern campus life, and Latinos, Latinas, and Native Americans do not enter the picture at all. One exception to this two-tone memory is Kathy's: "I did hear a lot of discrimination against Orientals from everyone. And it was because in [the Technological Institute] most of th[em] were [foreign students] working on their master's and Ph.D.s and they were TAs for courses. . . . And I know a lot of whites hated them more so than blacks. And they used to always complain, 'Oh, those chinks, they're everywhere' "(Kathy, NU '85).

The lack of experiences with white students, the largest racial group on campus, whether it be as study partners, as friends, or as dating prospects was so pronounced at Northwestern that 83 percent of my respondents explicitly characterized the campus as "two separate worlds," one white and one black. "I can look back and say I didn't have any [white] enemies, but I can't say that I could write anybody now or call up anybody who happens to be of another color. And that's possibly one of the sadder things about it" (Lynn, NU '83). In the absence of a norm that legitimated cross-racial friendships, my respondents claim that black and white students rarely socialized. Murray, who graduated in the mid-1970s, says that if he had not seen white students in class, he would have thought that he was "at a black college" (Murray, NU '76). He socialized with other black students so exclusively that, along with most of his fellow black alumni, Murray can not think of one white friend from college upon whom he could call today. Robert recounts a similarly representative story: "This one guy was in the tuba section which was right in my direct line of vision [as a cheerleader. When we met at the reunion,] I swear I had never seen him before. I mean *never* seen him" (Robert, NU '80).

A few Northwestern alumni adopt a confessional tone when describing the two separate worlds, citing their own "decision" or "choice" not to reach beyond the black campus community. They characterize the racial climate on campus as one in which blacks and whites "basically stayed to themselves" (Lou, NU '75). Deborah elaborates: "It was pretty segregated. The black students sat together during meals; they intimidated the white students a little bit; or the white students were intimidated *by* whatever. But I don't think there was any racial violence. You just stay on that side of the road and I'll stay on this side of the road. . . . I really, for the most part, segregated myself" (Deborah, NU '75). The characterization that several students offer that they "separated themselves" is worth noting. From all accounts, students entered a college community already highly separated along racial lines. Unless they were committed to interacting with white students, it is difficult to assess the extent of personal agency in the choices of teenagers doing what they were expected to do by both their black and white peers. It is likely that many black students, coming from segregated backgrounds, found the separate existence of blacks and whites commonplace. Indeed, it is likely that many may even have found the separation on campus comfortable. It is most likely, however, that many black alumni now describe their experiences with more agency or choice in the matter than they felt at the time they were students.

CONSEQUENCES OF SEPARATE WORLDS

I stayed almost exclusively in the black community. I've never had a close friend who wasn't black.
—William, Northwestern '88

Several alumni, though, remember their expectation that intellectual interests would triumph over custom and race prejudice, and that cliquishness would shrink in a university atmosphere with ideals of egalitarianism and rhetoric of colorblindness. "There were two worlds. And I often look back and wonder why. . . . You would think that this would be a time where people's minds are open, but I don't think it was that way. . . . It's as if you just existed in two different worlds, separate and equal" (Lynn, NU '83).

While few NU alumni explicitly blame the college for a negative experience, the university's complicity is questioned. After participating in what they believed was a random room assignment lottery, several black alumni remember that they found themselves with black roommates, with a disproportionate number of other black students on their floor, or assigned to dormitories that had a reputation for "where they put us all" (Christine, NU '78). Sophomore year . . . I . . . roomed with three people I never even knew before. And they were all black; it was weird. I don't know how that happened. . . . I was so young then that I didn't even think about it, but [now I think it was] more than coincidence" (Deborah, NU '75). Having made black friends freshman year, these students expected to be placed with nonblack students. Noting that separation between black and white students went beyond dormitory life, Jenny (NU '88) wonders why professors did not assign students to work together in or out of the classroom or why there were not more cross-racial rooming assignments for students from different racial backgrounds to get to know each other.

While notable exceptions exist, most respondents do not remember that white students at Northwestern initiated conversations, friendships, or study groups with them. "I would say," remarks Adam, a 1974 graduate of NU, "if anything, that the white community or the European community had a fear of the black community." According to respondents, white students appeared scared of, sometimes hostile toward, and usually indifferent to black students.

And while black students did not usually go out of their way to initiate interactions with whites—not surprising since so many mentioned the culture shock induced by the overwhelmingly white environment and as racial newcomers to campus—they also remember when sincere attempts to bridge the "two worlds" were made. Adam recalls one unsuccessful attempt: "[W]e put on a dance. It was a marathon dance. It was our specific goal to have this dance populated by both segments of the student body, and it didn't happen. I mean our advertising was geared to both communities; fliers, radio. We tried to really make it a neutral appeal to both, and it just didn't happen" (Adam, NU '74). With a hesitancy and quieter voice inconsistent with her gregarious attitude in the rest of her interview, Jennifer (NU '88) agrees. "It just seemed like, I don't know, I just thought that white people really didn't want to be bothered with black people, [pause] any more than the other way around, unless you studied together maybe." Ruth, too, rounds out Adam's and Jennifer's perceptions: "White people will not seek you out. . . . When you're just standing in line someplace and you just start talking to somebody for whatever reason, white people are . . . very indifferent to blacks—in other words, 'We realize that you have to be here.' I just felt like white people . . . looked through you, whereas, with their white counterparts, they might have struck up a conversation" (Ruth, NU '81).

Although many Northwestern alumni made lasting friendships in black clubs and organizations, some of these same individuals feel cheated, having believed that college was supposed to be a time and place to reach beyond the parochialism of the neighborhood and the neighborhood high school. These Wildcats remember expecting college to be a place in which bonds were forged in celebration of newfound commonalties, not only with other African Americans. Robert remembers what he expected before college: "I thought it would be this wonderful interracial world where I would meet all these white people and have all these great white friends and, you know, have some black friends. I thought . . . I'd be exposed to a lot of different kinds of people. That turned out to be true, but not as many of those different kinds of people turned out to be white; they turned out to be black" (Robert, NU '80).

Whether implicitly or explicitly hostile, then, the larger campus community encouraged a level of racial camaraderie, and even a survival mentality, among black students. And, while the presence of several hundred other black students was welcome to the alumni in my study, most expected a more racially diverse set of friends.

FICTIVE KIN: IN-GROUP AND OUT-GROUP TENSIONS

As I explained in chapter 3, I had felt on the outside at both Haverford and Spelman colleges. Still, I held on to an inchoate set of sentiments that turned on an axis relegating others to insider or outsider status as well: "pro-black" and "not black enough."

> A negative prejudice against someone not in one's own social group is often accompanied by a positive prejudice in favor of someone who *is* in one's own group; thus the prejudiced person will have negative attitudes about a member of an *out-group* (any group other than one's own), and positive attitudes about someone simply because he or she is in one's *in-group* (any group one considers one's own). (Andersen and Taylor 1999: 284)

Like all binary explanations of the world, this one was no less seductive in its simplicity. Although I felt that I had been misjudged by people who fell on both sides of this axis, I could not conceive of ordering the world any differently. Although many students today who identify as multiracial have challenged this binary axis, the desire to divide up the world into people who are racial warriors and others who are racial sellouts remains powerful among current college students.

While a couple of alumni like Jerry (NU '84) described the black community on campus as a very divided group, most black Wildcats use words like *kin* and *family* to describe the cohesiveness of the black campus community. Psychologists Signithia Fordham and John U. Ogbu (1986) describe the importance of close ties among African Americans. They are not, according to these anthropologists, based on blood or marriage ties. Rather they function as bonds among those "who have some reciprocal social or economic relationship. . . . [T]here is a much wider meaning of fictive kinship among black Americans. In this latter sense the term conveys the idea of 'brotherhood' and 'sisterhood' of all black Americans" (1986: 183, 185).[6] Christine's account is representative of how important to each other many of the black NU alumni were: "[I]t's hard enough that you're at [a rigorous and selective] institution. . . . And if you don't have that kinship and really know who you are, you can be totally confused . . . but if you have that kinship, you have a lot. . . . The friends I made in college are . . . like a second family to me" (Christine, NU '78). While there were more than 5,500 students on Northwestern's campus who were not black, over the twenty years the respondents for this study entered and exited the school, there were between 150 and 650 students on campus who were black. It is not surprising, then, that most of the black students at NU made many black friends. What is surprising is that the majority made *only* black friends.

I don't think there was a lot of racial tension at Northwestern's campus [during the late 1970s]. I think the races really got along well for two main reasons. They really did things very separately and [they] didn't think about intermingling. . . . [Y]ou had one or two people who did, and they were really Oreo cookies; they dealt with white people all the time and were never a part of the things that went on in the black community as far as FMO [For Members Only], which was the black organization for students . . . they were really, to us, white. They just had black skin. But I mean, you dealt with people—you know, there wasn't like racial incidents that went on. . . . I think we lived in separate and distinct worlds then. I don't think there was an actual blend of the communities. (John, NU '79)

The two separate worlds—while generating a feeling of kinship among most of the black alumni with whom I spoke—exacted penalties upon those at the margins of narrow intersection. As John, quoted above, implies, those black students who social-ized with whites were not considered members of the in-group.

In the 1960s, the United States embraced racial egalitarianism, rhetorically and legally. As many blacks have moved into the middle class, the narrative of what it means to be black and American is being reworked. In a community that has de-scribed itself as more alike than different, the upward mobility of some by its very na-ture predicts social tension. It is this particular tension that has captured the imagination of so many whites. African Americans, and, in this case, black students, sometimes negatively sanction each other as they achieve success differentially within predominantly white organizations. The sanctions—regardless of the politics of those making the observations—are real and often include epithets like "Oreo" and "sellout" for a range of behavior from socializing with whites to pursuing goals not deemed relevant to the black community by those making the judgment. Uneven mobility among blacks—greater opportunities for some, fewer for others—occurs against a backdrop of competing desires. These desires include the desire for accep-tance by one's own group and by the larger group, the desire to celebrate the changes in race relations that have occurred in the United States, and the desire for acknowl-edgment of all of the ways that the country remains racially stagnant.

Expanding Fordham and Ogbu's observations of oppositional culture, Richard L. Zweigenhaft and G. William Domhoff offer an additional explanation of this tension:

[O]ppositional cultural frame of reference refers to those beliefs and prac-tices that protect black people's sense of personal identity against the insults and humiliations of the dominant white group. Since these beliefs and prac-tices provide a defense against racism, they necessarily exclude certain white cultural traits as inappropriate, and some of these oppositional prac-tices help to keep whites at a distance when need be. Thus, the oppositional

cultural frame of reference creates unconventional ways of moving, gestur-
ing, talking, and thinking that are viewed as irrational and frightening by
whites. Ironically, the oppositional culture created as a protection against
white racism is then used as the primary rationalization by whites for rejecting black people—they allegedly lack the proper "culture," so they can't be
trusted. (1991:152)

Despite social tensions among blacks, however, the overarching historical theme of
racial penalty in this country is *not* one in which blacks penalize each other. Rather it
is one in which African Americans have been penalized *by* white institutions and
white individuals for being black. Furthermore, Americans of African descent have
had much less control than European Americans (unless they appear phenotypically
white and choose to identify as such) over who labels them, how they are labeled, and
what the consequences will be for their racial label.

College campuses, however, are unique spaces, in that the authority for declaring
authenticity and measuring racial identity within the black student community is in
the hands of black students. Unlike their fellow white students—or the larger white-
dominated society outside the college walls—black students often measure race loyalty (regularly abbreviated as race) by behavior or association and less by color or
ancestry. (These issues of racial authenticity and the performance of identity—that
is, identity based on behavior—are explored at greater length in chapter 8.)

Subordinate communities often find ways of reclaiming power, especially the
power to name self and others. And yet, naming, affiliating, or categorizing of oneself
and others is always a negotiation, dependent upon ascribed, acquired, and behavioral characteristics as well as the status one holds in the group and the larger society.
If one has higher status, more people will accept one's labeling of a situation, self, or
another than if one has lower status.

As in many subordinate communities, the camaraderie forged within Northwestern's black student community was, in part, a byproduct of an occasionally hostile,
and usually disinterested, larger environment. Participating in and shoring up the
boundaries of a subordinate racial community felt compulsory for many students. As
Charles Willie has observed, "When group survival is threatened, then group identity is emphasized. Robert Park recognized . . . 'The loyalties that bind together the
members of . . . the clan . . . are in direct proportion to the intensity of the fears and
hatreds with which they view their enemies and rivals'" (1981: 18–19). Alumni recall
the social "endogamy" that operated in reaction to being or feeling excluded by majority students socially or from university organizations. This subcultural constraint,
several respondents reported, presented them with confusing either/or options.

Katrina, the daughter of a physician and a graduate of the all-white college
preparatory track in her public high school, remembers the experience of trying to

"break into" the black community. After having passed up the summer program for black students, she made her first friendships on campus with whites:

> I kind of came in breaking the rules. . . . [I]t was a good year before I made some really good [black] friends. . . . I had pockets of friends from different groups, but I was never in a group. I was concerned about it, because I didn't understand the rules. . . . [The black students] might have perceived me as being an Oreo or really stuck up or something. I'm not really sure . . . it was something that really bothered me because I couldn't figure out how to fit in. It was such a tight [black] community. (Katrina, NU '81)

Although Katrina was more comfortable with whites than many of her fellow black Wildcats, Robert confirms Katrina's interpretation of events when he explains that fitting in was not only the anxious purview of the affluent, like Katrina, who had grown up in integrated settings. "I think you do expend an awful lot of energy just trying to find a way to fit in . . . [even] if you come from the kind of [predominantly black, working-class, urban] background that I come from" (Robert, NU '80). From Robert's point of view, coming to NU from a background like Katrina's was an advantage. But perhaps neither Katrina nor Robert pinpointed the cause of their unease. Both Robert and Katrina lost their mothers before they got to college. One can easily imagine that having suffered the premature death of a parent must have at least contributed another dimension to the insecurity of entering a new environment.

Deborah is an example of yet another variety of black student at NU. She grew up in a predominantly black environment but went to a predominantly white high school. For her, the adjustment to Northwestern was not a cultural shock, and she does not describe the social isolation from the group to which Tatum refers and which left Robert anxious at the start of his first year and Katrina ill at ease for all four years.[7]

While the self-protective expectations of NU's black student subculture are revealed by students like Katrina, who did not conform to them, even those like Robert, who seemed to thrive within its limits, admit its rigidity. Robert remembers that "[about] 90 percent of the black people were part of the black campus community." I asked about the other 10 percent. "Everyone talked about them, *everyone*. They were snubbed" (Robert, NU '80).

Although black alumni do not remember European-American students reaching out to them, neither do they characterize themselves as sitting idly by waiting for the outstretched hand of fellow white students. African-American students nurtured a world unto themselves, where rejection by white students and by the black students who socialized with them was rationalized, and that, in turn, justified their own separatism. For the most part, alumni describe themselves as independent and those black students who stood outside the group as sellouts.

The situation in which one was either in or out of the black community encouraged black students, in Deborah's words, to "choose sides" (NU '75).[8] Kathy expands the metaphor of "choosing sides" to include "no middle ground":

> Going to a white institution, there's no middle ground. . . . You either become more aware of who you are because of how you're treated, and you realize that you stand out and that you're [frequently] the only one, or you blend in more and try to conform to Caucasians. At least at Northwestern [that's how] it was. . . . [A]t Northwestern, there's an extreme: you were fully black and you hated white people—and I did feel like that when I was there—or you didn't deal with black people and you hung out with the white people. (Kathy, NU '85)

If there was no middle ground, most did choose sides. For some, choosing "the black side" was the path of least resistance. Jerry (NU '84) admits that his choice not to date across racial groups was based less on a political commitment to the group or lack of interest than it was on a desire to avoid "all the headaches and pressure and people talking about you. Who needs that?"

Those few alumni who seemed to straddle both worlds with success had already proven their allegiance to the in-group. Robert explains his own anxieties and the train of thought that led to conquering them:

> [M]y freshman year it was not the thing to go to University Theater productions. And there was a group of us who were really into music and theater. And so freshman year I never went to a university Theater production—didn't go to [the annual variety show], didn't go to concerts or anything. But sophomore year I started saying [to myself], "Well, wait a minute, I *know* I'm black. I went to a black high school, I lived in a black neighborhood all my life. I really can do this without risking my blackness." (Robert, NU '80)

While Robert does not consider himself to have been one of the people who successfully lived in both worlds (he graduated, he says, "not knowing many white people"), he did participate in organizations outside of the black student community. Still, it took him a year to work up the courage and a convincing explanation to others before he was able to do so.

WHAT'S RACE(ISM) GOT TO DO WITH IT?

My campus Big Sister [said] . . . "If you think that there's not gonna be racism here, you're wrong. But that doesn't necessarily mean that professors aren't gonna call on you in class." And I thought, "Wow! Why is she telling us this? . . . [T]hat couldn't be true, you know; [this was] the dawn of a new day . . . we were a generation away from all that."

—Ruth, Northwestern '81

Even among alumni who say they enjoyed the experience and would repeat it without hesitation, a resigned tone characterizes many of their voices when they describe the racial climate on campus. William is one such alumnus. He described an incident in which he returned to the place where he stored his bicycle one evening and found "NIGGER" written in peanut butter on the wall above the space where he stored it. After telling the story, he shrugged and added, "But I mean, you know, what the heck, they were as good as can be expected at a place like Northwestern, almost right in the middle of the North Shore . . ." (William, NU '88). His tone is resigned as he observes that expressions of racism are as likely to occur in wealthy white suburbs as in working–class white urban neighborhoods.

William's experience of being made to feel unwelcome in his own space comes up again and again a decade later in the work of Feagin, Vera, and Imani (1996). They observe,

> For these African Americans . . . [t]he experiential reality of *space* is at the heart of interpersonal ties and is a critical element of U.S. racial relations. The experience of the space around oneself, between oneself and others, and within oneself is deeply meaningful in many cultures. . . . The concept of *racialized* space encompasses a number of cultural biases that help define specific areas as "white" or as "for all," with the consequent feelings of not belonging or belonging. (Feagin et al. 1996: 16)

Sue saw a gendered breakdown when it came to expressions of racism: "[I]t seems like, if anything, the sororities are just snobs . . . they just stay away from you. But the fraternities, especially when they get drunk, [the] guys, they shout at you" (Sue, NU '81). Harold echoes the observations of William and Sue that bigoted attitudes did not have to be vocalized to become visible: "The whites with more education and background . . . don't think that blacks are equal and may not like you. But [they] don't feel it's incumbent upon them to say it, and may not even openly think it. But subconsciously, the attitudes are there. I think there's probably a lot of that going on, but I never had anyone run up to me and call me a nigger" (Harold, NU '81).

The fact that there was so little blending of communities exacerbated the problem of deciphering interactions with white professors and students. While alumni remember plenty of experiences that were clear evidence of bigotry, many experiences were difficult to interpret but left students feeling badly.

Because NU was at least a formally integrated campus, several students experienced dissonance between the informal reality of separate spheres and the formal ideal of a campus without racial boundaries. This made it difficult to distinguish racism from miscommunication or ignorance, and it undermined the ability of many alumni to trust both blacks and whites.

On several occasions, Northwestern respondents would label incidents or behaviors as racism with definitive statements, only to retract them later in the interview. Their thoughts on what caused or contributed to their problems in college have not clarified with time. Terry's situation is a case in point:

> My senior year was really kind of stressful. . . . I . . . was working from 5 A.M. to 12 [noon]; I was the president of the sorority; the dean of pledges in the sorority; [and] I was a resident assistant, which meant that I had a lot of paperwork to do for the university. . . . Blacks were not really accepted at all in the residential college that I was a resident assistant in, and—I think it was just really more like a game . . . —[the women in the dorm] were really silly. They would do things like put pennies in my door so I couldn't open it [and] I would be locked in . . . all kinds of childish-type pranks. . . . They were just a group of really spoiled kids and it was pretty much, "Okay, we don't have anything else to do; let's bother Terry." . . . I can't really say that it was primarily a race factor because I think they just wanted to bother the R.A., but I think I tended to get a little bit more harassed than some of the others. (Terry, NU '78)

Terry stands out as an example of someone uncomfortable with the possibility that the mistreatment she experienced had a racial basis. Although Fordham's work on black students in the 1990s looks at the high school level, the parallels are instructive. "In the school context [the black student] is committed to the meritocratic ideals promulgated there and does not want to have any information around her that might suggest that what she has learned, and perhaps is learning, in school is misleading or even untrue" (1993: 17).

Students of today's generation are caught between the negative situations in which they find themselves, although improved from previous decades, and the heightened rhetoric of equality in the post–Civil Rights Movement era that surrounds them. Ruth confesses her early expectation and subsequent disappointment: "[When my campus Big Sister warned us about racism,] I thought, 'It couldn't be that bad; she's just making an issue.' But then you notice subtle things. You know, [for example, my academic] counselor being so very, very disinterested in me. . . . The issues were all so much more subtle . . . hard to react to" (Ruth, NU '81). Without being sure where the blame lay, alumni had difficulty deciphering and confronting racial bigotry, and their memories are bound up with dashed expectations.

BEING A ONE AND ONLY

I was an engineering major in the early part of my career at Northwestern, and in many instances I was the only black student in a class. And that isolation took a tremendous toll.

—*Adam, Northwestern '74*

Coping organizations like formal and informal study groups meant a great deal to the African Americans who went through Northwestern. Those students who did not have these social and academic groups or organizations on which to rely were less likely to want to repeat their experience.

Especially for the few African Americans who were students of math and science, finding oneself as the only one in a class or laboratory section was a regular phenomenon.

[A]s a math major, I wasn't sitting in a class with a lot of black people. . . . I had always been in that separate world where I still had to rely on . . . other white people. 'Cause there was no way I was going to turn to a black kid in my Calculus B-40 class and go, "What, bro?" [There just weren't any black people in those classes;] I mean, Calculus B-40 had five people in it, one of which was me. (John, NU '79)

John faced a great deal of difficulty completing his degree. And while it would over-simplify his story to say that his lack of an academic support network was the sole reason for problems that he faced, it clearly contributed to them. H. K. Suen (1983) and Loo and Rolison (1986) found "that dropout behavior for white students was related to academic variables but that dropout behavior among blacks was due to feelings of 'social estrangement' as well as academic factors" (Loo & Rolison 1986: 60). Those students who came to college with rigorous high school training and success were able to spend more time on personal development and less time anxious about remaining afloat academically.

Many of the alumni depended on study groups composed of other blacks upon whom they were not embarrassed to rely. Tatum talks about the risks of not having a support system:

When one is faced with what Chester Pierce calls the "mundane extreme environmental stress" of racism, in adolescence or in adulthood, the ability to see oneself as part of a larger group from which one can draw support is an important coping strategy. Individuals who do not have such a strategy available to them because they do not experience a shared identity with at least some subset of their racial group are at risk for considerable social isolation. (1997: 70)

The majority of engineering students, for example, talk about the importance of the black engineering association to getting them through the major. Henry is representative of this group. He was one of the founding members of the NSBE (Northwestern Society of Black Engineers). "Peers can help you [study and focus]. Junior year we got a black engineering society together. . . . That created a networking and peer structure that enabled us to help ourselves. . . . [W]e studied together, and that helped me do better. Junior year, I started off bad, but then we formed the black engineers society, and things just [got better] from there" (Henry, NU '77). Henry speaks of NSBE the way loyal fraternity members speak about their house. In fact, he often uses the language of Greek-letter organizations to emphasize his loyalty to fellow engineers.

Some engineering majors—ten and fifteen years later—still seem to be recovering from the demanding experience of the major. Martin is a good example from this group. He went through the engineering program in the early 1970s, but became inactive in the various study organizations that existed during his junior and senior years. It was also during these years that he lived in a single dormitory room and failed a couple of his classes. After describing his NU experience as one of "pure tribulation," it is not surprising that he is among those alumni who would not repeat their experience at NU. Similarly, Henry ('77) said that his NU experience could be easily "summed up in one word: pain." And yet, his group of formally organized engineering friends acted as a support group, taking him through the most difficult third and fourth years in the major. In contrast to Martin, Henry speaks of NU with such good feeling that he acts as an informal recruiter for the school.

Study groups, or the lack thereof, became a mechanism by which one swam or sank. In addition, being a one and only emphasized the ways in which black students were not like majority students. Tatum explains, "The parts of our identity that *do* capture our attention are those that other people notice, and that reflect back to us. The aspect of identity that is the target of others' attention, and subsequently of our own, often is that which sets us apart as exception or 'other' in their eyes" (1997: 21). Black students on white campuses, then, and those who are alone in their classes, find themselves struggling with the material and preoccupied with that which makes them different. And their difference, as the work of Claude Steele has shown, is not neutral. Since all blacks are stereotyped as "not smart," those who are facing academic challenges have their concentration undermined simply because they are acutely aware of the stereotype. Even more so, the very isolation of those who are facing academic challenges without the benefit of a tutor, study group, or help from professors, renders them even more vulnerable to the effects of these stereotypes.

This said, it is just as important to recognize how profoundly being a "one and only" or one of a few can also become integrated into one's identity. A few individuals thrive when they are "on the spot" or exposed at all times. Jennifer, a Northwestern alumna, explains that she benefited from this explicit difference between black and white colleges:

> My personality is such that I tend to shine brightly in smaller circles, and at a black school I probably would have been intimidated by the large number of confident black students, to be honest. At Northwestern, I stood out naturally because I'm black. And then I might have stood out more because I'm confident and responsible and all that other stuff. So I had a natural edge that I'm gonna stand out more just based on who I am. At a black school, I probably am a little bit afraid that I would have had to work harder to stand out in a sea of black people. [Had I gone to a black college] I think that I would not have had the opportunities that I got at Northwestern. (Jennifer, NU '88)

Being a minority has become such a part of Jennifer's identity that to be in the majority would not be "natural." Similar to those who thrive because they are "big fishes in small ponds," part of Jennifer's confidence, she believes, is based on her racial uniqueness.

MENTORS, ADVISORS, PROFESSORS, CLASSES

The majority of NU alumni report that several of their professors were helpful, interested, and kind. Many professors were remembered as individuals who were friendly and supportive and whose classes alumni enjoyed. But few names came up repeatedly, and only one was considered to be a true mentor. A handful of white faculty, administrators, and students stand out for their honesty, compassion, and clear allegiance to black students. [9] A dean in the Technological Institute stood out for many black students:

> You know, this is really sad, but if I think back, I can't really think of any faculty or administrative people outside of the black community that were very supportive. . . . Oh, there was one guy who was the associate to the dean. He worked at Tech. He was very supportive of black [students]. Every black person who had problems at Tech would go to him. . . . He was the one [white] person who I would say was positive and supportive at Northwestern. (Kathy, NU '85)

Despite an initial positive response to the question of white faculty, eventually most alumni describe unpleasant experiences.

Other alumni describe Northwestern as a place that did not pamper students. A few students say they were glad that NU, as William ('88) put it, "didn't hold you by the hand." Most others, however, say they do not understand why the college admitted them and then acted with apparent disinterest. Alumni often came from homes where their parents had been intimately involved in their lives before college. When they left home for school, the freedom—combined with feeling like there was no adult they could turn to—felt overwhelming:

> [I]n high school, it wasn't just my parents making sure I did what I was supposed to do with regard to my classwork. There were also teachers. . . . Once I got [to Northwestern], it was: "If you don't do it, we don't care" . . . [M]y parents [had been] fairly strict with me and it used to amaze me that [once I got to Northwestern] I could be out and not have to have called back home. . . . Here it is past eleven, twelve o'clock at night and I don't have to call in and my mother doesn't know where I am. And it's just an amazing feeling and if you don't know how to handle it, it really screws you up. (Barbara, NU '81)

The parents of several black alumni had not gone to college or had not had similar career aspirations to those of their children. For these students in particular, advising played an important role in putting them on equal footing with their more privileged counterparts. "My girlfriend and I were talking," Ruth tells me. "She and I had the same advisor the first year. . . . I just remember the advisor being totally indifferent to me. She was just not helpful. . . . [S]omeone should be there to help you get an idea of what it is that you want to do" (Ruth, NU '81). The lack of good advising left many feeling out of control with regard to grades, what to major in, and postcollege planning. Lou begins his critique by describing what he wished he'd found:

> [I'm] talking about people that want to see you grow. Being with people that want to see you do well. In most cases, I don't think that was here. Either they don't care or, for the most part, they don't want to see you do well. So I think that [support] was absent here. One of the things that black kids need so much is—and I would say even black professionals, from when you're born to, most likely, when you die—some type of guidance from somebody that's already been there. If they could tell you, "Hey, these are the glories and these are the alligators that you can expect." I guess the current word today for that is mentoring, that exchange of information, making you feel—because so much of what we do is based upon how we feel about ourselves—making you feel like you're somebody, you know. And then maybe you begin to act like you're somebody and do things like you're somebody. So me and my wife, we decided that we wanted to send our kids in their undergraduate years, hopefully, to black colleges. (Lou, NU '83)

Michael T. Nettles has done research on factors that contribute to achievement among black students, and his work buttresses the importance of Lou's wish that faculty knew him as a student:

For Black students, frequent faculty contact outside the classroom, noncon-
servative teaching styles, and faculty with a high degree of satisfaction contribute to higher college grade-point averages. . . . Black students are less
likely than white students to experience faculty in frequent contact with
students outside the classroom. They are also less likely to have highly satisfied faculty members. (1991: 89)

In hindsight, students who went through the rigorous program of Northwestern's Technological Institute, especially, wonder why advisors—both white and
black—did not reach out to students they knew were failing.

> [My advisors] . . . knew that I was having problems 'cause I was [at the Black
> House for study sessions] every day. So they knew that I was going under. . . .
> But for the people that didn't come in, they never called them up on the
> phone and said, "Are you having problems?" or really reach[ed] out. . . . The
> people that are flunking out, they don't get the attention that they need . . .
> they never call the people that they know are in trouble. . . . At least so they
> know . . . you're really actually there for them. (Cheryl, NU '87)

Engineering majors were not alone in voicing their frustrations. Complaints about
advising, specifically, were not limited to any one discipline. They came from alumni
who had majored in journalism, economics, and math.

Indeed, first-generation college students in particular are not even sure that they
have a right to obtain guidance and advice, as this passing comment from Murray
demonstrates: "Coming there as a black student from another state, I'm not sure if
there was really anyone there looking out to help, just in little ways. Now maybe
that's an unfair request. Maybe there's no one there looking out for anyone" (Murray, NU '76). While careful and committed advising has always been more difficult
to provide in the university versus the small college setting, it is a crucial aspect of a
successful college career for many students.

> [During my junior year] I discovered that I was great with applied [math] but
> not as good with theory. So at that point, I had an ultimatum. [The univer-
> sity said,] "We will allow you to make the move to the College of Arts and
> Sciences" [out of the Technological Institute]. So I had to take Spanish, to
> [show] evidence [of] my proficiency in a foreign language so that I could, in
> fact, graduate from CAS. I'd taken Spanish I and I did okay; I got a C. And
> then, during the summer, I was taking Spanish II and III. Well . . . I didn't
> have any support from the professor. And it was the first time I'd ever felt
> that the university had set me up. At the Technological Institute, I just felt
> that people would bend over backward . . . to help you finish that program
> successfully. On the other hand, with CAS, the dean . . . had set me up for a

failure. The professor during the summer program was aware of my ultimatum—pass or get out—and he would not make himself available. I would have appointments with him that he wouldn't show up for; he just flat out wouldn't make himself available. And somewhere along the way, it became apparent that he knew of my situation, and at that point I could only conclude that he was trying to fail me. And so when I did not pass, I was academically dismissed—not because of my overall GPA, but—because I could not [transfer into CAS] without taking Spanish. And [the professor] wrote a report saying that he did not think I could ever pass. (Adam, NU '74)

Institutionalized racism often characterizes the atmospheres of larger schools that are both more bureaucratic and impersonal in their staffing and in their interactions with students who are regularly seen as clients. As Feagin and colleagues observe, "The institutionalization of racism means that certain hurtful ways of acting have become more or less routinized, as taken-for-granted actions linked to traditional ways of doing a professor's job" (1996: 94). When all is said and done, institutionalized racism is carried out by individuals. Advisors may end up making decisions that are difficult for students to live with, but such decisions are reconcilable when it is clear to students that they are made with care and attention.

While some students complained about the lack of academic advising, others voiced their concern for students who had not made it through Northwestern. It was rare, they said, but occasionally they felt the university was guilty of exploiting black students who were academically and emotionally unprepared for the college. Murray recounts having to look out for another black student who was brought in as an athlete, and, even after suffering a nervous breakdown from being unable to handle the combined pressure of athletics and academics, the school readmitted him the next fall:

I remember walking around with him to his room [at the beginning of fall semester senior year] and just saying to myself, "This guy's going to be back in a hospital." And sure enough, in three days he was gone. That was tragic. It's the first time that had ever happened [to me], and I never could quite understand what was wrong with him and why. He felt a lot of pressure on him, and I think it was because he didn't have the background that I, and some of the other guys, had. And he came to Northwestern and he just didn't have the training for the academic side, and he wasn't the type to just say, "Well, I'm going to work hard or just let it go." I think it just really ate at him, you know: "Why can't I do this?!" And it was really kind of the end of him. That was a sad story, 'cause he did end up killing himself, unfortunately. I remember that as being the beginning of senior year, which was kind of rough. (Murray, NU '76)

Obviously, this experience had a profound impact on Murray whose retelling of it was quiet and without drama. This was not unusual: when respondents told me about other black students who had not finished college or had nervous breakdowns, their voices grew quiet and resigned.

When alumni remember encountering unfairness in the classroom, it felt to many like betrayal. Although Henry is an avid supporter of his alma mater and would encourage other young black students to attend Northwestern, he says that he will never forget this frustrating experience with one white professor:

> There was one other black guy in the course. We studied together all the time. And we did well because we both knew something and together, we knew it all. We would study together, going over things in the Black House. . . . We were going over the communications devices—televisions, radios, and I knew how the television worked: from the receiver, the RF section, all the way down to the luminous and chromos. My friend couldn't get it, and I was going through it. I felt so confident. We got into the test and it was open book. We had [had] some people's old tests, and we had worked the problems that were on the old tests. So I *knew* I was getting an A. I had everything right. By test time, I knew that I was getting at least a B out of this course and my buddy may be getting an A because he did a little better on the midterms than I did. Well, [at the end of the semester] the professor tells me that he can't find my final. He looks in his book and tells me, "You got a C." I said, "How is that possible?" I wanted to look at my final and he says, "I can't find your final." He says, "It's gotta be here somewhere. But don't worry, you got a C; you did real well and your buddy got a B." That just floored me. I'll never forget that. (Henry, NU '77)

Jane's remembrance captures another negative experience with a European-American professor:

> We had to do a major project, and . . . [m]y group was an all-black group, but it was a large class so of course you had mostly all-white groups. And we wanted to do a project on discos—studying the ethos of discos at a point when discos were beginning to become the big thing—a multimillion-dollar industry. And we were studying the marketing and packaging. And [the professor] refused to allow us to do that project because he said discos were dead and it made absolutely no sense for us to do it. Well, the white students could do whatever they wanted. They could study the ethos of airports and things of that nature that would require them to leave the campus. . . . [But] his attitude was basically that you people just want to go and have fun and I'm not

going to let you do it. But with the white students, [they got to study] whatever project they chose—and there were fun projects that they chose to do: the ethos of country clubs [and of] tennis [clubs]. (Jane, NU '79)

An explanation for these experiences might not fall on the shoulders of racism; they may, in fact, only demonstrate unclear expectations or professional sloppiness. Of course, professional sloppiness takes on an air of agency and mean-spiritedness when the relationship is with those who not only have less authority and power vis-à-vis the professor but in the institution overall. These are situations, however, in which professors could have either challenged the prevailing norms (that is, that they have final say without explanation or apology) and in so doing contributed to making the campus environment feel welcoming and fair. For students already feeling embattled, experiences like these confirmed feelings of being under siege or humiliated and sometimes led to bitterness.

THE SPECIAL CASE OF BLACK FACULTY AND STAFF

Each [black faculty member and black student] is buoyed and embittered by the realization . . . that . . . salvation for the black in an integrated world really amounts [to] . . . nothing more than the salvation one might be expected to have in a segregated world: a younger black and an older black approach each other and say, in effect, "Who are you?" and, in Du Boisian eloquence, "How does it feel to be a problem?"

—Gerald Early

All my black faculty were supportive.

—Lou, Northwestern '75

Despite the cases described above, white faculty were not the only people with whom black students had negative experiences. In fact, both positive and negative experiences with black faculty and staff are conveyed with more passion. Black professors, even more so than most staff because of the regularity of interaction and their clear authority over students, readily stand in as objects of parental transference onto which students alternately project feelings of affection, anger, or frustration. Alternatively, and perhaps even additionally, black students maintain a skeptical distance from black faculty, even as they yearn for role models, guidance, approval, and agreement. Some black students are suspicious that the black person who has become a professor must also have given up pieces of his or her cultural identity in exchange for success.

Gerald Early deconstructs his emotions after a run-in with black students on the campus of Washington University in St. Louis, where he teaches literature:

the black professor and the black student at the white university sometimes confront each other over a gulf of precarious achievement and prosaic aspiration which can be bridged neither by revelation nor, certainly, by relief, but, in fact, only by a kind of pressurized disappointment: each thinking that he deserves a better fate than the other he faces while understanding that he has no fate other than what he faces in this moment. (1994: xv)[10]

Terry's story, below, offers a student's perspective on a disappointing experience with a particular black professor. Because the stories alumni tell about professors are among the more narrative and lengthy, Terry's will stand as an example of the emotional investment black students sometimes have in black faculty. Taking the time to introduce herself—politically, culturally, and economically—Terry begins:

[By senior year] I was no longer afraid. By that time, I was wearing this like really short afro, and I had turned really militant. My outfit consisted of earth shoes, overall pants, T-shirts, and caps. And I was just really into the Black House and really into "We're not going to let them turn back the hands of time!" 'Cause I was with the group that was marching on [the Administration Building . . . chanting,] "Stop investing in South Africa!" And we tried to hunt down a couple of [trustees] . . . it was, it was really stressful. I think I took on too much work; I was really stressed out. (Terry, NU '79)

After situating herself, Terry told me about the experience with her professor:

I was taking an independent study class for four credit hours, and two were coming from [one] department . . . and two were coming from [a class in another department]. And I was originally going to work with two other students, a white guy and a white girl. And [the professor] wanted us to do our project on . . . a group of elderly white women on Sheridan Road and North Shore. . . . I didn't want to do that. I said, "No" . . . I've gotten all these statistical classes, all this background in how to do a study. I want to do it on . . . the South Side of Chicago. You had to submit a proposal for what you were going to do, and that's what I wanted to do. And now that I look back on it again, [the professor] was right, to a certain extent. It was very difficult to get the train to the South Side of Chicago and to meet with [all of these people]. . . . But that is really what I wanted to do. He told me that if I did my paper on that subject matter, that he was going to fail me. . . . [We] never really hit it off. . . . At that point, I was very vocal, and I just couldn't keep my mouth shut, if it was something that I totally disagreed with. But his whole attitude was: "Everybody's entitled to their own . . . opinion." . . . His thing was, he was raising his child to know that he was a child growing up in America, not that he was a black child. . . . If someone asked [his son], "What are you?" he would say, "I'm a little boy." He wouldn't say, "I'm a little black boy." And I thought that that was just absolutely terrible! . . . [T]he thing that he was most proud of was being asked to go down to like Standard Oil and these other large corporations and speak to second- and third-generation [descendants of immigrants]. . . . And I was like, "Yes, that's something good to do, but you need to go back on the west side, from where you came from, and tell some of those [black kids] over there how you got a . . . scholarship to [a Big Ten university] and what you're doing now. Because that's equally as important as what you're doing. And how can you just totally lose your identity now that you're here and they've tenured you? . . . You can still stand up for who you are and still be black!" And we really got into it. And he said, "I'm going to fail you." And I was like, "I'm going to give you a paper that you will not be able to put an F on.". . . My political science professor gave me two As. . . . All the girls in my sorority helped me put it together. I had graphs; it was an excellent paper. It was about seventy-five pages. He had to give me two Ds. There was no way he could fail me. I didn't miss any classes, you know—the whole thing. But he told me that if it was left up to him, I would never go to law school. [*SSW: Oh, my goodness.*] Yes, he did, because [he said,] "You have the wrong type of attitude. . . . It's people like you, who are so militant, that make it bad for the rest of us." It was really bitter. That was really like a very, very stressful type of situation. . . . But it really, really hurt me, because I'm like, Is he here to help us, or is he here to harm us? And I knew that those really could not have been his true motives. . . . Something would not let me believe that. So then I felt maybe it was just something personal between him and I. (Terry, NU '79)

In this retelling, the stories of the assignment and the conversations beyond the assignment are overlapping and become conflated. It is difficult to pull apart which conversation happened when. With Early's observations as backdrop, it becomes obvious that black professors not only stand in as parent figures but shoulder many students' hopes and dreams. What is clear is that this professor became symbolic. Against such emotionally freighted expectations, black professors are bound to disappoint students—regardless of their politics or accessibility. And students may experience the disappointment as dramatically as a family betrayal.

If family betrayal is one script, family support and solidarity is another. Most of the experiences black alumni recall having with black faculty and staff were positive. "My involvement with [the Black House and the African American Studies Program] made the cost of Northwestern and that experience worth all the money. Although otherwise, if I hadn't gotten involved, I'd say Northwestern was a waste of money"

(Cheryl, NU '87). This sentiment continued to be shared by black students in college well after my interviewees. In *Battling Bias*, Sidel quotes one of her respondents as expressing a similar sentiment:

> Francesca Wilkinson, a senior at Tufts University, is an African-American woman from Washington, D.C. . . . . "It's good I came here, 'cause Tufts has to deal with my voice. The only reason I'm happy here is that I've made them deal with my voice. I can say what I need to say." When I ask if Tufts should perhaps get some credit for creating the kind of atmosphere that enables her to say what she needs to say, she responds, "I don't want to give Tufts credit for this. I give credit to Peace and Justice Studies, to the African-American Center, to the Women's Center, and to the Tufts Lesbian, Gay, Bisexual Committee. It was through these groups that I've gotten encouragement, support, and role models that I've needed to make it here." (1994: 110)

The staff members who ran the Black House are remembered by many Northwestern alumni as integral to their survival. One student remembers an African-American dean whose office was located there:

> I remember [during freshman orientation] they were always saying, "We're available if you ever need any help." We were so big-headed at the time . . . we were the top stuff in high school. And during the prefreshman summer program, upper-class students were saying, "Remember the address of the Black House." To have people throwing themselves at us, it seemed weird. And I remember [the dean I would encounter later] just emphasizing, "You're going to need us," as if there's something horrible waiting. . . . I always thought of myself as pretty independent. I never needed anybody. And I remember one day, going to him, just walking in and chatting because I was "in the vicinity." . . . But I remember confessing that "I've been working my ass off, harder than I ever worked before, and it doesn't seem like it matters . . ." And I just remember being so confused. How can you work so hard and have to always work so hard, and I just couldn't seem to make it with the grades? And he just . . . laughed and we had a real heart-to-heart talk about how difficult it is to try to make it in that type of setting. And for the first time I realized that I did need someone. I did need to know that there's someone who cared about me and who I could open up to. (Lynn, NU '83)

It was not only staff members who reached out to and impressed students; it was faculty as well:

I had an extraordinarily good experience with [Professor Z]. All of his classes. He was one of those professors, the kind of professor that I . . . knew in my mind existed, and [the kind] I found when I went to Howard [for graduate school]. But he was also a black professor, he really took a lot of extra time with the students. [He] really tried to push you the extra mile, just in terms of what the learning experience was. . . . [H]e tried to supplement what it was that you were learning in his classes with what was going on in your life and the environment as a whole. . . . He really was one of those type of professors that would really go to bat for the students. (Terry, NU '79)

TO REPEAT OR NOT TO REPEAT: THE BLACK COLLEGE FORGONE

I probably would have given much more consideration to a black college and may have gone to one . . . the environment and the surroundings may have been a richer experience. . . . [Y]our experience is always limited at a white university, I think, as a minority student.

—Harold, Northwestern '81

The answer to my question—*If you had the chance to do it all again, would you attend the same school?*—encapsulated the college experience for both Northwestern and Howard alumni. Previous research on this question (Gurin and Epps 1975, Fleming 1984, Allen et al. 1991) led me to expect that black students at white colleges would almost universally characterize the college experience as alienating. Much of this research, however, does not take into account the extent to which absolute numbers of black students—a critical mass—can affect student experience more decisively than high or low proportions of fellow black students.

The comparatively substantial population of black students, Northwestern alumni recall, allowed them to take advantage of the university without the alienation that many black students at smaller, more isolated, or simply less diverse schools often experienced. Northwestern alumni remember providing each other with opportunities for social life, acting as a mutual support system, and nurturing a community that acted as a buffer against a larger campus community that was often considered hostile or uninterested.

The experiences of Northwestern alumni suggest that a college or university setting with a numerically substantial minority population of students and faculty—that is, many individuals even if the proportion is low—may provide black students with advantages. Smaller colleges, isolated from urban settings with low absolute numbers—regardless of their percentage of the student body—, or large universities, with low numbers and correspondingly low percentages, may not.

Although a slim majority of the Northwestern alumni interviewed said they would repeat their decision to attend NU—seventeen of twenty-nine—at least a third of that group added tentative or lukewarm qualifiers to their answers. Ruth is representative: "On balance, my experience there was probably more positive than negative. And I don't think that any other choice would have necessarily been any better" (Ruth, NU '81). Most of the alumni who said they would do it all again factored in the prestige and opportunities that their Northwestern degrees have garnered. Jennifer explains: "Going to Northwestern, or any prestigious school, I think you receive opportunities that going to a Michigan State you wouldn't" (Jennifer, NU '88).

Forty percent of Northwestern alumni said either that they would not repeat the experience or they refused to answer the question directly, conveying how difficult it would be to make such a decision since they had made very good friends despite their unhappiness with NU. Robert explains: "I think I subjected myself to a lot of pain and agony that I didn't necessarily have to be subjected to had I gone to an historically black school. . . . But I say that hesitantly because my friends are . . . people whose friendship I can't imagine being without right now" (Robert, NU '80). The idealization of the historically black college is common among black Northwestern alumni. It figures prominently in discussions of comfort, confidence, and choices Wildcats would make for their own children.

Those alumni who would choose not to repeat their Northwestern experience are aware of studies that link self-esteem with a nurturing learning environment. Jill tries to put her finger on it: "It's kind of hard to explain, but [she sighs] . . . I don't know. The students that graduate from black universities seem to have a higher confidence level" (Jill, NU '80). Many alumni have made the connection between the underrepresentation of blacks in the student body, as a topic of course offerings, and among faculty and administrative staff and their own lack of confidence as adults. Lou's rhetorical questions are evidence that his observation reaches beyond college:

> [Northwestern] doesn't reinforce [building a positive self-image] for blacks. It may reinforce that for whites, but it's not something that is done for blacks. I mean the society really doesn't do that itself. If you read books, you read about [people like] Newton and . . . you begin to wonder: Where do I fit into this picture here, you know? Where are my contributions made? Where was my history at in the development of this total thing? (Lou, NU '83)

Lou's questions are a layman's version of what George Herbert Mead (1934) and Herbert Blumer (1998) argue: people build their sense of self from a process of interacting with and interdependence on others. Individuals are, psychologists have agreed, primarily relational (Gurin and Epps 1975, Chodorow 1989, Jack 1991, Brown and Gilligan 1992). That is to say, we build our images of self and possibility from those around us.

While a positive self-image is not necessarily based on being surrounded by others of the same racial group, racial categories in the United States correspond to a social hierarchy. Simply, they are not apolitical markers like eye or hair color. If one's race or gender group has lower status in the society and that group's history is erased, misrepresented, or underrepresented in the scholarship that everyone learns, it will be difficult to conceive of oneself as a full member of the community in which such scholarship is taught. As labeling theorists have long observed, if those around you do not see you as an achiever or potential achiever, it becomes difficult to convince yourself that you and people like you have been, are, and will be achievers. Many of the Howard respondents, as we shall see in the next chapter, remark on the importance of seeing black people all around them in their classrooms, in the administration, at the podium, and in their texts, not just at one lunch table.

Among the twelve respondents who would not repeat their Northwestern experience, three-quarters said they would consider a black college. And all of them wonder if they lost something valuable by choosing a predominantly white college. In this group, women who note frustrating social lives pinpoint the problem as a dearth of dating opportunities: "I can remember many days when we would sit around the dorm saying, 'What would it be like if we had gone to Howard? Would we have more boyfriends? Would we have dates?' But we'd made a decision not to, and you just live with what you had to live with" (Lynn, NU '83). The black women respondents in Willie and McCord's study and in Fleming's study note similar frustrations. In fact, the numbers of black men attending college dropped steadily until 1985 and then began to recover. After 1995, their numbers remained lower than those of black women. For the alumnae in my study (at Northwestern in the late 1960s through the late 1980s), their numbers were always greater than the number of men on campus (Sidel 1994: 42). The percentages of black men and black women *graduating* from college, however, have been very close. In the late 1980s, the numbers of black women enrolled in college began to climb, while men's numbers stayed the same. By the mid-1990s, there were roughly 45,000 more black women enrolled in college than black men, and that statistic began to have long-term effects as black women have edged out black men in completing college and beyond from 1996 on.[11] Even as black women begin to attend college in higher numbers, dogged by vestiges of patriarchy and white supremacy, they often have less fruitful college experiences: "Prospective Black female undergraduates face an especially difficult decision. At traditionally Black schools, males clearly fare better than females. But at predominantly white universities, the occupational aspirations of Black females appear to be more susceptible to depression from racism and sexism than do the goals of Black males" (Smith 1991: 125).

Those women who *would* go to Northwestern again are less likely to mention the lack of dating opportunities as a disappointment than their sisters who would forfeit the Northwestern opportunity. Women who would do it all again were more likely to offer the amorphous complaint that there was neither enough "spirit" within the larger campus community nor "cohesion" within the black community: "I guess I expected it to be more of an intellectual environment. . . . Socially, I expected more cohesiveness and more camaraderie. And there really wasn't a lot of that. . . . It's very cliquish here and I just expected [that people would] grow out of that situation when I left high school" (Sue, NU '82). In contrast, men who complained about unsatisfying social lives characterized the situation as a lack of camaraderie rather than a dearth of dating opportunities:

> [A]t this point, I would strongly consider going to . . . an all-black college . . . just the camaraderie would be greater than it was at Northwestern. . . . I would constantly think . . . "What would it have been like to have gone to an all-black school?" Because they have things that are kind of enduring. Although, as I said, some friendships have endured, because we were a small number and we were close. . . . You keep thinking that you missed something. . . . I always thought I missed something. I enjoyed Northwestern; I learned a lot of stuff; but I missed something. (Luke, NU '72).

The black men who attended white colleges in Fleming's study note similar feelings of social frustration.

In fact, among Northwestern alumni, there is the perception that a greater sense of community exists on the archetypal black college campus and that less energy is spent fighting the "battle" of countering the racism that one will have to face after leaving college. Paul explains why he would consider a black college today:

> I would take a real close look at [a historically black college]. Because, like I say, what I know now about self-esteem and self-image, I would be in the mode of building that. . . . I don't need to struggle that much, you know. A certain price, I don't want to pay. So if I can get what I want somewhere else, then maybe I can delay that fight until the inevitable; maybe I can put on more armor before I get into that battle. (Paul, NU '75)

The second-guessing their choice of college that my question raised for black Wildcats takes place even among the majority of those who said they would repeat the experience. While the sense of community, including the close friendships that have endured, is remembered fondly by most, it coexists with the belief that a black college campus would have offered (and may offer to future generations) greater racial comfort and less emotional energy spent metabolizing racism.

PRESTIGE AND TRAINING: THE COST IS COMFORT

*I would really be torn. . . . And now, I would really, really have
to think about it. Because I don't regret going to a prestigious
university like that, but I think I could have had more fun and
gotten more out of a black university. You know, the prestige
may not be there, but I think that I would probably be a better
person overall, you know?*

—*Jill, Northwestern '80*

The black college continues to be invoked when alumni describe their postcollege
lives as well. Many former Wildcats see their college experience as a trade-off. Only
four of thirty NU respondents insisted that they "love" their alma mater. Although
Henry (NU, '77) is one of them, remember that "pain" is the first word that rolls off
his tongue when asked for the one word that describes his college experience:

Henry: I loved my experience here. The good and the bad parts. I wouldn't
change it because of what I am now. I have no regrets.

Sarah Willie: When I asked you to choose one word to describe your college
experience, you chose *pain*. That might strike some people as contradictory
with what you've just said.

Henry: Right, but discipline is so important for all people to experience, because that's what gives you the ability to accomplish things. Without discipline, there can be no order.

For Henry, pain is a function of perseverance and discipline. And, having crossed
what he calls "the burning sands" of the requirements for majoring in engineering,
he will not forfeit his seat at the table where white Northwestern graduates also sit. "I
went to [the university president's] house for cocktails. . . . [He] knows me by first
name. . . . [T]he director of alumni relations . . . know[s] me. . . . All my friends are
[black] alumni; they're my extended family. I talk to an alumnus of Northwestern
University almost every day" (Henry, NU '77). Both Henry's social life and his status in the world are bound up with Northwestern.

While the place that NU has in Henry's life may be unusually central, he is not
alone in his perception of what a Northwestern degree means to others, especially in
the Midwest. "I was at an all-white university . . . prestigious, top twenty . . . so I was
getting a legitimate piece of paper" (Deborah, NU '75). Like the other seventeen
Northwestern alumni who said that they would repeat their experience, Henry and
Deborah emphasize the prestige they perceive an NU degree holds in the majority

world: "[T]hat Northwestern name means more. The value of that piece of paper is more in the business world. Those are the . . . facts" (Henry, NU '77).

Mary's postcollege experience buttresses Henry's and Deborah's claims that those whites with whom they are all likely to come into contact are duly impressed by an African American with a Northwestern degree:

> My boss [a Caucasian male and upper-level manager of the Fortune 500 company where I work] is just infatuated with my education. He tells people all the time . . . about [my Northwestern degree]. It's really a feather in my hat, more so than I ever thought it would be. . . . It's turned out that it's had a big effect on how well my career has gone since then. So that's really the most noteworthy thing about it for me. . . . The big thing that it affects now is how other people look at me and how wonderful they think it is. (Mary, NU '77)

Lynn adds to this chorus: "When I change jobs or I meet people, they hear 'Northwestern' and they go, 'Wow!' . . . [For] anyone who's never gone to it, it's almost like a sorority or a fraternity" (Lynn, NU '83). Alumni also say that surprise accompanies the acclaim they receive, revealing—they believe—continued prejudice. In any event, however, Northwestern's influence is as great and its stature as secure in the Chicago area as those of Ivy League colleges in the Northeast.

Even though Terry says she would go to Northwestern again, she is typical in her observation that a historically black college might have given her added confidence. She tentatively explains the trade-off of confidence for prestige in a manner common to other alumni in the study:

> I think NU helped more than it hurt. The only thing that I think that it possibly could have hurt is that . . . there really wasn't that cohesiveness in terms of the entire environment; everything was very competitive; and it was either you [succeed in it] or you don't. Depending on how you were raised as a person . . . you would really lose a lot of self-confidence at NU. . . . [O]n the other hand, if you were able to survive that kind of . . . sterile type of environment, then you would do okay. Where I think what really, really helped is that it's a good university with a prestigious name. And if you graduate from Northwestern, people think you really have something on the ball. (Terry, NU '78)

Terry's statement epitomizes the feelings of many NU alums. Indeed, frustration with Northwestern's competitive atmosphere and sterile environment are always mentioned in tandem with the esteem colleagues in the work world bestow upon those with a Northwestern degree.

The question with which many black Northwestern graduates continue to wrestle is whether the esteem they have garnered in the workplace is sufficient compensation for so much unhappiness during college. For Lynn, the trade-off may not have been worth it. I asked her, "Would you choose NU again, knowing what you know now?"

> God that's a tough one. I'm tempted to say I'd go to Howard. But I see Northwestern as kind of like a . . . microcosm of the real world. It truly represents a lot of the things that are tough about life: competition, unfairness, some happiness in the midst of all that. It is a *lot* like the real world. It's almost too much like the real world for an eighteen- or nineteen-year-old. . . . I just kind of wish it [had been] more fun. . . . I'm not that much of an advocate for the expensive schools. I think that you can find true happiness at [the] University of Illinois. I'm not into names, as much as I [used to be]. (Lynn, NU '83)

Below, Steve also articulates a clear trade-off between comfort and prestige. However, unlike Luke or Terry, who, as we've seen, wonder what they might have missed at a black college, Steve's choice of the school with the most potential for his career reflected his primary priority, outweighing the possible pleasurable aspects of college. When asked what he would say to a young person from a background like his, making the decision where to attend college, Steve advised,

> You need to realize that college is a sacrificing time. So you need to go to a school that'll give you two things: one, a school with the best reputation you can get into; and two, you need to learn how to manipulate white folks. You see, social graces for black folks are different than for white folks. You need to learn those things. For example, [Fortune 500 corporations are] looking for people who dress and talk conservative—in other words, Republicans. The sad thing is they'll never be comfortable with black people. So you choose a school with a sizable black population. That's why you don't go to Brigham Young. And you choose your education first. You want a piece of paper that will allow you to say what you have to say. (Steve, NU '79)

Steve is attentive to the necessity of attending a university with a critical mass of African Americans. That said, Steve's priority is graduating from "a school with the best reputation." He also believes that an undergraduate education at a predominantly black school will not garner the prestige or the social and behavioral lessons crucial to success in the white-dominated postcollege work world. Deborah concurs: "[At Northwestern,] I learned . . . that I could use what they offered as a stepping stone to get the things I wanted. . . . I learned how to manage the professors—white and black—and I just learned how to work the system" (Deborah, NU '75).

The alumni who would return to Northwestern all over again count the prestige that they now receive in the world of work as one of their primary considerations. Many of my respondents wondered whether the decision to attend a predominantly white school meant the forfeiture of romance, friendship, or a sense of comfort. At the same time, they are also sure that the salaries, promotions, and regard they receive from colleagues and supervisors is the result of having chosen, and been chosen by, a school of Northwestern's caliber and reputation.

ANALYSIS AND SUMMARY

*[Where is the] avenue that will enable us all to live peaceably and
fully within one political community without having to renounce
the specificity that ultimately makes our lives worth living[?]*
                                                    —*Darrell Moore*

Allen and his colleagues observe, "Of all problems faced by Black students on white campuses, those arising from isolation, alienation, and lack of support seem to be most serious" (1991: 5). On the other hand, Fleming (1984) implies that the responsibility of students for their college experience is equal to that of faculty. I would argue that faculty and administrators shoulder a larger responsibility for reaching out to and working with students, especially students who are different from them or who are members of an out-group on campus. "I look at [negative relationships with faculty] as a two-way street. I can't put the blame—total blame [on them]. I have to take responsibility for some of the things that have occurred. But then, some things are insidious, a little difficult to detect . . . those underlying currents may [have been] at work" (Lou, NU '75). Although relationships between students and their professors are interactive, professors are vested with the authority that the university bestows upon them and therefore have responsibilities that students do not have. It is our responsibility to facilitate classroom interaction, to set the tone in classroom discussions, to advise, confront, draw boundaries, and show confidence in and applaud our students when necessary. Furthermore, professors who are white have both formal authority and informal status over their black students. This demands additional self-awareness on the part of white faculty to anticipate what Freud would have called transference on the part of students, the developmental rebellions of late adolescence, and the centrality of students' formation of personal identity. Racial identity issues sometimes are worked out with professors standing in for students' parents. What faculty must keep in mind, and this applies to white professors in particular, is that they occupy the dominant-group positions in at least one but often two and three domains compared to their students. The responsibility for reaching out, therefore, and for conducting oneself in a compassionate and mature manner remain crucial.

Despite their frustrations with the campus community, black alumni cherish fond memories of NU. They talk of college parties, kinship with other black students, and friendships that have endured into adulthood. The Wildcats I spoke with recall with admiration those black students before them who fought difficult battles over racial issues with the administration during the late 1960s and early 1970s. "I was fortunate enough to meet and become close with an extraordinary group of black people," says William (NU '88). "I'll always be grateful." They list black alumni who have participated in their weddings and who continue to be central, if not daily, parts of their lives. In part because I formed hypotheses starting from my own experience and based on research on schools with smaller proportions or numbers of black students, I had not expected that the majority of students would repeat their experience at NU.[12]

Because so many alumni mention the importance of friendships with other black students, it is probable that the numerically larger minority community attenuates alienation on a predominantly white campus. Rosabeth Moss Kanter's work on minorities and majorities in corporate settings supports this conclusion. Her scholarship demonstrates the importance of a critical mass (15 percent or more) bringing a skewed group (under 15 percent) into greater social balance (1977: 209).[13] Kanter suggests that minorities are much more likely to be treated as stereotypes and to have a more difficult time in any organization when their numbers are below a certain threshold. "At least there were six hundred of us, and you could find a niche in six hundred people" (Mary, NU '77). Again, the work of Charles Willie and fellow researchers would suggest that the good feelings black students at Northwestern had were related to the critical mass formed by their numbers on campus and not necessarily by their proportion of the student body.[14] A larger minority community clearly compensates for, even if it fails to fully ameliorate, the degree of alienation that minority students experience from campus life.[15]

Of the twelve who would not go to NU again, eight say they would attend an HBCU. Of those seventeen who would repeat their Northwestern experience, nine say they wonder what a black school would have been like, and they consider historically black colleges very important. Seventeen out of the twenty-nine Northwestern alumni, then, are not only curious about, but laudatory of, historically black schools. A third of those even mention sending their children to black colleges. These findings reveal the importance of being in a place that promotes a positive racial identity. They also explain the faint praise that so many alumni use to describe their experiences.

Despite their characterization of the campus as "two separate worlds," the Northwestern alumni with whom I spoke argued that they learned the invaluable lesson of getting along with white people in a white-dominated world. Considering the fact that almost all of the African Americans I interviewed who attended NU attest to the separateness of black students' and white students' social lives, this would seem to be a contradiction. The classroom and the administrative apparatus of the school were dominated by European Americans, however, and learning to operate in such an organization is a repeated justification for having gone to a prestigious predominantly white college. John sheds some light. He considers living in a predominantly white world "a game that gets played from nine to five" (John, NU '79). Success, he adds, comes with knowing how and when to stop playing the game. Although Willa Mae Hemmons questions this assertion—"even on the white campus, the black college student is segregated" (1982: 397)—most NU respondents mentioned their ability to relate to white people, if only when they had to, as a consequence of attending a predominantly white school.[16]

While some, like Shelby Steele (1989), have argued that black students arrive at NU *choosing* to participate in the tight-knit black community, most eighteen-year-olds are busy coping with the changes of a new community, being away from home, and fitting into established social patterns on campus. To reach out to white students or white faculty was a risk, and this seems to have been especially true during the late 1960s and the early 1970s. Whether the attempt failed or succeeded, the cost was high and sometimes entailed rejection by the black community. Acceptance by those in the white community also carried with it the potential of undermining good relations with the black community. Certainly a rebuffed attempt could carry a double cost and, even today, is often enough to send one back to the acceptance of the smaller community. As Feagin and colleagues remind us:

> To be recognized as valued members of the campus community is important to all groups of students, but especially to those who are underrepresented on a large campus. . . . The omission of African American students from the yearbook [at a state university as late as the mid-1990s] suggests a general lack of recognition of the black presence and achievements on campus and hints at the low status the whites who prepared the yearbook apparently granted to black students. This kind of neglect encourages black students to congregate in their own groups and plan their own activities and publications, a reaction that may bring white condemnation of this black "segregation." (1996: 54)

The overwhelming majority of black Northwestern alumni talk about their friendships with other blacks who went through college with them. Black friends and black organizations offered invaluable support. Such support was, however, a double-edged sword: at times restrictive, at others liberating. Robert puts it well: "When you travel in that black community, as I did by and large, it cements you in such way that you don't get to know other people that well" (Robert, NU '80). Students need help to see options beyond the established social patterns that they often enter when they first matriculate.

The blacks who attended Northwestern sound wistful when they talk about forfeited expectations. I heard it when they expressed the belief that their relationships with other students and professors might have been deeper and more meaningful at a black college, or when they remember their excitement before arriving that college would not be like the racially cordoned-off spaces of high school. It comes across when they admit their disappointment at discovering that university life was not the cosmopolitan and racially integrated organization they had hoped for. These beliefs—that college would truly be a place of higher learning, garnering wisdom, above the pettiness and hurtful racism beyond its walls—reveals an ideal of academic life that has disappointed many American students of African descent in particular and students of color in general. In the ambivalence about returning to Northwestern that more than a third of my respondents voiced lies a quiet accusation of a promise unfulfilled.

Like most colleges across the country, Northwestern's campus changed a great deal from the late 1960s to the late 1980s. And, although the times changed, some striking themes run throughout alumni stories. Black students led a particularly separate social life from their white peers. Nonetheless, high absolute numbers allowed African-American students opportunities for social life. The black student community acted as a support system for its members and created a buffer against a larger campus community that was often considered hostile or uninterested.

Most black Wildcats would repeat their decision to attend NU if they could do it again, and most recall strong friendships that have lasted into adulthood. Experiencing racism was a nearly universal aspect of the college experience for NU alumni, although the incidents they describe were not constant and usually not overwhelming, and did not leave most black Wildcats feeling bitter in subsequent years. These findings offer a complicated picture of marginality, clearly an aspect that sociologists who pioneered discussions of marginality missed. In a society with increasing layers of stratification, contradictory class locations (Wright 1985)—a concept well articulated with the phrase "double consciousness" a century ago by DuBois—also exist. This was the situation of many NU respondents, marginal to the greater campus community, central to the black community, doubly conscious today of their status as Northwestern alumni and the cost of being such.

Faculty and staff mentors and advisors were especially helpful to student success, and black faculty in particular are noted for their support. Since it is clear that faculty and staff play important roles in the lives of students, the burden of helping students appreciate how to learn from and become friends with each other falls on the shoulders of such people.

Finally, the majority of alumni note the prestige that having gone to Northwestern has garnered for their careers. And while prestige is some compensation, so many black students should not have to continue to suffer through ambivalent college experiences where they feel largely unsupported as a trade-off for respect and higher salaries after college.

Some scholars criticize the presence of black Greek-letter organizations, black cultural houses, and black studies programs at predominantly white colleges and universities (Bloom 1987, S. Steele 1990, D'Souza 1991, Schlesinger 1998). They argue that these organizations encourage divisiveness, and they point to examples of racial polarization on campuses as evidence. What is clear is that the presence of several hundred other black students at Northwestern allowed the college experience to be less painful, less isolated, less depressing than it would otherwise have been had the number of black students been much smaller. Indeed, as Jackson and Swan note, "The more that Black male students attending white schools feel themselves to be a part of campus life, the better they will perform" (1991: 137).

What the data indicate unequivocally is that the presence of black Greek-letter organizations, a drama club, student newspaper, and choir provided forums in which to make friends and celebrate creativity and cultural specificity without enduring disinterest or rebuff by white organizations. What is also clear is that Northwestern's undergraduate campus was sometimes racially tense, usually racially polarized, and almost always racially separated. It is not at all clear that the cause of such division rests on the existence of black student organizations. Nor is it clear that the majority of black students simply wanted it that way. And finally—and perhaps most seriously—it is not clear what role the administration played in promoting or discouraging the development of these two campuses within a campus. What is clear is that its leadership role in promoting a multiracial community is conspicuously absent in the memories of the African Americans whom I interviewed.

THE EBONY TOWER: LIFE AT HOWARD

*Some students may choose a Negro college as a way of modulat-
ing and lubricating their escape from the segregated past to the
partially integrated future. Others will choose a Negro college
because they expect to move only from the old-style segregation
that characterizes so many aspects of contemporary Negro life
and see no reason to face the intellectual and social strains of an
integrated institution.*

—Christopher Jencks and David Riesman

Despite the changes brought about by the Civil Rights Movement, fifty years after
Brown v. Board of Education, historically black colleges and universities have not disappeared, as some predicted they would. However, they do struggle. In 1954, over 90
percent of black students were educated at historically black colleges and universities.
Although that figure today is between 15 and 20 percent, more than one hundred historically black colleges and universities are still thriving.

Black schools have always had a mission greater than the one all but dismissed as
passé by Jencks and Riesman in the epigraph above. HBCUs, despite their imperfec-
tions, continue to reach out to those who have been educationally disadvantaged,
they have mastered the art of remedial training (Monro 1978), and they have been
able to offer students collective success experiences crucial to healthy identity formation (Gurin and Epps 1975).[1] They offer a setting in which black consciousness and
expressions of racial pride are not met with threats or hostility, and demonstrate one
of the few organizational arenas of racial integration at the level of their faculties
(Fleming 1984). And finally, having never been racially exclusive, black colleges are a
milieu in which increasing numbers of white Americans have the invaluable opportunity to be in the racial minority (Willie 1987). At the same time, HBCUs struggle
with black nationalism as it plays itself out in campus politics and intellectual paradigms with new calls for racial exclusivity. One can always get a heated discussion

going on a black campus as to whether the goals of the institution and its students should be different from those of the historically white institutions and the students they serve.

I examine several themes in this chapter, including the importance of positive group identity, the influence of teachers who assume students can learn, and the presence of other blacks who are evidence of such confidence. On the other hand, Howard alumni voice a series of complaints that are interrelated, including the "nightmare" of everything from course registration to obtaining housing assignments and financial aid distribution to inflexible university policies and the alleged negative attitude of the employees who carry them out. This tension within the campus walls between students and staff is still further connected to a tension beyond its walls—the difficult relationship between the university, especially its students, and the poor black neighborhood that surrounds the school. Alumni describe this relationship as strained at best and confrontational at worst. As late as the close of the 1970s, interviewees continued to notice the institution's inheritance of colorism. This was reflected in what several described as a light-skinned student body that several assume was the deliberate creation of the admissions office. I have added colorism to the issues having to do with class because they seem to overlap in the descriptions given by respondents. And finally, remembering the "sense of ease," "comfort," "diversity of black people," and "inspiration" that they experienced "up on the yard," Howard alumni claim, with only two exceptions, that they would attend Howard again had they the chance. Despite the trade-off some feel they made by going to an HBCU—which garnered them less prestige in the majority society than they would have had if they had gone to a traditionally white college or university—they say they were provided with a clearer sense of their own mission. Its alumni contend that Howard is not *just any* HBCU; it is well known and highly respected both within the black community and within the country's dominant group. Below, African-American alumni of Howard offer memories of their undergraduate years.

WHO THEY WERE AND WHY THEY WENT

The majority of HU alumni with whom I spoke—seventeen out of twenty-five—evaluated themselves as good or very good students in high school.[2] The people who spoke to me chose to go to Howard from among a variety of highly selective schools for their postsecondary education. Alumni reported turning down offers of admission to such renowned, selective colleges as Columbia, Cornell, Harvard, Swarthmore, Brown, Stanford, Georgetown, and Boston University in order to attend Howard.

With such heady choices, a handful of their parents, some remember, were anxious about their children's choice of a black college when they had the opportunity to attend a predominantly white one. Betsy's story is representative of the three Howard students who mention this parental concern: "My father—it's interesting—at first he had misgivings about me going to a black university. He didn't think that it was a wise choice. I guess it's that whole thing about, you know, once you get out in the work world, you might not have the same level of acceptance among employers—that type of thing. But I went on anyway" (Betsy, HU '74). It's worth noting that parents of two Northwestern alumni interviewed had remarked to my interviewees that they were pleased their children chose Northwestern over an HBCU. Sue, a Northwestern alumna, told me about her parents' concerns:

> I did actually consider going to Howard, and I never applied. I let my parents talk me out of it. I grew up in a black neighborhood and I'd gone to an all-black school for a couple of years before they came in with a clean sweep and integrated everybody. [My parents] said, "Yes, [a black college] would be a more supportive atmosphere and it would be less of an adjustment for you, but you're going to have to make the adjustment one of these days. You're not always going to live in an all-black neighborhood, and you may as well learn how to deal with other people now while you're young and flexible." Yeah, I let them talk me out of it. I sometimes wonder if I should have let them talk me out of it. (Sue, NU '82).[3]

It is not surprising that parents would be concerned that their children get the best advantage in a competitive and still racist society. But respondents, and their parents, had different strategies for success.

Only seven out of twenty-six Howard alumni said that they were sure they wanted to attend an HBCU when they began the college-selection process. It was the financial aid package that the school offered—rather than the type of college—that was an important, if not the deciding factor, for most Howard alumni. More than half of respondents mention the financial aid package as an important variable in their being able to attend or continue at Howard. Fred's statement is representative: "[My parents] were real supportive. Obviously, since we weren't incredibly well-off, they were making sure I focused on all the financial aid packages" (Fred, HU '87).

Hannah remembers how much she was looking forward to attending Howard. What she had heard about it beforehand influenced how she thought it would influence her own sense of self: "One thing that really impressed me about Howard is . . . they have like the highest concentration of black Ph.D.s in the world, and I thought about the role models of having educated black people teach me. And I was really looking forward to that, 'cause all my teachers—although I went to black schools—all of them [had been] white, except for two" (Hannah, HU '88).

POSITIVE GROUP STATUS

*It was eye-opening because you were able to find out a lot about
yourself as a racial group. . . . I was able to learn so much about
us as a people.*

—*Stan, Howard '86*

Graduates typically talked about their professors' high and explicit expectations of them, and being inspired by seeing other black students pursuing difficult majors and professional careers. Once they saw themselves as worthy of those expectations and capable of those same pursuits, alumni appear to have become conscious of the extent to which the dominant society (as represented by television programming and a few high school teachers) had previously led them to limit their own expectations. The high expectations of faculty, combined with seeing black peers succeed, appears to have crystallized a sense of group identity among African Americans who attended Howard. Alumni remember having the sense that they belonged to a group with common interests, a common history, similar goals for the future, and the common enemy of racism. The majority of alumni with whom I spoke mentioned the importance of achieving this positive sense of group identity.

Many persons may assume that African Americans who chose to attend an HBCU must already possess a clear racial identity or unequivocal racial pride, reasoning that such students must all be aware of their African-American heritage before college in order to have chosen a black school.[4] However, most of the HU alumni with whom I spoke came to college without such positive group association, or with a tentative one at best. How is this the case? First, as Helms points out, the racial category to which a person belongs is not synonymous with his or her racial identity. "Many people erroneously use a person's racial categorization (e.g. Black versus White) to mean racial identity. However, the term "racial identity" actually refers to a sense of group or collective identity based on one's *perception* that he or she shares a common racial heritage with a particular racial group" (1993: 3). My respondents were aware of their racial categorization, and most even appreciated their shared heritage with other African Americans. At the same time, their awareness of the actual history of that heritage before attending college was lacking.

Second, black people are usually portrayed negatively by most forms of publicly decimated media. The majority of representations of African Americans exclude positive, healthy, and creative adaptations to life circumstance. Such representations are powerful in that they are nearly omnipresent. Even African Americans whose families give them the tools to fight such representations are unable to escape being influenced by them. One of the things that the positive support from faculty clearly gave the men and women with whom I spoke was a sense that they were a *group*.

I define *group* as a collection of people who share a common sense of history, common experiences in the present, including some common cultural experiences and goals, and an understanding of a common enemy that attempts to thwart achievement of those goals. I use *group* and *group consciousness* the way that Max Weber uses *class* and Georg Lukacs elaborates upon Weber's concept with *class consciousness*.[5] In Weber's scholarship, *class* captures the unresolved tension between class as an objective fact with material consequences (the way Karl Marx wrote about it) and as a characteristic about which one can be aware, and, if not transcend, manipulate. I expand Lukacs's concept of class consciousness to refer to a group whose situation lies between those of a caste and a class; group members have some potential for mobility while continuing to suffer stigma.

In the testimonies of Howard alumni, one can hear positive identification with the subdominant group, African Americans, and with the aspirations and values typically associated with the dominant group, European Americans. For HU alumni, success—defined as occupational prestige and high income—is not incongruent or incompatible with being African American. Remembering her days on campus, Betsy focuses on the unusual opportunity to associate being African American with being successful when she arrived at Howard.

> It was exciting from the very first day, just seeing that many black people who were . . . having a common goal there. . . . [A]t Howard, it seems, everybody was kind of there for the same reason, and that was exciting. . . . [The] beautiful thing about Howard that I enjoyed so much is that the people were really more positive—black people were more positive than I had ever experienced. And it was that they were there because of the dream or vision, and they were about doing that. And if you didn't seem to fit in to what they were doing, they didn't even bother with you about it. It wasn't a lot of cattiness or gossip or anything like that, 'cause people were really busy trying to work their own agendas. (Betsy, HU '74)

Despite Betsy's claim, several HU alumni described the university as cliquish and gossipy. This is not necessarily inconsistent with Betsy's characterization of the campus climate; her recollection serves as a measure of her sense of comfort, her own experience, and perhaps her desire to portray the institution she loves in the best light.

Although George was among those Howard alumni who described the campus social scene as cliquish, he explains how and why such an atmosphere at Howard was more palatable than at the prestigious small liberal arts college in New England where he spent his freshman year:

Howard has its cliquish elements and everything, but at least people could find people who they wanted to hang around with. At [the small New England college where I started], you hung with the blacks 'cause you were black. And there are so few of you, you couldn't choose—you couldn't make your choice on geographic distinctions, or common interests, or anything. It's like, well, you're black; [let's hang]. (George, HU '85)

George's reminiscence about his year spent at a predominantly white college recalls the sense of sticking together against an outside enemy. A critical mass of students can alleviate that sense of isolation.

The importance of needing and developing a positive group identity emerges from several things—the realization of previous ignorance about one's history, the desire to believe oneself equal to white citizens in the present, and the wish to leave a legacy to others in the future. As Randall Robinson has argued in *The Debt: What America Owes Blacks* (2000), naming the places where the contributions of African Americans have been omitted in the national narrative indicts our national institutions and finds them culpable of endorsing a profoundly erroneous, simplistic, and disingenuous history. Again and again, Howard alumni reveal their shock at discovering their legitimate claim to a dignified history, as well as their sense of betrayal by white primary and secondary school teachers who, they feel, should have been part of making this discovery happen earlier.

Maybe it was something about hearing that Pushkin was black. Maybe it's just something that boosts you up subconsciously because all your life you're not hearing anything about black people except for that one . . . black history month. So everybody knows [Martin Luther] King but there's so many other things that you just didn't know—like the inventor of the stoplight was black, or the first cowboys were black; [not knowing] all this kind of stuff probably does something to you. 'Cause all the while they're telling you [that] you have no history, and all of sudden you find out [you do, and] you're like, "You liar!" So you just [start] to look at everybody like, "You've been lying to me all this time." (Lucy, attended HU in the '80s without graduating)

These discoveries encourage a more holistic understanding of the past, but they also contradict the negative expectations of the present and the future, as Peter explains: "I think for a black person to go to a black school, . . . it's very important because you learn about yourself, who you are in society, and you're around your own people and you see what they can do. Because so often we're not told what we can do. We're only told what we cannot do" (Peter, HU '84).

Students inspired each other simply by their collective presence:

[G]rowing up in an all-black situation, black people tend to tease one another: you know, "[Are you going to Howard because you] want to party?"

and all of that. And [before I got there] I'm thinking, "Oh, God, I don't know if I can take that." You hear all these ideas, "Oh, white people are more serious." But, you know, it didn't turn out to be the case. Because I went to . . . an all-white summer school, and people are basically the same. So one thing that really surprised me freshman year was just the fact that these people [at Howard] are serious . . . like seriously competing for grades, and [internships], and the mentality was different. . . . Whereas the [white] people that were in my classes [during summer school] . . . were like, "Oh, I'm just going to hang out [after college], work in a diner, whatever." (Hannah, HU '88)

Hannah explains how she was introduced to the possibility that the stereotypes were wrong: the black people she knew were in fact more serious about school and career than many of the white people that she knew. Karl echoes this observation, telling me how seeing black students around him who were making the most of their academic experiences, working hard, and succeeding provided him with a positive institutional context:

It was a lot of people who had a lot of dreams and high hopes, and it was great just being there because there were so many people in higher education. There were black dentists, black doctors, all types of health majors, business, engineering, you name it. Graduate [students in] programs like you're in: psychology, sociology [getting their] master's degrees, Ph.D.s. All these intelligent [people] out there just really striving. It was great. It was very motivating, and that was exactly what I needed. I felt like that really influenced me to do well, because all my classmates were jammin'! (Karl, HU '89)

The fact that even African Americans who had grown up in predominantly black settings did not have a more balanced sense of the past, present, and future is both surprising and disheartening. Their experience reveals the extent to which being excluded from one group contributes to feeling good about another aspect of their identity. In this case, coming from a group without class privilege plays a role in undermining positive racial group identity. This warped view of past, present, and future also reveals how profoundly people of African ancestry are mis- and underrepresented in school curricula, television programming, and in every arena of American life except entertainment and professional sports.

Being cut off from a fuller sense of one's cultural humanity was not, however, limited to alumni from poor or working-class families. Many respondents from middle-class and affluent backgrounds had a sense of what was achievable occupationally, but had little sense of a positive history of the African Americans who had come before them. Matthew, for example, a middle-class student who grew up in a predominantly white environment, feels his eyes were opened at Howard:

> I can't think of [just] one thing that made college [great] for me except to think back and to think, "If I hadn't gone [to Howard, I wonder] what kind of person I'd be?" And I just look at my poor little brothers and hopefully they'll come around . . . there are just so many things that you cannot know until you meet a variety of black people from different backgrounds. . . . To think that now I know myself a lot better. I know my people. I know what some of us have to go through. I was just the most naive person ever going. I tell my little brothers now, you know, they think they're so worldly and they're not. They grew up in [a small town in the Midwest] and one of them goes to [a big Southeastern university] and I mean, he'll never see a lot of the things that I saw. And I think that I'm a lot better a person for it. (Matthew, HU '86)

Finally, one aspect of a definitive group identity is the recognition that one belongs to a group because of a common enemy. In this case, the common enemy is racism. Below, Harriet makes a compelling case for recognizing shared group status. In addition, she defends the right (she might say necessity) of people who are disadvantaged by racism in the larger national society to absent themselves during college from the relentless racism in American life.

> I think of all these white students who go to white colleges or universities who don't encounter any kind of racism; why aren't people telling them, "That's not the real world"? No one's looking down their noses at them or saying they're inferior, giving them funny looks or anything. But if we're in an atmosphere where no one's looking down at us, then "That's not the real world." [It's not the real world] because we're not encountering racism?! It's almost like they're saying . . . "[Y]ou *have* to encounter racism in order to be a normal individual." How come we can't [be normal individuals] . . . going to this black school, [be] just as happy as those white students who aren't encountering any problems? It's the same thing for us . . . why go and endure it? . . . Don't get me wrong; I'm not saying that we, as blacks, don't have to deal with racism; but at least [not] in college. 'Cause you're going to deal with it on your job or wherever. At least in college, give the people that: to just have four years of a happy experience without that stuff being thrown in their faces. . . . I'm sorry, I get really emotional when I talk about it. (Harriet, HU '86)

Harriet's voice takes on a pleading quality to it at the end, incredulous that people can't see the importance and health of an atmosphere free of racism. Forming positive visions of the past, present, and future is closely linked with forming positive visions of one's own worth, abilities, and potential.

THE GIFT OF ANONYMITY AND INDIVIDUALITY

What the Howard environment allowed was the development of a common identity coupled with more room for individuality. At Howard, because black students were in the overwhelming majority, they were allowed the freedom to simply be students. (The freedom to be anonymous is noted in other work about black college students, including that of Willie and McCord, Exum, and George Napper.) The size of the black student population offered both the comfort of anonymity and the celebration of particularity that a small, mostly white college (and to a lesser extent Northwestern) could not provide. Fred, who went to predominantly white secondary and postgraduate schools, explains:

> You stand out in a predominantly white school. For good or for bad, you're going to stand out solely 'cause you're black. And then you have to prove that "I'm good." . . . [I]f I'm going to stand out, let [the fact that I'm good] be the reason I stand out. At Howard, it would have been very easy, if you chose to, to just kind of be anonymous and blend in. Nobody's staring at you when you walk down the campus. . . . Howard is a cosmopolitan type of place. I mean it's right in the middle of northwest D.C. . . . I remember feeling at ease. It wasn't that strange sense of tension that I had known the twelve years before or the four years after . . . where somebody's staring. . . . It was just a sense of calm. I really felt at ease. (Fred, HU '87)

This relief of anonymity is echoed by George, who also spent the final years of his secondary education at a predominantly white high school.

> In those days, very, very few people went to college from a black high school [in my town]. And [the teachers at the school where I transferred to] wanted to see if the quality of the education in the black high school was equal to that of a white high school. So I was kind of like under a microscope, and they were watching to see if I could do it. And I did it. . . . [But] I knew, after those two years at [a public magnet high school] that I didn't want to go to a white school for college. (Joseph, HU '71)

Alumni who have spent time in predominantly white settings explain that in the majority-black setting, one not only has the opportunity to "blend in," but one also has "a chance to have a broader base of friends and contacts" (Martin, HU '73). Joseph (HU, '71) echoes Martin's observation:

Sarah Willie: Were there any experiences that really stand out for you during your college experience?

Joseph: Freedom. Freedom and a sense of belonging, you know. A sense of achievement, that we actually achieved something. . . . [There was] a common bond . . . a common enemy. So [among today's youth] you have all this fragmentation, you know; you can't get it together. Then, everybody was focused. We knew what to do, knew what had to be done, and everybody was right on it.

The concept of group identity itself can discourage us from appreciating the differences among individuals who fall within it. Having a group identity, however, is not understood as being the same. Respondents frequently countered the accusation that going to an HBCU necessarily circumscribed their ability to relate to a range of people. Ann speaks to this question most succinctly: "A lot of times people say . . . 'You're going to a black school and that's not how the world is . . . the real world is not all black; you're gonna have to deal with white people.' But if you go to Howard and you deal with *those* black people, you can deal anywhere, baby!" (Ann, HU '79). Matthew elaborates on Howard's diversity:

I mean, I never knew that black people came in some of these shades and colors and hairstyles. . . . Black people from every socioeconomic background, from the very rich to the dirt poor. . . . And you think of the history behind it and all the prominent people who have gone to the university and what they've made of themselves and how you've become part of that legacy by also going to that school! I don't know, to look back on it, it's really awesome to be part of that and to know that . . . I'm not like a weirdo because I didn't grow up in the inner city. (Matthew, HU '86)

Kirstin, on the other hand, speaks for the minority of HU graduates who suspect that different communication styles and different kinds of cultural knowledge are both absent and needed at HBCUs. Describing how the predominantly white workplace has been her proving ground, she intersperses her story with some tentative observations: "I figure there are some things you just don't always learn in the educational process [at a black school]." Kirstin goes on to describe her own situation:

[F]or fifteen years I worked in low-middle management. And there were a lot of times I clashed with my managers or coworkers. But I think not understanding the politics, or how to play politics in corporate America, how not to get so emotional about things [was the problem]. . . . There were many things that were impersonal kinds of things that I took very personally. And I think—maybe I'm wrong, but—I see it as something that blacks in general have a problem with. Because when I talk to other people that I know who work at corporate jobs, they feel pretty much the same way I do. We can sit down on any given day, and we all start talking about similar kinds of experiences . . . that we felt were negatives or how our bosses related to us.

So I think there's still a sufficient amount of racism around that we do need [help] to develop skills in how to cope, how to talk to whites without really sacrificing—I don't mean being [an Uncle] Tom or even eating crow. [But] you can learn skills that help you effectively get around some of that stuff without sacrificing your personal integrity. . . . I don't know how to deal with it or how you learn those things. (Kirstin, HU '74)

Kirstin understands, after graduating from college, that there are things she could do differently to help her reach her goals without participating in her own oppression or clashing with others.

THE IMPORTANCE OF TRUSTWORTHY PROFESSORS

Howard—through its professors, administrators, and students—offered a crucial challenge to students' ideas of what it meant to be a black person in America. The school endorsed the acceptance of subdominant group status, reframing it as a status that was not inherently inferior, but a marker of perseverance, intelligence, spirituality, intelligence, and pride. Peter, who transferred to Howard from a predominantly white university, puts it this way:

I think my entire couple years at Howard just stood out as extraordinary. It was a period where I got to see *us* in control and what *we* could do and what we're trying to do. People believed in me and showed confidence in my ability. And I didn't have to prove that I could [do it] because I was black; I just had to prove that I could [do it] because I wanted to. . . . [The whole experience] gave me confidence; it prepared me. (Peter, HU '84)

Like Peter, Stan transferred to Howard from a small predominantly white liberal arts college. He argues that Howard professors had high expectations of their students and conveyed the belief that students could succeed:

[O]ne of them was Dr. [Y], and he was tough, you know. I remember I had to do a paper and I did it in two . . . or three days . . . and I didn't . . . have a chance to proofread it before I handed it to him. He was like, "Stan, this is the worst work I've ever seen you turn in," and that touched me, you know. I was like, "Wow!" . . . [T]he difference in going to a white college and a black college is that you have more black professors, and they have more faith in what you can accomplish. And they know that you're like either sliding or not doing your best. Whereas when I was at [a predominantly white small liberal arts college my freshman year] and I [was a] political science major, I had this professor, Dr. [W], and I was the only black in that class. He wrote his dissertation on the genetic inferiority of the black race. I swear that he did that. It just hurt me to know that this man was in charge of my grade. . . . [I]mmediately when I walk into the class I'm [considered] genetically inferior to him. So there's nothing that I could do that would impress him more so than any other quote-unquote nigger would. 'Cause [supposedly] this is in our blood. . . . [W]as I to count on him to [have] wholehearted faith and [take me] under his wing? (Stan, HU '86)

One of the successes of a racist system is the insecurity that the structural inequity of racism imposes on those who are members of the stigmatized racial group. This insecurity, as Claude Steele's work has shown, undermines the ability of students to perform to their potential. Alumni from Howard do not say that their black professors were all free from negative racial stereotypes about them, but alumni *assumed* that their professors were. And this assumption appears to have made all the difference.

Most Howard alumni believe that few racially motivated problems arose between students and faculty—whatever their racial background—because those faculty who chose to teach at a black college, so they reasoned, were already committed to the education of black people. Betsy maintains that the predominantly black atmosphere, coupled with the mission of the college and its students, was a deterrent to racism. In answer to my question "Was there any racial tension on campus?" she responds, "No, 'cause I had several white teachers. . . . The [white] people being there for a [positive] reason—I mean, it cuts a lot of the monkey business out. It really does" (Betsy, HU '74).

Lucy describes how any infrequent racial tension that existed was isolated: "[T]here was one professor there, but she didn't last too long, I think because of her attitude. . . . [I]f people wanted to go on to, let's say, graduate school, she would tell them that they shouldn't try that, that they should try something else" (Lucy, attended HU in the '80s without graduating). Lucy implies that at Howard a professor who doubted the potential of his or her students based on race would not be encouraged to stay.

Enjoying the trust of one's professors distinguishes Howard's black alumni from their Northwestern counterparts.[6] Shirley explains: "[Howard] helped me because I had teachers who were very caring, who made me feel like I could do anything. They'd fail you in a minute, but yet . . . they were still behind you" (Shirley, HU '89). While not every alumnus and alumna believed that every professor had their best interests at heart, Howard students had a markedly different relationship to their professors than did Northwestern students. When professors did not appear to be trustworthy or appeared to harbor racist attitudes, students protested, sometimes to the professors directly and sometimes directly to the administration. George (HU '85) provides an example from the economics department:

> *Sarah Willie*: Was there ever any friction between nonblack faculty and students?

> *George*: Yes. Lots of times. Like in Econ, when the professor would propound, say, a conservative economic theory or something like that, or bootstrapism, or the failure of the welfare state . . . they would jump on him and they'd say, "Well, you're not black, you're white [or] you're Asian [or] you're Indian—whatever—and you can't know."

When asked about the few white students who attended or the many white faculty who taught at Howard, alumni say that they never had to second-guess people. "If they're coming to a predominantly black environment," several said, "they have to know where they stand, and it can't be against black people."

There were only a handful of white students that a few alumni recall were enrolled at Howard. Like the nonblack professors, these students are also remembered for their comfort with black students. Joseph says, "I knew one guy named Dan. I remember Dan [was] from San Diego. He was in my class. I don't remember any others. But Dan was a 'brother.' He even dated black women" (Joseph, HU '71). Those white Bison who did not socialize with other undergraduates may have gone unnoticed by the people I interviewed.

Several studies of minorities and women in coeducational college, graduate school, and the professional world (Kanter 1977, Blackwell 1981, Charles Willie 1981, Fleming 1984) have noted mentoring as an important aspect of success. The dictionary defines a mentor as a wise and trusted teacher. First generation college students and students distracted by their sub-dominant status have often had difficulty learning how things work and how to succeed at college. If no one in one's family has had experience with higher education, or if fellow students regularly remind outsiders of their difference, success can be undermined. Mentors can play an invaluable role in helping students who feel like outsiders to become a part of campus community, or at least to get the most out of their experience.

That said, Howard alumni are less likely to mention mentors than are NU alumni, but neither do they bemoan their absence. "Okay, [professors acted] not so much as mentors, but they impressed me in such a way that they made me believe in myself so that I could complete school" (Stan, HU '86). Indeed, Stan's observation points to a larger finding by Walter R. Allen et al.: "[W]e found that students on Black campuses had a tendency to solve their own problems to a much greater extent than did students on white campuses, who relied more on their families and institutional mechanisms" (Allen et al. 1991: 14). Without hand-holding (and in some cases without even directional signs), students figured out how to make it through and still felt supported by their professors.

On the other hand, Karl describes relationships with two of his professors whose advice to him could be considered mentoring:

> I developed some relationships with a couple of professors who really, sincerely seemed to care and were interested in me. [At Howard] there were just a lot of tips about how to deal with the world . . . from the point of view of black people who had been there. . . . [Howard professors] always gave more than just what was the class material. A lot of times teachers would just [be] talking about the subject and say, "When you get out there, don't expect this and that." [They would let us know] just how it's going to be dealing with a white-dominated society, being a black professional out there. And . . . that's something . . . that I probably wouldn't have gotten from a predominantly white college—people just breaking it down realistically, how it's going to be. (Karl, HU '89)

Karl's professors at Howard were giving lessons in life, not just academics. No doubt these lessons added an element of pragmatism, allowing students to see the links between real life and their studies.

The attitude of the professors and the school's general climate of acceptance fostered a sense of ownership among the individuals I interviewed—that is to say, as students, they felt as if it were *their* school. This is in distinct contrast to the students at the predominantly white state university who were interviewed in Feagin, Vera, and Imani's 1996 study. For many, it also fostered a sense of responsibility to other African Americans. But, as we will see a bit later in the chapter, establishing and maintaining the positive link with the surrounding community—a community of working-class and poor African Americans—was difficult.

THE BUREAUCRATIC NIGHTMARE

Although most Howard alumni describe negotiating the bureaucracy of the administration (financial aid, dormitory room assignments, and course registration, for example) to be "a waking nightmare," they also assured me that it was one worth enduring for the sense of confidence and dignity that they say they took away. Howard graduates told sometimes harrowing stories of administrative red tape, incompetence, rudeness, and neglect. The bad experiences, however, rarely seem to squelch the alumni's enthusiasm for or gratitude to the school.

Mark is an example of a student who endured several bureaucratic hassles. At the same time, he did not want me to interpret his bad experiences as evidence that the university was negligent: "A lot of things happened that were not always positive, but like anything else—I'm a positive-minded person—I think things which happen to us in our own lives [happen] for a reason. . . . I'm trying to be careful about my words. I want [them] to adequately reflect how I feel about Howard University. It was a wonderful experience for me" (Mark, HU '76). Like Northwestern alumna Terry in chapter 5, who was hesitant to label mistreatment from fellow students as racist, Mark is hesitant to name the shortcomings of Howard. Terry was caught in the contradiction of formal equality and informal inequality. When selected as a resident assistant for her dormitory, Terry found that her white charges at NU regularly mistreated her with impunity. Mark, too, is caught in a contradiction: Howard gave him opportunities, and its atmosphere nurtured his positive sense of himself. At the same time, he was also a victim of what others refer to as bureaucratic incompetence. After vaguely referring to things that were "not always positive," Mark manages to deflect attention away from the question and tells me his own life philosophy—"Things happen for a reason."

While the majority of Howard alumni interviewed for this study agree with Mark's positive assessment of Howard as a wonderful place during which they had a similarly "wonderful experience," they are also more explicit about their frustrations. Although I did not ask about housing, registration, or financial aid difficulties during the interview, the majority of respondents mentioned at least one of these things of their own volition.

> [O]ne thing about Howard, they were real bad with financial aid, as far as getting people's money to 'em. You know, you'd have all your stuff there . . . but they'd take so long that classes would start and people wouldn't have money. . . . [F]ortunately I was working, so I could take care of myself. But as far as people who were solely dependent on financial aid, a lot of times people wouldn't have money, (Karl, HU '89)

Some of the experiences of long registration lines and problems with financial aid, I learned, stem from the fact that the school depends on multiple private and public agencies to handle students' financial situations. Former students argue, however, that good old administrative incompetence might also have been operating. Suzanne (HU '87) explains:

> *Susanne*: Howard doesn't hand you anything on a silver platter; you have to deal with them face-to-face on every issue, especially getting back in school and money issues. They don't take checks [and] you have to stand in line to register . . . lines at least two hours long.

Sarah Willie: They didn't take checks?

Suzanne: No.

Sarah Willie: So you mean you had to bring cash or a money order?

Suzanne: Right. And they might have sent you a letter telling you, "You owe this amount." And by the time you got up there, it was another amount, and you couldn't just say, "Oh, okay, let me write you a check [for the difference]." You had to go and call home and say, "Mom, I need this, and I need it in cash or a money order." So, I guess it helped me deal with people, [but] it was a big headache. I don't think they were very well organized in that way.

Many alumni recall having difficulty as students believing that other African Americans were treating them with such seeming indifference. Even today, black people negatively judge each other for becoming too "full of themselves," "forgetting where they came from," "forgetting who they are"—in other words, for ignoring their shared racial status and history. Thus, the cultural dictum within the black community is to treat each other as equals. Often, alumni confided, they had difficulty living up to that dictum when they felt others were not doing the same. Christopher explains,

It was chaos when we walked in the door, because the administration is so fucked up. I don't like people who think that they're doing you a favor by being there at work. I have a real problem with that. When I pay my tuition, I pay their salary, and you had better act like you're doing me a favor. I mean, I'm doing *you* a favor [just by being here]! So we had a problem when we got there with ignorant administrative people. (Christopher, HU '87)

The additional variable that gets thrown into Howard's mix is the importance of the college to the community that surrounds it and is employed by it. As alumni remember, Howard had a wide range of students, some of whom were affluent and a few of whom were arrogant. When this latter group in particular came into contact with staff members, who often came from working-class backgrounds, some of whom resented privileged students, a negative attitude expressed by an employee could be interpreted as a passive form of resistance.

LESSONS FROM THE 'HOOD

The relationship between neighborhood and school was often marked by resentment, tension, misunderstanding, and mutual distrust. Many former students invoked

DuBois' concept of "the talented tenth" to describe themselves. This elitist attitude haunts the campus, for the tension between campus and community has its basis not only in crime perpetrated *against* students but also in notions of social superiority perpetrated *by* students. Many alumni saw the source of their problems with the surrounding neighborhood as the responsibility of the university's administration or the staff people who work there. Staff people were occasionally lumped with the "neighborhood people," with whom alumni recall tensions. Matthew (HU '86) for example, begins this section of the interview by talking about the administrative problems at HU, which he quickly labels the result of "ghetto mentality." He then elucidates this phrase by relating an experience he had at a fast-food restaurant adjacent to the campus. His frustration seems based on middle-class expectations of polite behavior.

Matthew: There are drawbacks to going there, just like any other school. But the drawbacks are a little different.

Sarah Willie: For example?

Matthew: They screw your money up a lot; you stand in line and the clerks are usually from the [local] area and they're illiterate and they hate you. They're just like, "Oh, these stuck-up kids, I don't have to be nice to them." You're dealing with ghetto mentality. Like I never understood ghetto mentality until it [was] forced upon [me]: You go to McDonald's and the girl is like popping her gum saying, "What do you want?" And I worked at Burger King when I was sixteen and if we didn't smile and say, "Welcome to America's Burger King. May we take your order, please?" and just be extremely giddy and happy, you got fired. And I'm sittin' here and this girl is acting like I'm bothering her. There's no "Thank you"; there's no "Have a nice day"; [and] the food's shoved at you. I mean, when I first got there everyone was just pounding on me: [snarling] "Whatchou want?!" and I'm like [he uses a falsetto voice] Oh, my God. "Well, I was this and I want that." Toward the end, you learn to adapt to the environment and learn to survive. [So] one day, I went up [to McDonald's] and I had ordered a root beer and the girl puts the thing under the tap. I could tell that the soda was running out and you just get seltzer water. And I'm just like, "Excuse me, I don't want that anymore. Just get me an orange [soda]." And she just pops her gum and looks pissed and she tells the manager to get it for me. So by the time he comes to the counter, I've waited and waited for this. So I have my hand out [ready to take the soda] and he was just like, "I come up to the counter and people have their hands out. I can't believe this!" And I was just like, "Look, I really don't have time for your ignorant ass. Just give me my pop. I paid for it, [and] I really don't have time to sit here." And he just went on. So I said, "Well,

that's probably why you work at McDonald's and you're forty-five years old."
He just forced me to be rude to him. [When I told my mom, she said,] "Well,
that's why they hate the Howard students, because you guys come off as if
you're so much better." But I'd just reached a breaking point. And there's a lot
of tension between—we call 'em block boys—and the people at the University.

Sarah Willie: Is there?

Matthew: Yeah, because we're the best blacks that there are. We're the
bourgeoisie. We have all the money and we just come and trample on them,
and we haven't done anything to make their lives better.

Realizing that he must sound arrogant, Matthew admits by the end of this diatribe
that, from the perspective of the locals, he may have a different role in this drama
than the one he considers having played. But despite this assertion, it is not clear that
Matthew understands what he calls ghetto mentality, considering how quickly he ab-
dicates his code of politeness if it's not immediately returned. It is further interesting
that being rude back to people (not the people alumni refer to as the "block boys"
who hang out on the street corner, but those working at McDonald's) is what he calls
"learning to survive." Few other Howard alumni went into as much detail as
Matthew, but almost all of the respondents characterized the relationship between
the school and surrounding community in negative terms.

Most respondents gave me answers like the following two from Stan (HU '86)
and Gwen (HU '75).

Sarah Willie: What was the relationship like between the neighborhood
around Howard and the campus?

Stan: Are you serious?! Wow, they hated us. They used to think that
Howard students were rich snobs because, like—let me give you a for instance. . . . Howard was in the middle of all of the crime, all the oppressed
blacks. It was like one of the worst neighborhoods, with the exception of
Southeast. . . . They sold crack, loveboat, all this stuff on the street corners
right around the school. . . . And people would smoke that and it would get
'em real high and they'd act crazy. Case in point was that in one school year,
I had at least one, two, three, four of my friends attacked and stabbed just by
walking to and from school or parties.

No other alumni told me that they had had four friends stabbed in one school year by
people from the surrounding neighborhood. But Stan's recollection, even if hyper-
bolic, reveals the palpability of the tension.

On the other hand, many Howard students participated in community service in the neighborhood, and while they noted the tension they did not blame the people in the neighborhood for it. A few even blamed the university and the students there. Gwen (HU '75) is one such Bison.

> *Gwen*: [A] friend of mine who lived in my dorm, we would often walk downtown, which was about a one- or two-mile walk. And we would have to go through the community. And we would have our jeans on and just some regular nondescript blouses or sweaters on, and men from the steps would yell, "Y'all, we know y'all from Howard. You bitches! You think you so great." I mean we would get that, believe me, every time we would take this walk downtown. And every now and then there would be forums to try to air these grievances out.

> *Sarah Willie*: Do you think there was anything that the university could have done to make it better?

> *Gwen*: I'm sure. I'm sure, but the university really didn't care. The university's main concern was providing a secure place as far as the campus was concerned for the students. Because there were some incidents involving off-campus people. But as far as trying to resolve the issue of how D.C. residents felt towards Howard, the university wasn't concerned about that at all. And frankly, most Howard students weren't that concerned either. . . . And [it's] not as if everyone at Howard came from a wealthy background; there was a lot of diversity there. So we understood that situation out there. But we were all too concerned with our own agendas to really do much about it.

Gwen's analysis admits the disinterest of students once they had made it to college.

Stan identifies only superficially with what some would call his "community." More so, he identifies with what it means to be "in college," the way college is often represented on the television shows and in the movies. Howard's campus would be perfect for Stan if it remained all-black but were situated among rolling tree-covered hills, like the photographs in admissions brochures of many bucolic colleges that are also, incidentally, predominantly white. He elaborates:

> I was all for tearing down the surrounding community and putting in rolling hills. I don't think that we should have been accosted by the neighborhood. But my classmates' feelings are that we are part of our community and we shouldn't tear it down. That's what the Establishment does with our people. Where are they gonna go? But I don't know. I figure that they would go

somewhere. I mean the university can put up nice housing in other places for them, but I don't think that we should have to be around that. (Stan, HU '86)

Stan exemplifies someone who has reified his particular class-race location, and would probably conform to what E. Franklin Frazier most despised about the black bourgeoisie. Stan wants to enjoy his college experience without facing the complicated reality of living as a black person in this society. Without turning Stan into an ogre, it should be remembered that he only wants what so many white students go to college to find, the last years of adolescence or fun, without having to confront the painful contradictions of the larger society.[7]

Finally, Karl is someone who observed the tension between fellow students and the members of the surrounding neighborhood; he also observed what happened when students refused to participate in the local folk culture and the bad feelings it precipitated.

> There were certain individuals who, I guess third-generation Howardites . . . just thought they were so high and mighty, compared to the poor people in the community. . . . Howard students tended to have a little paranoia about the community people, because [HU] people would get robbed [or] they'd hear about people getting robbed. And people from the community just thought, "Those Howard women, they think they are this and that. They can't even talk to me." . . . [W]e'd hear that a lot. . . . I guess people felt like they thought they were too good. . . . [T]he Howard students were too good to deal with the people in the community, as far as dating and just speaking to people, you know. 'Cause I think that's something that I notice about D.C., especially around where the school is, there's a lot of people from down south. [Strangers] tend to speak [to each other], you know. They just say hi to people on the street quite a bit . . . that's where they typically migrate from, North and South Carolina. . . . So I would hear them speaking, and the women wouldn't say anything [back], and there'd be a lot of shouting after that, calling names. . . . But there were quite a few people who were involved in the community . . . sororities and fraternities . . . sponsoring things to help out the community. And even in the School of Engineering there were people who were tutoring in the schools. . . . So there was outreach. (Karl, HU '89)

From these excerpts, it is clear that Howard and the neighborhood are characterized in particularly feminine and masculine ways. Howard, as represented by the young women who refuse to speak to neighbors when spoken to, is seen as both vulnerable and arrogant. The neighborhood, as represented by the young men who become agitated and verbally abusive when their greetings are ignored, is both predatory and hospitable.

Several respondents were not critical of any system except that of race. Even when they have been disadvantaged by other forms or systems of oppressions—the economic/class system, sex/gender bias, or the political system—individuals described racism as the root cause of other ills. Echoing DuBois, Zweigenhaft and Domhoff argue that "those who are mistreated by a society develop a healthy skepticism about its culture and pretensions. They develop 'double vision' and as a result are able to discern sham and hypocrisy more readily" (1991: 101). This is certainly true when it comes to African Americans and racist behavior. It is not clear, however, that double vision, or, as DuBois called it, double consciousness, leads to critical vision of other oppressive systems.

THE PAPER BAG TEST: COLOR, CLASS, AND GENDER

While Howard was for the most part free from racism perpetrated by white individuals against black individuals, the effects of the racism in the dominant culture continued to influence people's lives, and this is especially visible in alumni's memories of the presence of colorism. As Karl remarks, "There were a few people on campus who thought they were better than—you know how it is with the light-skinned people and the people who want to be" (Karl, HU '89). Colorism—the valuing of people with light brown skin over people with dark brown skin—within the black American community varies by family, region, and class. The paper bag test refers to the alleged colorist ideal that a black person was most attractive if he or she was the same color, or preferably a lighter shade of brown, than a paper bag. In Karl's remarks, light skin is a trope or proxy for wealth and arrogance. While it may in reality only have been, as he says, "a few people on campus" who exploited their light brown color and just as many students who behaved rudely toward neighborhood folks who were not light-skinned, Karl dubs the latter "the people who want to be."

Light skin is both a representation of a status that distinguished people of African descent in the past and a reality that remains in the hearts and minds of many blacks as an unfair and painful marker of beauty or attractiveness. There were many examples of people with light skin (and presumably a white father) facing the same kinds of hardships as those with dark skin during slavery. At the same time, people with light skin (and obvious biological relation to whites) had color-based privileges in certain areas of the country (especially Louisiana) and in certain white slave-owning families. Several studies contend that light-skinned blacks continue to receive disproportionate recognition and opportunities from whites. Although these privileges were (and continue to be) inconsistently offered, the association of light skin with whiteness, white supremacy, dominant ideals of beauty, the ability to pass as (or pretend to be) white, and racist notions of genetic superiority through hybridity are still painful and contentious topics for African Americans.

Like whiteness, light brown skin can operate as a privilege whether the person who is so marked is conscious of it, wants it, or fails to exploit it actively. The light-skinned person who is conscious of it does not exploit the privilege, puts no stock in the assumptions surrounding its many myths, and shows his or her loyalty to the group is both embraced and forgiven by the group for what he or she cannot control.

Below, class, color, and ideals of attractiveness current in the dominant culture combine with geography to form a complicated picture of the role that Karl believes physical appearance played in who was admitted to the university.

> I think a lot of people were perpetrating that they were from L.A. But a lot of them . . . would have their hair weave and always be dressed up and playing the role like "I'm from Hollywood," and they were just too good. . . . I noticed that at Howard there weren't that many dark-complected people . . . outside of the people who were like from Africa. . . . I noticed most people were tending to be light-complected. I mean, I'm kind of middle ground myself, kind of brown-skinned myself, on the lighter side. But the majority of the people were either my complexion or lighter . . . and I talked to people. I said, "Why is it that it seems like that?" And they said, "Because the dark-skinned people know what it's like. People have a perception of Howard, like it's all the pretty people." A lot of the women who don't tend to be very attractive don't want to go there, 'cause they don't want to go with that . . . which made it highly competitive when it came to looks and stuff . . . people trying to dress better than other people. A lot of people would say it was a fashion show . . . prancing around with their finest on during school. But that was limited to certain majors. . . . Like the School of Business, they really tended to be the fly types . . . the guys would be wearing suits. . . . But the School of Engineering, everybody was in jeans. (Karl, HU '89)

Lucy's experience in the School of Engineering adds further nuance and emphasizes the overlapping aspects of how people looked and what they majored in at Howard. She talks about the consequences of majoring in a technological science and its relatedness to her presentation of self. Her experience is not peculiar to Howard, however. The women who pursued college careers in the natural or technological sciences in both universities echoed her confusion and loneliness.

> *Lucy* (HU n.d.): I didn't [make a big deal about dressing] and you could get away with that more so in engineering. . . . All the while I was in school I would always wear like eyeliner and lipstick and girls in engineering would make some little comments about how I would wear eyeliner and lipstick all the time [saying], "*I* don't have time for that!" And since I didn't have the grades, they would . . . make little snide comments like, "Too much time on

your physical and not enough on your grades." . . . And then outside engineering, people would come and be like, "These girls do not take care of
themselves. What is their problem?!"

Sarah Willie: Sounds like you couldn't win?

Lucy: Yeah, and I usually, you know, I didn't change myself. I wasn't going
to. I probably went more in the opposite direction [of what anybody said]
because I felt like there was pressure to be one way or the other.

Conservative feminine gender expectations tend to be salient at Howard, even as
women outnumber men in graduating from college and pursuing careers. Those
women pursuing technological or science degrees, however, were exempted (or exempted themselves) from such preoccupations because of their pursuit of majors traditionally dominated by males and customarily defined as financially practical, or
"nerdy" in common parlance. This fits Hughes's [1984] argument (explored in
greater depth in chapter 9) that persons with subordinate status who achieve prestigious careers often attempt to resign from their subordinate status by minimizing the
characteristics that so label them. Kanter (1977) argues that numerical minorities are
often pressured to conform to dominant-group expectations—whether those expectations are to be like the members of the dominant group or fill a proscribed role of
difference that is acceptable to the dominant group.

All of these issues that have to do with color, gender expectations, and attractiveness have implications beyond the superficial. Indeed, when it comes to being a
woman in the classroom, Howard students face some even harder choices than do
Northwestern Wildcats. Gail E. Thomas's examination of studies on black men's
and black women's college experiences led her to conclude that "Educational expectations and college racial composition . . . significantly impact Black females'
selection of college majors" (1991: 70). Echoing Fleming's work of a decade earlier,
Thomas also found that "being male is the most important determinant for majoring in the natural and technical sciences for Blacks who attend public predominantly Black colleges" (1991: 71). And A. Wade Smith expressed his concern
further still:

Sociodemographically, not much matters at white schools except gender,
where males clearly get the best of things. At Black schools, males generally
out-performed females in the classroom, and usually also have higher occupational aspirations. There may simply be more sexism at predominantly
Black universities. But, while this could explain Black males' classroom advantage, it would not explain the relatively limited aspirations of Black females. (1991: 123)

The road for women with high career aspirations, especially in the natural and technical sciences, appears to be a difficult one at the coeducational HBCU.[8]

TO REPEAT OR NOT TO REPEAT

[Going to Howard] changed any lack of confidence I may have had into something that is almost unstoppable. I firmly believe that I can stand up against anybody from Harvard or anywhere else of those, quote-unquote "good" universities and probably outdo them because I have more heart.

—Jack, Howard '89

While I expected that the majority of Howard alumni would say they had enjoyed their experience, I also expected that a sizable minority would have found the experience unhappy. Although several Bison noted specific incidents in which they felt they were treated unfairly or suffered long periods of adjustment and frustration, the desire to repeat the experience was almost universal. For the most part, Howard alumni did not describe their experiences as "happy" or "enjoyable." Rather, they were satisfying or worth repeating. Alumni talked about the overall mission of the college and their ability to find a place in the life of the institution. Harriet speaks succinctly for the majority of respondents: "Socially you were welcomed . . . no one was a misfit at Howard" (Harriet, HU '86). Karl extends her observation with his own that Howard was a diverse place where anyone could find a place: "There were a lot of people who were just like me and a lot of people who grew up in the suburbs; a lot of people from everywhere, you know. I met people from all over . . . who carried themselves a different way and looked at life a different way" (Karl, HU '85).

Allen's observations buttress the sense that Karl and Harriet have that, at Howard, no one was an outsider:

> Students on Black campuses . . . operate within an institutional setting that provides a broader range of choices for satisfying basic social needs. . . . Indeed, Black students on Black campuses are commonly assisted in feeling good about themselves and about their places in the university community through favorable interpersonal relationships with their fellow students. . . . Unity and sharing among students on Black campuses may not be ideal, but the institutional setting and the likelihood of common geographical and socioeconomic characteristics enhance their probability of occurrence. (Allen et al. 1991: 156)

Harriet extends Allen's analysis with her own story: "Howard put a lot of happiness in my life. And I think when you're happy you do better at the things you're doing. It seems like when you're sad or troubled, you don't put as much effort into your studies. But because Howard surrounded its students with a happy atmosphere, I think that did help me in my classes, which, of course, helped me to become an attorney" (Harriet, HU '86). A happy atmosphere, it becomes clear, is not synonymous with perfection. When I dug a bit deeper with the questions "How would you describe your college experience in one word" and "Knowing what you know now, would you go to the same school again?" the responses were overwhelmingly positive. Only two of twenty-five Howard respondents said that they would not go to Howard again.[9]

The reasons given for choosing to repeat their experiences at Howard were multiple, but, invariably, the primary reason alumni mentioned was connected to race. Howard offered them, they said, the chance to learn about the range of fellow African Americans and an opportunity to be part of something larger than themselves. It gave them the chance to be members of an organization with a dignified history clearly related to their own. And finally, they had the chance to spend time in a place where they could see greater possibilities of what they could become through the role models of Howard's faculty, administrators, and graduate students. Mark's comments are representative:

> If I had to do it all over again, I would go back to Howard University. I would. . . . It helped me to live in a world that sometimes doesn't always readily accept you, [it helped me] to let people know that certainly I am to be valued and that I have as much to offer . . . in this life and the life of the community as anyone else. Howard taught me in many ways to be taken seriously as a leader and as a person. (Mark, HU '76)

Howard has a reputation that all respondents were familiar with as "the mecca of black intellectual thought" and "the best of the black colleges." In addition, HU is remembered as a place that offered its students the opportunity to set—and then meet—new expectations of themselves while living up to the higher expectations of others. Lydia explains,

> I was raised in the ghetto in New Jersey. And I think you'll always hear, "Niggers can't do this and niggers can't do that," and "Niggers ain't this and niggers ain't that." Looking up there and [seeing them] standing around on the corner. And it was just so uplifting to go to a black institution that has been there for over one hundred years. And it's still standing and it's operating day to day and you're turning out the *crème de la crème* of black society. So we must be doing something right! . . . [I]t's very positive and uplifting. And that was part of the excitement in being there. And it was good to be a part of that. . . . I was excited to be a part of history, because I felt connected to everybody that had been through there. And you can take

me to Howard right now and take me up on the yard and I will fall out crying. Because I can just feel them all just moving through me. It's wonderful. (Lydia, HU '79)

Lydia's testimony is a reminder of the points made above about the importance of positive group identity.

PRESTIGE FOR CONFIDENCE—A TRADE-OFF?

When people have the opportunity to go to a better school, to better themselves, and then they choose an historically black college, I don't understand. People who go to HBCUs either couldn't go to any place else for financial reasons, or their grades are too low, or they go there because they want to be around black folks. But you'll be in trouble if you're good but you don't get a degree from the best school you could.

—*Steve, Northwestern '79*

There is more than one grain of truth in the comment above, but they are grains of which most historically black schools are not ashamed. HBCUs have often accepted students who were ready to perform in college but whose high schools were unable to offer the resources and challenges (such as Advanced Placement courses) commonly available to suburban public or private high schools. But HBCUs have also been a beacon of pride and a symbol of accomplishment carrying on a tradition from when racial apartheid was commonplace in the United States. In fact, the tradition is so strong that comments like the one Northwestern graduate Steve made above were occasionally made by Howard students about Northwestern students as well: "I can't see why anyone would go to NU or another white college," remarked one Howard alumnus.

At the same time, Howard alumni noted—sometimes with visible anger, other times with resignation—that Howard did not elicit as high a level of admiration from others as they might have expected.

[W]hat irks me the most is the fact that people really don't give my credentials from Howard their just due. They feel oh, you're from a black institution and your education is inferior. I remember when they were trying to get me to come to Northwestern [for the graduate program in journalism]. They were even trying to say that I should come out for a summer program. Now I have a [an undergraduate] degree in journalism and you want me to come to a summer program at your school?! I'm like, no way! That was the ultimate insult. No way! I did not go. . . . [T]o me it was a psychological ploy to browbeat [me and my other Howard friends] and maybe even make them think that their education wasn't really up to par. And it's crazy, because Howard taught me to be resourceful, okay? And to look at things with depth, [to] go beyond what is on the surface. I think anybody can just run out and get the who–what–where [of] . . . a story. But Northwestern would have the black students feel that because we had our degree from Howard that we couldn't do that. [O]ne of my girlfriends did the summer semester and she had to stay there a semester afterwards [as well]. And she was a good student. But like I say, to me it was . . . psychological battery. (Ann, HU '79)

Whether Northwestern offered this to all of its incoming master's degree students or whether Ann's recollection is correct that Northwestern offered a summer session only to students who had come from historically black schools is not clear. In either case, the invitation was perceived as insulting.

Most HU alumni agree with Betsy (HU '74) when she says, "I didn't exchange anything, in terms of academics, by going to Howard." At the same time, a few are willing to acknowledge that—even when they were satisfied with the rigor and breadth of their education—others do not always see education at a predominantly black school the same way. George has had mixed reactions since graduating.

[A Howard degree] certainly doesn't help that much in Chicago. On the East Coast, I found that people, in general, have heard of Howard and have good feelings toward it. White colleges can offer their graduates—especially name-brand white colleges—can confer a degree of legitimacy on their graduates that even the best black colleges . . . cannot. If you manage to get plugged in to all the advantages and resources that these institutions have, they can give you a great boost in your career and ultimately in what you'll be able to achieve if you're of that mind to give back to your community. For instance, my old girlfriend, she went to Penn and she got close to a lot of faculty there. She's gotten a lot of her jobs through contacts that she made at Penn, and she also went to [Northwestern School of Business], and those schools just have resources in the outer world that black colleges, in general, don't. (George, HU '85)

A small but vocal minority of HU alumni describe predominantly white schools as obsolete. "I don't think white institutions are needed to educate black students. . . . I just have to be blunt. I just think that all black students should go to black colleges. I just believe that" (Harriet, HU '86). But the overwhelming majority of Howard alumni agree that people should have the choice of what kind of a college to attend.

Some HU alumni argue persuasively that they should not have had to go to a black college to learn about black history and black culture. Christopher, who started out at a predominantly white college but transferred to Howard, believes that his Howard education was more rigorous than the small liberal arts college he attended in the Midwest. He also believes, though, that the differences in priorities between the two kinds of schools can be eradicated, *if* white colleges make a good-faith effort. Mixed with Christopher's observations below are also prescriptions:

> I think there's a place for predominantly white schools, if they make a real serious attempt at educating black students. [T]here are cultural things that white colleges can't even touch. Or they could if they had the proper faculty or tried to touch, but I don't think they really do try and touch those things. They don't try . . . because they don't think it's that much of a concern. They feel as though the students will try and blend. But it's not that easy . . . to be accepted if you're black at a white school. (Christopher, HU '87)

Others are less sure that black colleges are the answer and wonder if the trade-off was too great:

> [T]here are trade-offs. . . . The trade-offs had to do with what the advantages were economically [after college and] career-wise, not only getting maybe a more rigorous academic curricula [someplace else]. . . . In going to a different kind of school [you might have the opportunity to] make contacts with a broader population that might strongly influence your outcome in terms of career choice . . . that is a trade-off. (Sally, HU '74)

And at least one Howard alumnus is at odds as to whether black support networks were a major or minor contribution to his experience. While Stuart's statement below appears to call into question Howard's uniqueness, it simultaneously reflects his attempt to demonstrate to skeptics that Howard is comparable to any predominantly white college:

> I think Howard's a great institution; it's not for everybody. They don't give you anything; it's reflective of the nation. What you get is what you take; or what you're willing to work for is what you get credit for—no different from the rest of the country. The illusion is that, because it's a predominantly black institution, that in major ways they're going to do more for you. I would say in minor ways they do more for you, because the environment is not nearly as hostile as it is when you're an undergrad going through a majority-white situation. (Stuart, HU '83)

Stuart's ambivalence about just what he wants to communicate about this HBCU is evident. While he does not want to paint Howard as an institution that offers an undeserved advantage to African-American students, he is unsure what likening it to

the "rest of the country" means: "What you get is what you take; or what you're willing to work for is what you get credit for." Obviously, those two sentiments have different implications.

Several Howard alumni, like Kirstin conveyed earlier in the chapter, appreciate
that the white-dominated corporate business world has narrow standards by which it
judges people. If one wants to play in that game, one has to play by at least some of its
rules, as Fred argues in concert with Kirstin:

> As much as I love Howard, had I gone to B[usiness] school at Howard, I
> wouldn't be [a corporate banking officer] now. Because . . . there are certain
> schools that corporations recruit at, and they only recruit at predominantly
> white graduate business schools in the top twenty. . . . I guess it gives you
> some degree of credibility in their eyes if you go to an Ivy League school. . . .
> If your options are some of the Ivy League schools, credibility comes with
> that. (Fred, HU '87)

Bruce also chose to attend a predominantly white business school, and he elaborates
upon Fred's points: "[I]t's a predominantly white environment. . . . The very fact
that I have competed with people in [a predominantly white] business school and did
well and beat a number of my majority [colleagues] is helpful; it gives [me] a tremendous amount of confidence. . . . [A predominantly white business school] is like your
green card in the business world" (Bruce, HU '79).

A handful of Howard alumni simply believe that black and white colleges offer
students different experiences and different skills. Paula (HU '81) speaks for this
group when she observes, "A black institution, I think, teaches you more confidence.
A white institution . . . teaches you more to interact."

SUMMARY AND ANALYSIS

Howard alumni are almost universally excited to tell the story of their school. They
restate the school's role in producing important alumni, and are pleased with the
sense of self-confidence and African-American history with which they left. Kanter's
work on utopias, which I explore further in the next chapter, helps to explain the
extraordinarily positive memories that discussing Howard University evokes from
so many of its alumni. Still, it would be intellectually and pragmatically dishonest
to minimize the importance of the absence of racism, the presence of explicit assumptions about student potential, and the sense of a dignified history that were all
profoundly significant to the experiences of these alumni. HU alumni expressed
frustration about the slow and poorly run administration in terms of admission, financial aid, housing, and registration as well as the negative relationship between the

university and the surrounding neighborhood. Even these, however, are not enough to keep Howard students from singing Howard's praises for giving them a sense of African-American history and of their own worth as black people.

Unfortunately, the tension between the university and the surrounding neighborhood is especially poignant considering the kinship with which most African Americans describe the American black community. While Howard appears to do a great job of instilling a sense of group pride among its students, it does not appear that the university has encouraged students to be critical of DuBois' concept of the talented tenth. This is ironic, for Howard has more students than Northwestern does from financially and educationally disadvantaged backgrounds. As Gwen noted earlier, in the section titled "Lessons from the 'Hood," most of the students had some experience with poverty or hardship. There seems to be a fine line between instilling pride in students and encouraging arrogance. Some would argue that one could not go too far in helping students who are racially denigrated in the larger society to feel good about themselves. This kind of education for self-confidence must maintain a delicate balance by offering students the sense of social and academic entitlement that often presages their success while at the same time demanding that students critique the structural inequality that has shaped the world from which they were previously excluded. In other words, teaching an alternative history means examining the very assumptions behind the accepted history and the present goals that accompany it.

Clearly, Howard has given its alumni a sense of self that is founded on an understanding of history as well as of possibility. Less explicitly, however, it appears that some of that sense of self is achieved at the expense of an awareness of and compassion for fellow African Americans who have not been included in the part of the American dream Howard has facilitated for its students.[10]

CODA: "EVERYBODY USED TO BE RADICAL"

*We might have been one of the . . . last classes that had a lot of
lower-middle-class black students coming in.*
—Edward, Northwestern '79

INTRODUCTION: COMPETING NARRATIVES AND IDEAL TYPES

Many of the alumni I interviewed characterized their experience at either Howard or
within the black community at Northwestern in utopian terms: they were part of a social group, they remembered, in which they shared a vision of "harmony cooperation,
and mutuality of interests" (Kanter 1972: 1). When they did not describe the utopian
nature of the black community, their explanations seemed to describe archetypes.

Alumni of both institutions remember participating in the protests of the day.
Northwestern alumni, however, remember feeling that the campus was continuing to
lose urban, working-class, and radical students, and alumni who graduated over a
twenty year span also made this comment. That sense of anxiety and loss is a regularly reiterated theme. "Urban," "working-class," and "radical" alchemize into a
trope for the idealized black student with which many Wildcats identify. This parallels the trope of the light-skinned, arrogant, and wealthy student with whom many
Bison fear their school is associated. Each school has an ideal type upon which loss or
anxiety is projected. While there are surely students who fit these descriptions
throughout the last thirty years on each campus, their presence in the narratives of
alumni who do not resemble these types points to the fact that different challenges
and anxieties face students who choose different kinds of schools. I have already discussed the archetype of the wealthy, light-skinned, and arrogant HBCU student in
chapter 6. Below, I discuss the shift that so many Wildcats remember from the
plethora of urban, working-class, and radical black students on Northwestern's campus to their sense that there were fewer and fewer of them. I offer a few ideas about

the reasons for NU alumni's differing narratives and briefly examine the radicalism at Howard that is confined in most Bisons' memories to the 1960s.

NORTHWESTERN

CHARISMA AND NOSTALGIA

Stories told by the NU alumni I interviewed invariably began with a description of cohesion among blacks on campus when they were first-year students and ended with a description of fragmentation, disunity, and the erosion of a working-class urban base of students by the time they left. *Whether one began school in 1968 or 1986, this aspect of most respondents' recollections is strikingly similar.*

Paul was at NU from 1971 through 1975. Like all of the alumni in this study, he pinpoints the transition from cohesive utopia to social disunity during his first two years.

Sarah Willie: Was the black community on campus cohesive during your time there?

Paul: Only during my time, it was cohesive. . . . However, let me add a caveat to that: a huge, a huge rift occurred at Northwestern after my sophomore year. Between '69 . . . and '73—and this probably wasn't just Northwestern, it was probably typical nationwide—is when you got your influx of inner-city blacks. [Not] one or two, a trickle, I mean a real handful. [And then] all of a sudden, my junior year you see these freshmen coming in wearing designer clothes, you know [driving expensive cars] and stuff like that, and they don't feel any compunction to identify with the black students. . . . It was a clear rift. And, as I said, it wasn't just at Northwestern. 'Cause I had friends at Stanford and Columbia and they said the same thing.

Sarah Willie: What do you think was behind that?

Paul: I think it was a plan. . . . I know that the educational aristocracy in this country said, "Hey, enough!" . . . It had to be, Sarah, because it was just too definable; it was palpable. . . . You could just smell the dichotomy.

Paul believes that university administrators were tired of protests about racist incidents, protests for more black students, black faculty, and black studies courses. He believes that the protests were, in the minds of university administrators, associated with working-class African Americans from cities.

Although Terry started Northwestern the fall after Paul left, she, too, describes a change in the black students that the university was admitting:

It was like, this could be a really good experience if everyone allows it to be. And we knew that everybody could really work together, but we also felt that Northwestern was losing a lot of the commitment that they had had in the '60s—commitment and promises that they had made to try to reach out to inner-city students. I really felt that my class was one of the last classes that really came from the inner city, 'cause we were *all* inner city. We were from Cleveland and Chicago, Philly, East Orange, New Jersey, you know, Los Angeles. We were *really* from the inner cities. We were not predominantly from the suburbs or anything; we were really from the inner cities, and we had gone to either private schools or really good college preparatory [public] schools. Primarily everybody there, you know, was qualified. They could do the work. But there were a lot of bad experiences that people had. We lost a lot of the males—a lot of guys [that] came with me did not graduate. (Terry, NU '79)

If the "palpable" change, as Paul puts it, came in 1973 and yet Terry insists that her class, which entered NU in 1975, was one of the last full of working-class and urban blacks, how the black community was experienced may not have depended on when one was there.

Another NU alumnus, Edward (NU '79), locates the "time of transition" from idyllic cohesion to cacophonous fragmentation several years after Paul and about year later than Terry remembers the change. Yet Sue, who graduated three years after Edward, insists it was the election in 1980 of Ronald Reagan as president that marked the transition.

I noticed a change on campus. Not really political reaction, but I did notice that the people changed. Almost overnight it seemed to go from people who wore jeans and were ordinary . . . to people who dressed up and wore pearls on campus. The last couple of years I felt like the people who were like me were close to a minority. . . . [And] it wasn't just that they had money. . . . These people were ostentatious. . . . They drove their BMWs and their Mercedes and they wore their cashmere sweaters and their furs and pearls and they got their coiffure. And it wasn't like that when I first came in. (Sue, NU '82)

Finally, Jennifer's testimony demonstrates that it really didn't matter when one entered the undergraduate college to have observed this transition. Notice the similarities between her portrait of Northwestern in the mid- to late 1980s and that of Sue above.

I would have called it cohesive my freshman year, and progressively less cohesive as I moved up. When I was a freshman, in between classes . . . you could always go to the Black House and catch a really good discussion going on. . . . There were people in there all the time, always using it. . . . [By] senior year, there was nobody there. . . . When I was a freshman, people who had hung around the Black House were kind of known as militant. . . . When I decided to pledge [a sorority], they were like, "Jennifer, you've decided to pledge?! You're gonna join something?! Oh, be yourself." [A]lthough it was petty on one side, . . . they *did* have a point [and they got me to ask myself]: "Should I really be joining a sorority? What are my reasons for joining it?" Gosh, when I was a senior, [underclassmen would say things] like, "She's *not* wearing Guess jeans! Where's her Coach [handbag]?" (Jenny, NU '88)

Regardless of when one began college, the feeling of cohesion faded for students as they progressed through school.

I would argue that these differing interpretations of the loss of black student cohesion have several causes, some of which are buttressed by other observations below. It is not difficult to imagine the changing attitudes of faculty, administrators, and board members whose desires went from knowing that they needed African-American representation on campus to being uncomfortable with the implications of such a presence during the late 1960s and early 1970s. Their changing attitudes were likely passed down to or simply intuited by college admissions offices. Those schools that were able to attract blacks to campus were likely to have changed their priorities from "get some blacks on campus *now*" to finding black candidates who conformed to the culture of the school or, more crudely, who conformed to the social characteristics of their typical white candidates. Some of the change people I interviewed experienced might have been due to the increasing diversity of African America, including more middle class since the gains of the Civil Rights Movement.

As Sidel corroborates, there was indeed a retrenchment of sorts from the mid-1970s to the mid-1980s:

According to a 1992 report by the American Council on Education, the percentage of black and Hispanic high-school graduates enrolled in college declined sharply during the 1980s. . . . [T]he percentage of black high-school graduates between eighteen and twenty-four years of age who were enrolled in college dropped from 33.5 percent in 1976 to 28.1 percent in 1988. . . . The percentage of comparable white graduates enrolled in college rose from 33.0 to 38.1 percent. . . . Since the mid-1970s, the college participation of African Americans and Hispanics has been a picture not of progress but of major regression. In the late 1980s, however, the percentage of African-American high-school graduates attending college rose. By 1991, among eighteen-to-twenty-four-year-olds, 31.5 percent were attending college, up from a decade low of 26.1 percent in 1985. Though most of the increase was among black women, the attendance rates of black men increased 6 percent between 1985 and 1991, reversing a decline over the previous eight years. . . . During the same period of time, the rate of white high-school graduates attending college rose from 34.4 percent to 41.7 percent. (1994: 42)

The sense of close-knit family described at length in chapter 5 about NU alumni's college memories appears to have followed students out of the passionate days of the Civil Rights Movement when black students were, for the first time, more than one or two faces appearing on traditionally white campuses. Because this positive group identity was not only the result of simply being a minority but also of de facto segregation and heightened awareness facilitated by the Civil Rights Movement, it was (and continues to be) vulnerable to the effects of time. When the passion of the moment dies down (and in this case, the Civil Rights era is such a moment), so too does the strong sense of the group begin to fade. Max Weber observed more than a century ago in *The Protestant Ethic and the Spirit of Capitalism* that social movements based on passion do not endure indefinitely. Such movements and admiration of their leaders must be made routine and institutionalized to ensure that they last as passion wanes in the banality of daily living.

And finally, one aspect of the "rift" or "change" that former students describe may have been a result of their close ties with those who were in school with them. Indeed most seniors, of all colors, begin to look back at the "good old days" of their first year and begin to see younger students and the college as "not like it was when I started." Alumni I interviewed recognized the ambition and what they called "middle-class goals" of the black students who were two and three years younger than they. At the same time, it is quite possible that their own difference from those ahead of them was not as apparent to them while they were in college.

UTOPIAN HINDSIGHT

Kanter's work on communal utopias helps us to understand the height of expectation that many, if not most, black alumni tell us they brought to each other on NU's predominantly white campus. While the range of black experiences is diverse, the shared history of oppression leads many African-American students to anticipate shared experiences, shared compatibility, and a future complete with shared goals. This may all be amplified on the campus with an insufficient critical mass of black students.

Kanter's observations buttress the feelings of many students:

The argument runs that when communal groups effect harmony between members and develop a smooth, intimate, cooperative life, they often achieve this at a terrible cost to the individual. . . . To the extent that these issues bear on communal orders, it is important to remember the general

features of communes: they are voluntary social orders, based on free en-
trance and exit, regardless of how much pressure the group may put on the
individual to stay. (1972: 232)

I know of no black student community on a white *or black* college campus that has
ever been characterized as smooth, intimate, cooperative, and harmonious (but I
would welcome hearing about one from any reader who has had such an experience!).
Clearly, Kanter's work goes only so far in describing the situation of black students
on the mostly white campus.

Even the explicit conflicts between black students and white administrators that
took place on college campuses across the country during the 1960s (Exum 1985) and
again in the 1980s were not marked by complete solidarity among black students.
Black students who are small in number or proportion on a campus are usually aware
of one another's personal lives, frustrated that they are so dependent on one another,
and cognizant of their differences from one another. These factors undermine constant cooperative spirit and harmony. Although the analogy to Kanter's utopias is
further complicated by the disparate reasons that account for black student attendance at a particular college, her work is useful in noting the toll of maintaining a
united front, even when adversity calls for one.

HARDLY UTOPIA

While college may not mirror a utopia, once one has been accepted to a college, it
would seem to be a place that one can freely enter and exit. This is really true, however, only for the relatively wealthy. From the moment of a student's acceptance by a
college—and more so for financially disadvantaged students—the delicate negotiation between each student and the institution begins. Black students (who are still
disproportionately from working-class or poor backgrounds in the United States) are
often caught in what feels like a nonnegotiable situation in which they must play by a
very particular set of rules, all the while hoping that rewards will follow. Students
who are economically disadvantaged, regardless of race, are acutely aware that a college education, especially one that has been paid for by scholarship or fellowship,
may be their only chance to escape poverty or to pursue a career that is both satisfying and financially rewarding. For the student whose grade point average slips, there
is the threat of a withdrawn scholarship. For the student who has never known privacy at home, a mismatched roommate can be tormenting. For the student who must
work thirty hours a week, college is rarely, if ever, about football games, parties, and
late-night bull sessions. For the student whose parent dies or whose parents divorce
during college, life is an uncertain tightrope that requires emotional and financial
balance. In other words, for many students college life is far from utopian, and yet

leaving college before graduation raises pragmatic fears that one will permanently forfeit the opportunity to lead the advantaged life of plenty and security promised by the American Dream and widely advertised by the American media.

To freely exit college or suspend one's pursuit of a degree, along with the relationships that came with the black student community there, was not a possibility for many of the Northwestern and Howard alumni with whom I spoke. Lynn is representative.

> [By junior year] I was tired of my roommate. . . . I wasn't truly involved in any organizations. . . . I didn't feel committed to anything, outside of just getting my degree. By that time, I was sick of Northwestern, so the only thing that made sense was to finish my degree. I remember going to some [professional counseling] people at the time, because I was feeling so frustrated. . . . I remember sitting down and talking to this lady and her saying, "Have you ever thought about just taking time off, getting to know yourself outside of an academic setting?" And that was just a mind-blowing thought—that I was a person beyond a student and that I had a right to have a life beyond just being a student. And that stayed with me, and I often thought, "Well, could I take off a year? Or not even a year, maybe a quarter?" And I debated that for an entire year. The next thing I know, the year was up, and I was working another summer job. But I always thought about it during my junior and senior years, just taking off a quarter. But then I saw so many people who were forced to leave for academic reasons, who were forced to leave for financial reasons, and I kind of thought, "If I don't finish this, something's going to knock me out of the game," you know? I don't want to [risk that]. I just want to stay the course and get the paper. Because if I go away, maybe I won't come back, or maybe the [financial] aid won't be there. I was just too fearful of stopping what I had already started. I had never really given up on anything, so it's kind of hard to give up and take a break and admit that you're tired. And I just couldn't admit that I was burnt out. (Lynn, NU '83)

Since college is most African-American students' best shot at financial stability and occupational mobility, taking time off is often understood as risking self-expulsion, and the choice seemed foolhardy to many.

These fears were not without cause or concern. *The Statistical Abstract of the United States* provides data on the relationship between unemployment rates and educational attainment. A comparison between 1992 and 2000 is instructive.[1] In a time of higher unemployment, 1992, just over 14 percent of blacks were unemployed and looking for work with only a high school diploma. The unemployment rate for those blacks with some college education was 10.7 percent; the unemployment rate for those blacks with a bachelor's degree was only 4.8 percent. The unemployment rates for whites who had attained the same levels of education were consistently lower than for African Americans: 6.5 percent, 5.3 percent, and 2.7 percent, respectively. By the year 2000, when unemployment was at an all-time low, the stark differences by educational attainment and race remained in effect. The unemployment rate for blacks with a high school diploma was 6.3 percent; with some college it was 4.3 percent; and with a college degree it fell to 2.5 percent. For whites in that year, the unemployment rates were about half that of blacks: 3.6 percent, 2.7 percent, and 1.4 percent, respectively. Staying in college was and continues to be unequivocal insurance for future employment. In short, blacks simply have fewer degrees of freedom, as compared to whites, when it comes to choosing to follow dreams without, versus with, a college degree.

RADICALISM AT HOWARD

At Howard, the story alumni tell is different. In contrast to the repeated perceptions of collegiate decline attributed in each successive year by NU alumni, Howard alumni agree on a particular moment in history as being the one radical time. The late 1960s and early 1970s were times of tumult, protest, and change, after which the campus returned to business as usual. Business as usual, however, included a built-in sense of being able and willing to critique the status quo if it was called for. True, there were student protests over the *Bakke* decision in the 1970s, American investment in South Africa in the early 1980s, and protest against the appointment of Republican Lee Atwater to the Board of Trustees in the late 1980s. At the same time, Howard alumni—contrary to their counterparts at Northwestern—all agree on Howard's radical era.

> During the early '70s . . . Howard had just come through a very difficult period where there were a lot of student protests in the late '60s and a lot of changes that were made. . . . By the time I got there [the protests] had all blown over and all those issues were pretty much resolved. But during that time, there was a much higher level of consciousness, about many issues, than I think exists on these campuses today. (Gwen, HU '71)

Kirstin (HU '75), who entered Howard just after Gwen was leaving in 1971, remembers:

> *Kirstin*: [When I was there] it was pretty quiet. I think it was kind of a time in between all of the things that had gone on [during the Civil Rights Movement] and I think at the time it was pretty quiet.

> *Sarah Willie*: How would you characterize the campus community?

Kirstin: Cliquish. . . . Yeah, people were pretty much into their own little worlds.

Karl, who attended Howard several years after both Gwen and Kirstin, speaks about student demonstrators during his era as a marginal clique.

It was . . . a group—what do you call? I made fun of 'em so much that I forget what they're called. Oh yeah, it was Progressive Student Movement. I used to call 'em PMS. They were PSM, but I used to call 'em [does not complete thought]. But they were always trying to raise issues. It was like a lot of brothers who acted like they wanted to do something, but they were pretty much all talk. (Karl, HU '85)

Joseph (HU '67), however, remembers the days of radical change. During these days students protested the single-sex dorms and the strict visitation rules that accompanied them; they protested the lack of black studies courses, and what several referred to in antebellum terms as "the Big House" mentality of Howard's president. Alumni remember protesting the presence of ROTC on campus and taking over the administration building. This was a time when students prepared themselves for protest battle by covering themselves in petroleum jelly to protect their skin from tear gas burns. "Things were just wild. I mean everything, all demands, were met. We got a new president, Dr. [X.], and President [Y.] was gone, and the whole atmosphere changed. Overnight, it changed" (Joseph, HU '67).

At Howard, the radical moment is not an ongoing sense of loss, felt anew by each class as it progresses toward graduation, but the close of Civil Rights Movement era. Current students who are committed to progressive causes and social activism are often seen as one more clique, rather than a sign of the times.

CONCLUSION

NU alumni remarked that students behind them seemed to be moving further away from blackness. There are at least four reasons for this perception by alumni. First, passionate movements, like the Civil Rights Movement, become institutionalized or routinized. Each generation of black students is further away from the height of activism of the 1960s, and the urgent necessity for protest and change dims. Second, after the protests that shocked so many campuses nationwide, including Northwestern, admissions offices—although few may admit it—began to prioritize "good fit" with the campus as much as, if not more than, the presence of numbers of African Americans. Third, students grow, shifting their priorities, and are often unaware of this while it is happening. While this kind of looking back was not a feature of the interviews with Howard alumni, further research is needed to uncover whether this feeling of loss as one matures is psychologically developmental and, therefore, likely to occur on black campuses as well. And finally, neither African Americans nor institutions of which they were part were immune from the growing conservatism of the country that began in the 1970s following the end of the Vietnam War. For Howard alumni, however, the college experience, except for the protest days of the late 1960s, is still described in utopian terms. So protests similar to those on Northwestern's campus took place, but they occurred a few years earlier, and alumni's stories do not include the loss of working-class and radical students in their memories.

The grain of truth to the narratives of a utopian environment at both campuses, the working-class, urban, and radical student at Northwestern, or the light-skinned, wealthy, and arrogant student at Howard (though the latter was mentioned less frequently), can easily become our distraction. The focus should be the campus climates that facilitate the generation of such idealized types and the reasons that utopia, while hardly a reality on most campuses, so easily becomes the nostalgic characterization of the past.

RACE

The effort to constitute the race concept theoretically as some-
thing neither apparitional nor tangible, as neither true nor false,
so to speak, is a daunting task, but a necessary one.
                                                    —*Howard Winant*

THE CONCEPT OF RACE

Most people in the United States understand race to refer to biological difference, the way sex is understood to refer to biological difference. People who share certain phenotypic characteristics such as skin color, shape of eyes, nose, and mouth, body type, and hair texture, for example, are said to belong to particular racial groups. In the United States and throughout the world, Winant (2001) argues, racial groups mark social and political difference as well. The categories themselves are increasingly contested, since millions of people do not fit neatly within one of this country's four or five major groups. These groups have been designated by the U.S. Census and other government agencies as African Americans, Asian Americans, Native Americans, Caucasians or European Americans, and Latinos/Latinas (although the latter is, for some purposes, recognized as a nonracial category, overlapping with other groups). The corresponding colors—black, yellow, red, white, and brown—have at different times been used as epithets, simple descriptors, or appropriated by members of racial minority groups as proud self-designations. Furthermore, the majority of people that *do* identify with one of the racial groups often do not share phenotypic characteristics supposedly common to the group. Phenotypic characteristics are seen as racial, and each racial group is associated with and signals expectations about ethnicity, class background, and a particular relationship to the dominant culture.

Race and *ethnicity* have occasionally been treated as synonyms. Considering the confusion about race and racial categories, their conflation with other concepts, like ethnicity, their association with racism, and the ideological baggage they have bequeathed, some people have jettisoned them altogether as unnecessary, of an earlier era. Race experts Omi and Winant explain that the impulse to dismiss racial categorization is not only based on righteous frustration. It also coincides with the attempt of contemporary social conservatives to undermine efforts to achieve racial egalitarianism. Sensing all of this and being confused by much of it, many Americans in good faith would like to move beyond race into an era of colorblindness while others have elevated racial identity to the most important aspect of self. Omi and Winant caution against both extremes: "There is a continuous temptation to think of race as an *essence*, as something fixed, concrete, and objective. And there is also an opposite temptation: to imagine race as mere *illusion*, a purely ideological construct which some ideal nonracist social order would eliminate" (1994: 54). Neither position, they argue, serves us well. In fact, the one thing that should be transcended is this bipolar and rigid characterization of the debate. Although their research shows that the symptom of race has been color-coded bodies, its meaning changes over time and from place to place. "[R]ace is a concept which signifies and symbolizes social conflicts and interests by referring to different types of human bodies. Although the concept of race invokes biologically based human characteristics . . . selection of these particular human features for purposes of racial signification is always and necessarily a social and historical process" (Omi and Winant 1994: 55). While our racial experience of reality is significant, then, race is even bigger than individual identity, for it also exists at the level of groups, institutions, the state, and throughout the culture. In short, race is one of several social systems that organize the social body (Weber 2001: 17).

Race is a relatively recent concept developed by European social philosophers of the seventeenth and eighteenth centuries. They elevated phenotypic differences between peoples for several reasons, not the least of which was justifying their differential treatment by attributing to them differential worth. By the early twentieth century, American social scientists had largely moved beyond Social Darwinist perspectives that made erroneous distinctions between "species" of people and embraced the less racist but still arbitrary categories of Caucasoid, Mongoloid, and Negroid. Sociologists of the period (for example, Park, Burgess, and McKenzie 1928, Wirth 1938) focused on ethnic differences between groups in the United States. From 1945 through 1970, racial minority groups seeking political and social rights in the United States began to challenge the ideals of assimilation or the great melting pot implicit in the focus on ethnicity (Omi and Winant 1994). Sociologists began to follow their lead, examining race more critically even if they still conflated it with ethnicity. Since the 1970s, scholarship on race has been more prolific, authored by members of racial minority groups as well, and has shown that the assignment of individuals and groups to racial categories has changed dramatically over the course of this century alone. It reminds us that race has no unchanging or stable meaning over time.

In their book *Racial Formation in the United States* (1994), Omi and Winant observe that over the course of the last century conceptions of race were usually examined as constituent of other paradigms that scholars saw as broader—ethnicity, class, and nation, for example (9, 12). Nonetheless, because race was and continues to be such "a fundamental axis of social organization" (Omi and Winant 1994: 13), these same scholars found themselves interpreting, representing, and explaining racial dynamics in efforts to influence the way the society was racially organized and the way resources were distributed. Omi and Winant describe these activities as *racial projects* (1994: 56). Groups and individuals from one end of the political spectrum to the other—and from one end of the color spectrum to the other—have engaged in racial projects throughout the country's history.

Acting Black is one such racial project, focusing on the college experiences of racial minorities for the purpose of improving racial dynamics and advocating inclusion of racial minority groups on any college campus that has a racial majority group. In the next sections, I offer an explanation of race that decouples physical attributes from behavioral and social expectations in an effort to further undermine ideologies of white supremacy. In attending to behavioral and social issues, a range of disciplinary perspectives—theories on sex roles, racial identity development, power, and performance—provide additional ways to think of race in general and blackness in particular.

SOCIAL CONSTRUCTIONISM AND SYMBOLIC INTERACTIONISM

> *[T]he relationship between the individual and the objective social world is like an ongoing balancing act.*
> —*Peter L. Berger and Thomas Luckmann*

A vision of the world as socially constructed emerged from anthropology. Field workers who had visited several societies appreciated that concepts as diverse as cousin, depression, and childhood have quite different definitions and expectations from one place to the next. Anthropologists, therefore, tend to take the social construction of reality for granted. It is those sociologists accustomed to studying Western societies who have needed the reminder that meanings change within the systems we analyze. In *The Social Construction of Reality* (1966), sociologists Berger and Luckmann argue that human life is a negotiated symbiosis. Their observations lead them to understand society as a huge organization in which individuals and institutions, groups, and political climates shape, influence, and contribute to each other. Within sociology, most scholars agree that the definitions of marriage, illness, crime, and sexuality, for example, take their meanings from the contexts in which they are embedded. For our purposes, the meaning of race is understood to change depending on the social context (Gossett 1965, Osborne 1971). This view is social construction-ism. The respondents in *Acting Black* revealed how the meaning of blackness—as a social group and as an individual identity—changed for them over time, by place, or within social interactions.

Symbolic interactionism is an application of social constructionism that focuses on the interaction between people. Interactionists argue that the meanings people at-tribute to each other's behavior—for example, body language, dress, and speech—are perceived symbolically and in turn influence their interactions with each other (Thio 1994). For example, an unshaven motorcyclist wearing heavy boots, a metal-studded leather vest, and bandana may well be "seen" as rough, violent, and threat-ening; but the same individual, clean-shaven and dressed in suit and tie at a wedding, might well be "seen" as approachable. In the same way, each person's apparent racial category also has symbolic meaning for every other one of us, and—depending on the context—can signal a range of possible meanings from danger to trustworthiness or low status to kinship. In chapter 9, we will see examples of this in action.

POWER AND RACE

> *To historicize the question of identity . . . is to introduce an analysis of its production, and thus an analysis of constructions of and conflicts about power; it is also, of course, to call into ques-tion the autonomy and stability of any particular identity as it claims to define and interpret a subject's existence.*
>
> *—Joan W. Scott*

Power, like race, has also been treated as a binary variable, present or absent, one or zero. From the German sociologist Max Weber, who wrote during the 1800s, power has been understood economically and dichotomistically—one has it or one does not have it, and if one does have it one will be able to accumulate more of it. Ger-hard Emmanuel Lenski defines power in the Weberian tradition "as the probability of persons or groups carrying out their will even when opposed by others" (1966: 44).

Michel Foucault, however, encourages us to think about power as multidimen-sional: "What makes power hold good, what makes it accepted, is simply the fact that it doesn't only weigh on us as a force that says no, but that it traverses and produces things, it induces pleasure, forms knowledge, produces discourse. It needs to be con-sidered as a productive network which runs through the whole social body" (1980: 119). There are multiple reasons that people respond to power and find it acceptable and that do not include fear or virtue, as Foucault implies. What is useful here is not whether Foucault's conception of power is complete, but whether his admonition serves as a model for an examination of race.

Race has also been used both positively and negatively to sanction individuals in American society. In fact, like race, power is multiple in its forms, continuous rather than discrete, and shifting depending on the context of the relationship rather than reducible to money, prestige, or the abuse of authority or will. Foucault observes that, in much of the world, power has been understood as repression. Even radical scholars have interpreted power almost completely as juridical and negative, outside the reach of the subaltern, desperately desired, and infinitely corruptible. To this Foucault responds, "It is precisely [the] positive mechanisms that need to be investigated, and here one must free oneself . . . [from] all previous characterizations of the nature of power" (1980: 120–121).

What if, in the same spirit, we were freed from previous characterizations of race and could imagine race in different ways? That freedom would offer us some new possibilities for meeting the challenge of living with the important differences over which we have no control as well as revealing the places over which we do. Indeed, in the next chapter respondents demonstrate that race is not only a badge of insult, as Anthony Appiah has described it (1992), a mark that separates people, allowing for their unjust treatment. It is also a network that defies the modifiers positive and negative and runs through the whole social body.

To examine the multidimensionality of race compels us neither to ignore the oppressive conditions under which the concept of race was generated nor to deny the negative implications its genesis has had for world culture and individual lives. Suffering has not been the only experience of those persons disadvantaged by systems of race categorization. Those advantaged by such systems have not only exploited, ignored, or benefited from them. People have grabbed hold of race, precisely as Omi and Winant have observed, and attempted to manipulate its boundaries and definitions. Perhaps by carefully examining the places where race generates community, responsibility, and dignity as well as the places where it fractures community, exonerates responsibility, undermines dignity, and offers false notions of superiority, perhaps then we will understand race better. This exercise may also lead us to appreciate how race functions as symbol, status, expectation, social construct, and performed role. Race is a structural imperative, a historical legacy, *and* an experiential identity, context-dependent and sometimes malleable.

FROM SEX ROLES TO RACE ROLES: THE PERFORMANCE OF A LIFETIME!

Once I was able to accept my role—as distinguished, I must say, from my "place"—in the extraordinary drama which is America, I was released from the illusion that I hated America.
                                                    —James Baldwin

Sociologists have often characterized social life using the language of performance or dramaturgy (Mead 1934, Berger and Luckmann 1966, for example). In *The Presentation of Self in Everyday Life* (1959), Goffman uses performance as a central organizing theme around which he proposes a theory of human action. Many scholars, including Hughes, Robert Ezra Park, St. Clare Drake, and E. Franklin Frazier, have previously alluded to race as a role, but few have used role theory to describe or theorize racial identity or behavior. This is likely because many sociologists over the past century saw race as a symbol whose power would eventually disappear as people of color assimilated into American culture both phenotypically and culturally. Additionally, because the idea of roles implies an acquescence to the status quo or neutrality (Connell 1987), some scholars have probably been keen to avoid suggesting that racial minorities were in permanently subservient or unequal roles. Ironically, race has continued to be the apparent reason for the lack of full political and economic integration of certain groups into the U.S., and role theory might have shaken if not undermined the idea that racial categorization is fused with particular roles.

The subversive power of treating race as a role lies in the implication that race is not solely phenotypic, but is one way of behaving, a place to be entered and exited, a garment to be put on and taken off, impermanent, calculated, and chosen. Indeed, the voices of the men and women quoted in the next chapter show the unpredictability of performance. No performance is identical to the one it precedes or follows (Phelan 1993). If role theory is going to continue to be useful, however, appreciating the ways in which roles themselves can quickly come to seem natural and conform to the hierarchical (and sometimes oppressive) aspects of the culture they inhabit is also necessary.

Scholars of sex/gender systems have used the analogy of performance to examine and expose how much human behavior has been dictated by socially constructed roles rather than by biologically determined roles (Rich 1980, Connell 1987, Andersen 1988, Stoltenberg 1989, Butler 1991, Fuss 1991). It is this work, in particular, that has encouraged my understanding that sex difference is not only about reproductive difference, but also about ways of behaving that people are taught. So, too, the work of scholars theorizing sexuality has revealed that sexual orientation is about more than erotic desire, that it is also about how erotic desire is demonstrated and how we demonstrate ourselves demonstrating it. Similarly, race is not only—or solely—about phenotypic difference, but also about which differences match up with the behaviors that are expected from each racial group. Indeed, regardless of how much our behavior may contradict racial stereotypes, we each still have to navigate the expectations of others.

Monique Wittig is one scholar who does not take for granted the social structural arrangements between men and women and their accompanying roles. In her essay "The Straight Mind" (1992), Wittig argues that the lesbian is "not-woman." For the majority of people, woman is synonymous with specific social expectations of the straight, adult female[1] in Western society. Since the lesbian does not conform to these expectations, Wittig characterizes the lesbian as a "not-woman."

Wittig's ideas provoke me to think beyond the situation of persons who defy culturally proscribed sex expectations, and to then think about defying and conforming to race expectations and race roles. The ways in which the people interviewed for this project spoke about race encourage me to think about the African American "not-black," or the person of African descent who does not conform to social expectations of a black person. I have been led to broader thinking about how much black and white (and red, yellow, and brown) are also roles in the personal and institutional dramas of race, rather than simply markers of biological difference, signifiers of ethnic traditions, and expected behaviors.

The work of Butler (1991) continues to push my thinking. Her focus is on the institution of heterosexuality and the ways in which the roles of sexuality are played out. She argues that performances are repeated for the precise reason that the role being performed is unstable. In other words, to approach permanence, it must be repeated continually. By emphasizing that sexual identity is continuously reinstituted and reinvented, Butler provides us with a model for understanding that racial identity, too, is also continuously reinstituted and reinvented. Butler's appreciation of identity's fragility implies two things: first, that changes in an actor's routine depend on the audience, and second, that an uncertainty exists in the mind of the actor that betrays the instability of the racial or sexual identity at which the actor is "playing."

Using sexual orientation, Butler makes these ideas concrete. She discusses heterosexuality as a role and an institution that is compulsively played out:

> [I]f heterosexuality is compelled to *repeat itself* in order to establish the illusion of its own uniformity and identity, then this is an identity permanently at risk. . . . If there is, as it were, always a compulsion to repeat, repetition never fully accomplishes identity. That there is a need for a repetition at all is a sign that identity. . . requires [*sic*] to be instituted again and again, which is to say that it runs the risk of becoming *de*-instituted at every interval. (1991: 24)

In the very need or decision to repeat the performance compulsively, the actor betrays the nature of the characteristic in question as, at the most, unreal, and, at the least, incoherent and unstable. That characteristic might be straightness, masculinity, or whiteness; it might also be gayness, femininity, or blackness. To generalize from Butler's point, persons with dominant-group characteristics (who also enjoy higher status) are compelled to remind others of their dominant-group characteristics again and again in order to prove themselves to seem more real, more healthy, or more normal. In other words, part of why they repeat the performance compulsively is to prove to others that they are more worthy of or more securely possessing that high status.

Butler's point should make us question not only the performances that many people tend to think of as deviant or unusual but *all* performances. We all repeat the performances of our identities, whether our identities are relatively stable or unstable, and whether aspects of our identities increase or decrease our social status. Butler's distinction between the stable and the unstable identity is not always clear, and to focus on that alone seems a bit beside the point. All identities are evanescent.

When the aspect of our identities under discussion is not an occupation, like "professor" or "waitress," but even closer to one's core self-definition—like religion, race, sexual orientation, or biological sex—distinguishing between role and essence becomes more complicated. Performance is still involved, but it no longer carries with it the connotation of imitation or act. Most people do not think of themselves as *acting* when they behave in ways that feel natural and normal. With the following questions, Butler demonstrates the limitations of the performance metaphor:

> When and where does my being a lesbian come into play, when and where does this playing a lesbian constitute something like what I am? To say that I "play" at being one is not to say that I am not one "really"; rather, how and where I play at being one is the way in which that "being" gets established, instituted, circulated, and confirmed. This is not a performance from which I can take radical distance, for this is deep-seated play, psychically entrenched play, *and this "I" does not play its lesbianism as a role* (1991: 18, her emphasis).

Here, Butler chafes at the analogy between human behavior and drama. Indeed, Butler's use of italics signals her conviction that she is not playing at being a lesbian. Though her attempt to turn heterosexuality on its head by treating homosexuality as *not* play and *not* pretend is admirable, Butler's seeming inability to (or her decision not to) highlight the instability of *all* identities is a limitation. Goffman recognized precisely the ways in which we play the roles of our identities: *we are all performing all of the time.* For Goffman, performance has broader meaning than the desire to make one's identity seem stable; for him, performance needs to be neither compulsively repeated nor deceptive. He argues that we are always behaving for an audience because we can never escape the presence of the social world. Rather than an accusation that we are all inauthentic, "playing" our roles is what makes us authentically human (1959).

PERFORMANCE AND THE PROBLEM OF IMITATION

The fact is "black" has never been just there either. It has always been an unstable identity, psychically, culturally, and politi-

*cally. It, too, is a narrative, a story, a history. Something con-
structed, told, spoken, not simply found.*

—Stuart Hall

Since white people have understood themselves to be the norm in American society, through white dominance, white people have (in the United States and in other
colonialist societies) implied that being anything other than white and yet having
good values must indicate mimicry of whiteness. In the United States, it is obvious
that black, brown, and red people, and to a lesser extent yellow people, are—when
they become materially or occupationally successful—understood to be acting
"white," and are often referred to as Oreos, apples, bananas, or simply sellouts. Discussions of racial mimicry can be found in the work of Franz Fanon (1968), Aimé Césaire (1972), Albert Memmi (1967), and many others. Each racial minority has a
particular relationship to whiteness and attendant stereotypes that explain success
and failure in ways that emphasize the group or the individual, depending on the context. But whiteness, though seen by many European Americans (and nonwhites, too)
as the standard, the norm, and the goal, is itself context-dependent. Whiteness is only
occasionally the standard, the norm, and the goal. And it is itself a bundle of expectations that whites, as well as nonwhites, find themselves trying to meet and to perform,
even when they do not acknowledge that bundle of expectations in racial terms.

A NOTE ABOUT PSYCHOLOGY

*Unraveling and reweaving the identity strands of our experience
is a never-ending task in a society where important dimensions of
our lives are shaped by the simultaneous forces of subordination
and domination. We continue to be works in progress for a lifetime.*

—Beverly Tatum

In racial identity development theory,[2] a model in which individuals are understood to develop toward greater psychological health as they come to terms with the
implications of their own racial identities, the focus is on the individual's progress
from one stage to another. Furthermore, identity is considered to be relatively stable
by most theorists (Helms 1993: 41).[3] People have the potential to move through various stages of personality maturation over the course of a lifetime, but I would argue
that race, sex/gender, religious, and class affiliations are constitutive of personality
rather than personality being constitutive of any one of these.

The interviews with African Americans in this study reveal that racial attitudes
and ideas about the self are open to change and challenge, are negotiated, expanded,

and contracted. "Open to change" is not synonymous for me with "unstable." I do not argue that persons whose interviews I return to in the next chapter had unstable racial identities (though examining the variability of identity is my focus). Rather, it is my position that although identity is relatively stable, it includes a slightly different bundle of attitudes and ideas for each individual. One's ideas about race, gender, sexuality, class, and religion, regarding self and others, are included in that bundle and influenced by one's first family as the self is mirrored back through others, then by the neighborhood or school, and by increasingly larger groups of people. In other words, individuals' ideas about self and others can go through radical shifts without their personalities seeming to change willy-nilly depending on their environment. This is because racial identity, like sexual identity or gender identity, is only one aspect of one's relationship to the world.[4]

Psychologists who espouse racial identity development theories have, as compared to sociologists or anthropologists, already become comfortable with the notion of individual change, since the psychologist's primary unit of analysis has been the individual system or the individual within a family system. While most sociologists also admit individual change, theorizing at this level has not been the focus of the discipline, for our primary unit of analysis has been the group or the social system. That said, most work in this area of psychology, while including an appreciation of social structure and cultural meaning in the very focus on race as a crucial aspect of identity, tends to treat the individual's life through the lens of development or progress. I contend that one can find oneself in an environment rather arbitrarily and that the environment and its culture can alter that construction, status, or performance of one's identity in the same way that our personalities shift when we speak a different language.[5] Such a shift, then, may be less a fact of development than of context.

SUMMARY

Having received my training in sociology, I have tended to focus on the ways that racial identity emerges as a result of structural forces. The discussions of respondents in this study pushed me to appreciate race through the lenses of anthropology, economics, and psychology. I became newly familiar with race as status, as interactive with socioeconomic class, as context-dependent, as an identity that can described by developmental process, and, finally, as a characteristic that—like all characteristics assigned to us—can be manipulated, played with, or performed. College alumni reveal all of these aspects of race in the next chapter.

BLACKNESS[1]

*I was on both sides. I remember when you couldn't call me black.
You know, Negro was acceptable; nigger was okay. Negro was
just a nicer way of saying it. But we went from that to Black,
and everybody had to accept Black. And Black was cool, you
know.*

—*Joseph, Howard '71*

This study began as an interest in the college experience, but it quickly became apparent there was much to be learned about race at this moment in the United States by taking it seriously and examining it at the micro level of individual experience and narration. The interviews with these men and women show many things, in fact, too many things to analyze in one chapter or one book. Their words reveal the ways that race is indeed shaped by and overlaps with class, stratification, and sex/gender explanations of inequality and oppression, and how racial identity is socially constructed by contexts as wide ranging as historical era, campus climate, neighborhood, and conversation.

The women and men of *Acting Black* came of age after the heyday of the Civil Rights Movement and were, therefore, positioned to enter corporate and educational institutions that had already begun to open their doors to racial minorities and women. While many white Americans were able to embrace the legal changes that no longer discriminated against nonwhites, just as many were unable to translate those changes into their personal philosophies. The result has been a combination of informal discriminatory behavior and a conservative and status quo interpretation of many of the legal changes that have taken place. Despite formal changes for the better, many African Americans, including my respondents, have experienced mistreatment on a continuum from the discomfort of their peers to harassment, abuse of authority or disdain by professors, and violence. Their descriptions of college and postcollege life sometimes reflect, therefore, contradictory experiences and confusing times. They describe living in a state of formal racial equality while informal racial inequality persists.

All of the approaches to understanding race to which I referred in the previous chapter help to interpret the situation of post–Civil Rights era blacks in college. In this chapter, several important points about race, and blackness in particular, emerge:

- People of the same apparent phenotypic racial identity do not always agree on a definition of that identity. In this case, African Americans are not always in agreement about what blackness means.
- People encourage each other to expand and contract each other's definitions of what it means to be a member of a racial group, whether or not they realize they're doing this. In our case, African Americans may discuss what blackness means with each other consciously or they may engage each other less explicitly in broadening or narrowing its definition by sharing personal experiences that push the boundaries of their own definitions.
- People may affirm or defy racial expectations in the interest of the group or self. In this study, African Americans report consciously playing to and against the racial expectations that others had of them.
- Racial and gender identity appear to influence each other.
- And finally, the men and women with whom I spoke reveal awareness that the racial expectations others have of them influenced their success or failure at being able to avoid, meet, or transcend those expectations. Some of the examples presented are new, while others will be recognizable from earlier chapters. Where examples are repeated, they are used for the purpose of revealing the multidimensionality of race.

RACE IS SOCIALLY CONSTRUCTED

Hearing Malcolm [X] analyze the dreadful psychological consequences of black self-hate had a transforming effect upon the consciousness of African-Americans. They began to think black and act black, because Malcolm, through the power of his oratory, helped them to realize and to accept their blackness as the essential element in the definition of their humanity. "All of us are black first," he told African-Americans, "and everything else second."
—James Cone

The argument that race is socially constructed is not new (Hamilton 1949, Berger and Luckmann 1966). The words of Northwestern Wildcats and Howard Bison go even further to suggest that simply having as one's primary reference group or being physically surrounded by persons of the same racial heritage is not sufficient to guarantee a similar understanding of or way of talking about race.

Henry and Robert are examples of the fact that African Americans are not always in agreement about what it means to be black. Said another way, they define blackness using different metaphors and emphasizing different things. In the following excerpt from Henry's interview, he reveals his awareness that blackness is at least in part associated with expected behaviors. Since he knows that the behaviors that describe his own life are not associated with blackness in the minds of most people of every color, he (re)defines blackness for me so that I will not confuse his behavior with a repudiation of his African heritage. Moreover, he distances himself from those African Americans whom he perceives—and perhaps whom he supposes I also perceive—as materialistic, status-mongers.

I'm not a bona fide buppie; I don't have no BMW. I drive a Volkswagen . . . I don't need a BMW. All I want is to be happy and have peace of mind. And that's what I have and school gave me that. School gave me my lifestyle. Everyone has to do it their own way. . . . There's something for everybody. I know people who get lost in school. And I guess they happy, but I don't think they are 'cause it's like they're always puttin' on. They're not real to me. I have this thing about being real. That's why I work on my lawn. I have to touch the earth. Because it's real. It's some substance. And you go and take a good look at it and you think it's just dirt, but this is life. This is what life is really about, believe it or not. It's not about the *Wall Street Journal* and what the stock market is doing. Life is in the ground. This is dirt. This is the base, where everything comes from and where we all will return. And we miss that sometimes; we forget about it. I try and stay in touch with that. I come home sometimes and cut my grass and dig in the lawn to keep my roots and know who I am. It's just like being Black is not just wearing your hair a certain way or changing your name or going on different marches or reading this and caring about what they did in South Africa. That is not the basis of being Black. We have a culture and a way we talk at times, but what's more important to me is where we're going. You know, I think my definition of the Black Race is a certain pride: I am a Black Man and I can achieve. I am doing my best and I'm still Black. I'm still Black. I was very radical in school—I mean sandals, dashikis, I didn't cut my hair for three years. I cut it during my junior year and I didn't cut it again until I was working. That was the way it was. I'm a corporate soldier now. I won't lie. I have the uniform. I mean, I will admit it if anybody asks me: I'm a corporate soldier. (Henry, NU '77)

What counts in Henry's definition of racial identity is less who his parents were or where he grew up and more who he is now—"I am a black man and I can achieve." But he also locates his sense of what it means to be black, indeed what it means to be human, using the metaphor of lawn care. Indeed, many people find peace and creativity in the ritual of caring for their lawns and tending their gardens. Because Henry's description is almost synonymous with home ownership in the American lexicon, his choice of metaphor implies a desire to move away from behavioral and ideological definitions of race and toward the less racial associations of blackness as American or human. Indeed, his "confession" of being a corporate soldier can also be interpreted as a declaration of pride. The measure of his success is that he has earned a place in a corporate world that a generation ago would not have accepted him.

In their famous study *Black Consciousness, Identity, and Achievement*, Gurin and Epps observe that "the problem of how to integrate the personal and collective levels of identity is not dead or dated" (1975: vii). Henry's unsolicited soliloquy demonstrates the continued relevance of that statement. While his description may initially strike some as superficial or arbitrary, Henry's improvisational metaphor serves several purposes: first, it allows him to define who he is now; second, he is able to include race in that definition; and third, he avoids rejecting where he came from.

Fordham explains that for anyone whose identity is under construction, by the larger society or in their own eyes, Henry's description makes perfect sense. "Ad hocing or improvising one's life suggests constructing an identity that, on the one hand, does not violate one's sense of 'Self,' while, on the other hand, enhancing one's sense of fit within a given context" (Fordham 1993: 12).

Like many other post–Civil Rights era African Americans, Henry wants to be seen as an individual.[2] And yet, he is not willing to give up the concept of racial identity—"my definition of the Black Race is a certain pride." Still "blackness" is now described by the nonracial, indeed typically American, metaphor of tending to his lawn and garden. Its meaning, subsumed within the homogenizing rubric of property ownership, has clearly changed dramatically from the days of the Black Power Movement. This move away from physical or ideological definitions of race and toward "just-like-everybody-else" definitions that finally are indistinguishable from the identities of middle-class white people, is one of the things of which Frazier (1957) accused middle-class blacks in the 1940s and 1950s. (That said, middle-class whites very seldom feel compelled to search for metaphors to describe themselves racially.) And yet, as opposed to Frazier's arrogant status-mongers, Henry balances his description of "pride" with humility, obvious in his biblical allusion: we all start as dust and to dust we will return. Finally, because Henry knows his behavior may also be suspect to both blacks and whites, he implies that his choices are at once examples of racial pride and at the same time beyond race.

In contrast, Robert, also a Northwestern graduate, reveals his understanding of racial identity while answering a question about campus participation. In chapter 5, Robert's experience served as an example of the separate social lives of blacks and whites at NU. Here, it is as an example of an alternative definition of racial identity:

> [M]y freshman year it was not the thing to go to University Theater productions. And there was a group of us who were really into music and theater. And so freshman year I never went to a University Theater production—didn't go to [the annual variety show], didn't go to concerts or anything. But sophomore year I started saying, Well, wait a minute, I *know* I'm black. I went to a black high school, I lived in a black neighborhood all my life, I really can do this without risking my blackness. (Robert, NU '80)

For Robert, racial identity is defined by the associations of his recent past: parents, neighborhood, high school, and friends. He distinguishes his racial identity from his broader, one might say extraracial, interests. He remembers the confidence he gained when he realized that his identification with the black community was clear enough to himself and others in that it conformed to what most people *expected* of black people. As he says, he grew up in a working-class home, lived in a racially segregated neighborhood, and attended an all-black high school. He had an arsenal of associations to respond to any accusation of not being authentically black. Robert figured that his background—as someone who grew up in a working-class black neighborhood—fit with others' expectations enough to allow him to participate in unexpected activities without being threatening to either blacks or nonblacks. By conforming to racial expectations in some arenas, he gained a greater ability to challenge them in others.

In the same way that definitions of blackness are arrived at and justified differently, it meant something different to be black and from the city than it did to be black and from the suburbs. Hannah explains,

> [My first year] was hard 'cause me and my roommate didn't get along. She . . . grew up in predominantly white schools and she lived in suburbia. So even though we were from the same area—they try to put people from the same city together—we still didn't get along. 'Cause she thought I was a hood', hoodlum, and I thought she was prissy. So we had problems. But by the second semester, it was cool. (Hannah, HU '88)

Hannah and her roommate learned that to be African American and from the same region did not guarantee a common understanding of what it meant to be black. While they never became best friends, according to Hannah, they learned that one need not conform to stereotypes to be truly black. Like Henry and Robert, Hannah's story reveals a consciousness of what others—black and nonblack—expect of African Americans and how those expectations are usually measured. Robert, Henry, and

Hannah reveal their awareness of what others think, and their behavior—or at least how they explain their behavior—is shaped (or performed) accordingly.

Hannah remembers that she and her roommate were aware that simply being black and from the same region did not guarantee friendship or even shared culture. Hannah's discovery is one that Matthew, who also went to Howard ('86), made his first year. Below, he describes his anxiety about attending a predominantly black college after having grown up in a predominantly white town.

> *Sarah Willie*: Do you remember having any expectations of what college would be like?
>
> *Matthew*: Scared to death. I was absolutely petrified. . . . In high school, you grow up around all white people and none of them are going to Howard. In high school, my biggest problems came from black people, because I was class president and they saw me as being too white. . . . And I'm like, Oh, my god, I'm gonna go to a black school and these people are gonna harass me and I'm gonna hate it. And then I got there—and Howard is in a lower-income area—and I was petrified. I had never even seen a [housing] project before. . . . I guess I had very low expectations in terms of me getting along with people. I thought that everyone was going to like hate me, and that everyone was gonna tell me that I talk like I was white. . . . It was a lot easier than I thought it was gonna be, because, I'd say, probably about half the students came from similar backgrounds [to my own]. . . . I thought American Top 40 [music] was gonna be laughed out of the dormitory, and you know, I'd walk down the hall and hear [the heavy metal rock group] AC/DC and I was like, Oh, maybe I'm not that weird after all. Or you know [some] people would assume I was from California or something. And I was like, no, that's [just] how people talk in suburbia. You know, it's not just a "valley" kind of a thing.

We learn several important things from Matthew in this memory: one, he believes he was successful in convincing other African Americans of his own authentic, if different, black experience; and two, he learned that some black people have even less stereotypically black tastes than his own. With these observations, he reveals how race is socially constructed, even at the level of individual interaction. He demonstrates that, at Howard, black people—like Hannah from Philadelphia and her suburban roommate—were able to introduce each other to expanded understandings of what it means to be black in America. In other words, he is telling us about individual participation in broadening the definition of blackness. And third, by confessing his own precollege anxiety, Matthew shows us the anxiety that many blacks have about meeting the expectations of authentic blackness. Conscious that his background was not understood to be normative for African Americans, he neither had to change his behavior nor leave the setting because the spectrum of what it meant to be black, at least at Howard, was broad enough to accommodate him.

Unlike Matthew—who was at Howard in the early 1980s—Debbie argues that Northwestern in the early 1970s was still feeling the repercussions of the Black Power Movement (BPM). A few blacks that were middle class or affluent felt keenly the expectation that "black people are urban and working class." Those students who entered college in the late 1960s and early 1970s were doing so just a decade after Frazier's scathing characterization of the black middle class, *Black Bourgeoisie* (1957), and during the height of the movement. The BPM implicated whites as undeservedly privileged and challenged the country's class hierarchy. It also characterized blackness as the distillation of a few specific characteristics that included identification with the poor and working class, an embrace of racial separatism and a particular brand of African-American culture, distrust of dominant-group cultural practices and rejection of legal authority. When, suddenly, "Black Is Beautiful" and it became a point of pride to have come from a working-class family, those few middle-class blacks (overrepresented at elite colleges) must have found it difficult to acknowledge their affluent upbringings. Debbie remembers, "[W]hen I was in college, I think half the people were probably pretending to be something that they weren't. I knew I was middle class, [and] there were a lot of students there who were not, but there were a lot of students there who were but who would not own up to it" (Debbie, NU '75).

Of course, the desirability of coming from a working-class background was often in the eye of the beholder. Many working-class students say they gained a new understanding of what black could mean by meeting affluent black students. Eventually, meeting fellow African Americans from such radically different class backgrounds broadened their definition of blackness as well. At first, however, many alumni told me that meeting affluent blacks threatened their conceptions of self. Paul describes his reaction as a first-year student:

> I knew white people had money and were privileged, but I had never encountered wealthy blacks, well-to-do blacks. I mean Sammy-Davis-Jr-and-Aretha-Franklin-wealthy. But *it blew my mind* to see blacks who were able to ski the Swiss Alps during spring break and stuff like that. And [one woman] went to Paris on a shopping trip. I mean, we had to go collect pop bottles so we could pay for next year's tuition. It just completely blew my mind. I mean there were guys who'd order pizza for the whole dorm. Just blew me away, just blew me away. I had never been in contact with blacks who were well-to-do. That was the biggest adjustment for me. 'Cause that was the first time I ever had any self-doubt. I'm not ego-driven, but I'm a pretty confident individual. . . . I mean [this one guy] had a different kind of car

every year: a Benz, a Porsche. . . . [I remember wondering,] Why do they have this and I don't? 'Cause I remember coming off this ego trip from high school in which I got almost everything and all of a sudden this kid has everything. . . . I mean, I thought I had everything. I mean, it was a real mind-blower. (Paul, NU '75)

Robert describes a similar discomfort:

[That first year at NU] I was exposed to more solidly middle-class black people than I had ever been exposed to before. You know, everyone *I* knew pretty much had gone to public school in Chicago. And all of a sudden, I was exposed to all these black kids who were incredibly talented, incredibly smart. . . . [So] I did very little [in the way of extracurricular activities that first year.] I was so intimidated by feeling . . . [let me put it this way,] the worst school in the city that all these [middle-class] black kids were from was Lindbloom. Lindbloom is like a magnet school that pulled the *crème de la crème* of kids from the city. The rest of the kids who [I met in NU's pre-freshman summer program] were from . . . lots of Catholic and private schools. It was just incredibly intimidating for me. Everyone played the piano and flute and talked about trips to Europe with their parents. And these are the black kids! I was just completely and totally out of my element. And I was also pathologically shy. . . . And so all these forces converged to make my freshman experience incredibly miserable, I mean just really, really bad. . . . I just didn't feel comfortable with myself. (Robert, NU '80)

Affluent black students, then, ended up stretching the ideas of what was possible for working-class black students, often without being conscious of doing so. Of course, there were probably many things that working-class students taught affluent blacks, but my focus here is on expanding definitions of blackness. Affluent black students were, after all, already aware of the existence of working-class and poor blacks.

Expanded understandings of who black people could be and what they could achieve was not limited to material advantages or occupational opportunities. Lynn, for example, had thought of herself as "the exception" because of her underexposure to the range of black people. Her conceptions of African Americans were greatly broadened at Northwestern in terms of intellectual ability, charisma, and talent:

[I]n college, for the first time in my life, I'm seeing a lot of *black* women, like women *who are so smart*—smarter than I could have ever have imagined—because I was always the top shit, you know, in my own circle. And to see women coming from all around the country, majoring in engineering and psychology—you name it—just *incredibly brilliant* people, I was just kind of in awe. I just had never seen so many black women who were so smart, who were *so attractive*, who had all these different writing skills and music abilities. It blew my mind. (Lynn, NU '83)

The things that Lynn stresses above and Betsy mentions below—achievement, intelligence, and physical beauty—are precisely the characteristics that have historically been and continue to be misrepresented in this country's ambivalent portrait of African Americans. "And just knowing the variety of black people and that they can *achieve*. I mean you really see it firsthand, that they're *bright* and they're *pretty*, and all of that. It was very inspirational" (Betsy, HU '74). Furthermore, while both Betsy and Lynn convey their surprise, Betsy from Howard describes expanded horizons as something that inspired rather than daunted her.

SOCIAL CONSTRUCTION IS CONSTITUTIVE OF OTHERS' EXPECTATIONS

Expectation is also part of construction. As Hughes argues, "people carry in their minds a set of expectations concerning the auxiliary traits properly associated with many of the specific positions available in our society" (1984: 144). The only qualification his observation needs is that stratification is even more obscured today than it was sixty years ago. It remains inarguable that people carry in their minds a set of expectations concerning the auxiliary traits associated with stereotypes of racial, ethnic, religious, class, and gender groups.

Several alumni mentioned high school guidance counselors and teachers who revealed their prejudices by expressing low expectations of them. Hannah's story is representative of alumni of both schools who recall coming up against the low expectations of their teachers. With the help of their parents or their own willpower, these alumni fought others' expectations that they were not able to go to college.

> The [counselor] in my high school told me I should go to beauty school. Can you believe that? That was her advice . . . and my English teacher was the same way. She was like, "You'll never make it through your freshman year in college. Your writing skills are terrible." And they were. Freshman English was the hardest class in my life, but I mean it really wasn't encouraging. . . . They kind of pushed along their few favorites, and the rest of the people [were on their own]. (Hannah, HU '88)

At the time of the interview, Hannah was working as a corporate manager for a Fortune 500 company. Obviously, negative expectations can be debilitating and disheartening. Hannah's experiences conform to what sociologists call the labeling theory, which is based on research revealing the power of expectations, either positive or negative, on behavioral outcomes for persons who are the objects of such expectations.

Expectation was crucial to students at Howard and Northwestern being able to see possibilities for themselves and by extension to expand their own constructions of what it meant to be black. Both of the Northwestern graduates below talk about internships that introduced them to affluent black people and the cultural rules of predominantly white corporate America:

> It was the greatest year because I had an opportunity to do an internship with IBM . . . and it was just a tremendous experience because it introduced me to things I'd never seen, even all the time being at the Northwestern campus. It put me in touch with minorities that owned sailboats and had prestigious jobs and lived a suburban, traditional kind of lifestyle, earned great sums of money, certainly by my standards. . . . [F]rom my perception it was just really outstanding, and it just gave me a different sense of what one could truly accomplish. (Adam, NU '74)

Adam notes the new possibility of being black and wealthy, while Jennifer notes the experience of being introduced to the affluence of corporate culture:

> I was an intern at [a Fortune 500] corporation downtown in their corporate affairs department. . . . It was a really good internship. I wrote a lot of biographies of the senior vice president for this and [the senior vice president] for that. They do a weekly newsletter that goes out to their employees— they have about a thousand employees—and I wrote that. But it was more eye-opening not in terms of the work experience but in terms of the cultural corporate experience. Because like I got to go to the annual meeting, and I got to go out to dinner several times, and I got to go on a boat ride—I had never been on a boat—sailing, and all that kind of stuff. And I got to see how you're supposed to act when you're standing around human resource people; how to make small talk with people you could care less about. So it was enlightening in that way. (Jennifer, NU '88)

Zweigenhaft and Domhoff followed graduates of the ABC (A Better Chance) program for their study *Blacks in the White Establishment*. They came away with similar findings: "[I]n addition to the formal education they had received, many had acquired at least two skills that became part of their cultural and social capital: the ability to talk with anyone about anything, and the ability to benefit from the access to influential people they had gained as a result of attending elite schools" (1991: 107). For Jennifer and Adam, experiences with wealthy and successful people in settings to which they would not otherwise have gained access offered them more life lessons as well.

Those alumni who were not privy to such experiences in college are aware that they are missing something, not something genetic, not even wealth itself, but what is learned by growing up within the culture of the wealthy:

I think some of the things that happen in the corporate world, it's more typical of what white kids get in their home life than a black kid, because our parents are not part of the corporate structure of wealth. There are more blacks who are a part of the corporate structure now and they can impart some of that stuff to their kids. But before, we didn't have a clue. It's like, you grew up in a household where your mother is a maid and your father is doing construction work, some menial kind of job. They don't have a clue . . . the kinds of things that you talk about in your household have no bearing on that. . . . I think especially if you're going to a black school, [this is] an issue that might need to be dealt with specifically. (Kirstin, HU '74)

Kirstin understands that there are things one cannot know without exposure. Clearly, expectation and exposure are fundamental to allowing elasticity to the roles people may play within a racial designation.

Elasticity of expectation was fundamental to helping many of the respondents in my study form broader expectations of themselves and an enlarged definition of blackness. Joseph reveals that there are ways one cannot see oneself without exposure to the possibilities:

[T]here's really no limits to what [a kid from a background like my own] can do. I've seen people in every capacity. There's not an area of any profession that I haven't met [an African American] there who's doing it or excelling in it. So don't be afraid of any area. Don't let the fact that people think that . . . black people can't do it because they're not smart enough. . . . A lot of people don't know that there are a lot of black people in a lot of different areas. . . . [You] don't necessarily have to meet someone; just realize that [you] can do anything that [you] want to do. (Joseph, HU '71)

For Joseph, just knowing about the possibilities is more than half the battle of pursuing dreams and realizing options.

Especially for those people who had grown up in situations where they only saw a couple of options for their lives, the chance to go to college, especially a black college, provided them with a broader understanding of what it might mean to be black. Karl echoes Joseph's observation: "I just realized that I can do a lot of things. There's really no limit to what I can do. . . . I think I got a real good idea [at Howard] of what it is to be black in a lot of different parts of the country, and to realize that people can do it. No matter where you are, where you're coming from, you can aspire to be something" (Karl, HU '89). Karl's remarks imply that African Americans need a variety of ideas of "how" to be black, since there are such limited black roles on television, in the movies, and even in some peoples' neighborhoods. In addition, Karl's remarks show that college taught him that to be black in Detroit was not necessarily the same thing as it was in New York City, Cincinnati, or Seattle.

Lucy recalls her perception that expressing low expectations of students at Howard was not tolerated. This implies that people at the institution understood how important expectation is for their students: "[T]here was one professor there, but she didn't last too long, I think because of her attitude, where if people wanted to go on to, let's say, graduate school, she would tell them that they shouldn't try that, that they should try something else" (Lucy, HU n.d.).

People behave according to the expectations of others and also have their own expectations of how others should behave. In other words, not only did students have to "live up to" or "strive against" the expectations of others, they also developed their expectations of how professors, particularly black professors, should act. Like Terry, the Northwestern Wildcat in chapter 5 who was frustrated with her black professor for not meeting her expectations, Howard alumnus Stan (HU '86) recalls a particular African-American professor who did not fit his expectation of what it meant to be black.

> *Stan:* [T]here was this one professor . . . he was from Harvard. And I'm not talking about [everyone] who goes to a white college . . . but he was a nerd. . . . This guy, he came into class [with] flood[pants], smoking a pipe. He wore the same thing every day. And the way he spoke to us was like, "You've been slightly culturally deprived of knowing how to even talk to your own people." And I'm not faulting him for that because I saw people who tried to be white. And it's like, okay, you can try to be white, but you can cool [out] up here at Howard. There's no need. The city's ninety-eight percent black and the school is almost one hundred percent black. No need to be white down here!

> *Sarah Willie:* Maybe that was just natural for him.

> *Stan:* Maybe it was.

> *Sarah Willie:* Or did it seem like he was putting it on?

> *Stan:* Well, I have no idea. Because if you've been trained a certain way for ten, fifteen, or twenty years, don't expect for that to turn around in two years. If you're a drug addict for fifteen years, you're going to be a drug addict for the rest of your life. I mean, you're going to be an alcoholic or whatever for the rest of your life. You're recovering. . . . He was a recovering black white man. [We both laugh.] I don't even know if he was recovering yet.

In contrast to Stan's expectations, Gwen rejects the notion of an authentic black way of being: "I wasn't the typical Northwestern student. I just could not be categorized; there was no place for me, so I didn't get stuck in a rut. . . . [M]y friends were mostly other oddballs. Just a little bit off center, really! Not your typical black student, not your typical white student, not your typical anything!" (Gwen, NU '81). Although Gwen refuses the idea of "true blackness," like many women she does so implicitly assuming the burden of that rejection by referring to herself as atypical. Similarly, Lucy argues that what it means to be black is multidimensional:

> [A]ll the black people [at Howard] were . . . not unified in any one course or under our skin color; we are not going in the same direction; . . . there are as many view points as there are people; . . . that's how [Howard] was. And I didn't expect that because I thought that if we were "the talented tenth" we're supposed to know better than to buy into all that other social stuff [including making a] big deal about dressing. (Lucy, HU n.d.)

At the same time that Lucy observes this diversity, she is disappointed by it. Invoking DuBois' notion of "the talented tenth," she expected blacks at Howard to not only be bright and ready for leadership, but mature, less cliquish, less judgmental, and more politically unified. The discontinuity between her expectations and the reality she found is quickly attributed to her own shortcomings. She did not graduate. When asked if she would like to return, she says, "I'd like to go back and change me, not change anything about Howard" (Lucy attended HU in the 1980s without graduating). Like Sue, in the end, Lucy attributes the problem to herself.

Simone de Beauvoir once wrote, "One is not born a woman, one becomes a woman." In the excerpt below, Sally suggests that one is not born black, one becomes black by learning the culture of black America. And "becoming black" for Sally was a positive thing:

> [T]here's no question there's a lot to be gained from a black cultural experience. . . . There are sort of black traditions in [the] closed system [of black culture] that are acceptable [and others] that are not acceptable. . . . This was probably the first time in my life that I really got to know all these black folks. And so it was learning a lot about the culture, but it was learning by doing. I had never really been in a system that was predominantly black. . . . And so, for that reason, I would certainly try to advocate to send my children to Howard or a Howard-like school. (Sally, HU '74)

If one is phenotypically black and therefore racially subordinate, one needs to be fluent in both the subculture and the dominant culture for the sake of survival.

Biculturalism, Joseph (HU '71) implies, is not necessary for the success of white students. Below, he elaborates on Sally's point.

> *Sarah Willie*: Since you are a Howard graduate who'd choose NU instead of Howard if you were to do it again, do you think it matters whether kids go to a black college or a white college?

> *Joseph*: I think it matters for a black student. If a black student has a black background, he should probably experience a white environment. And if a black student has a white background—like my son went to [the local racially mixed] high school, and that's pretty much all he knew. Well, you've got to realize that things are different. Things are not the way they are at [the local] high school [here where blacks and whites all know each other] because they go to the same school. They *have* to [know each other]. Given a choice, they probably would segregate. So I think he went off [to college] thinking that every thing was just fine, and he's finding right now that it's not. He's twenty-one years old and he's in the job market and he's seeing that the point of view [of white people] is different.

Joseph wonders if his son should have gone to a predominantly black college to be better prepared for—ironically—the self-confidence to deal with white people.

It wasn't just Northwestern alumni who remember consciously constructing their identities. Howard alumni, as well, give examples of performance, or consciously constructing an identity:

> There was this image that one had to have [at Howard]. The image was, "I don't wear blue jeans or T-shirts to campus; I wear three-piece suits and dark glasses" kind of thing. . . . And then . . . [there] were like photographers for [the campus newspaper, and although they were also] Greeks, come to think of it, they were the "blue jean ones" . . . more political, you know, "I'm here to make a statement." (Sally, HU '74)

Making a statement is something that most college students participate in at one point or another during their college careers. For black students, the recipe began with the roux of race.

If blackness has had a history of being understood as the complement to, lack of, or on the margin of whiteness (like femaleness and homosexuality to maleness and heterosexuality), what does it mean to come of age in an era when blackness undergoes a social revolution? What happens when you grow up with one construction and then have to live as an adult with another? What happens when one's own transition to adulthood is precisely in step with the larger society's racial transformation, as contested and tenuous as that transformation is? How does one negotiate that transition period if one is black?

Joseph remembers trying to embrace the roles or constructions of "Black radical" and "ROTC student" simultaneously. What he remembers keenly is the poorness of the fit:

[I]n 1966 . . . all male students had to be in the ROTC for two years. . . . That was true of all land grant schools. So it was pretty much like a plantation. We were young adults—most of us were paying our own way—[but we] were treated like kids. . . . Every Thursday we had to dress up in our uniforms—they had to be like World War I issue . . . awful, heavy wool, in Washington, D.C., in the summertime. Hot! Every Thursday we had to dress up and we had to be army people. . . . [W]e didn't know from army; had to salute and all that stuff. And nobody wanted to. . . . [W]e had another issue at stake, and that was we had to become recognized; we had to be people first. And we couldn't very well become full-fledged, accepted people in our culture with our ethnic identity and still have to do this every Thursday. Well, in 1967, we decided to rebel. . . . Afros, Blackness, [all of that] was just starting to catch on, and Howard was the hub. The activity was right there. You could feel it. In Sociology class, for example, you're sitting around going through the routine, and then all of a sudden Stokely Carmichael comes in and asks can he talk to the class. We go, "Yeah! Great!" And he would sit down and he'd give us all the rhetoric and get us thinking and we'd go, "Yeah, that's right!" . . . So leaders were starting to identify themselves and things were starting to happen. . . . Well . . . the first thing we did was we burned down the ROTC building. [We just said] "We're not going to do this anymore!" . . . [It was] stupid: We had to [carry these] World War I guns; you'd go out in the field and you had to do all this . . . and it just didn't feel right, you know. . . . [I]t was hard to demand our identity when we were having to do this sort of stuff, you know—put on the uniform. You can't feel very much like a radical if you've got to do that, you know. "Enough!" We burned down the ROTC building with all the guns and all the uniforms and then there was no more ROTC. (Joseph, HU '71)

Burning down the ROTC facility was the beginning of the radicalization of Howard students in the memories of alumni with whom I spoke. Eventually, they took over the administration building, demanding that administrators add black studies courses, eliminate student visitation rules, and include student voices on decision-making committees. Clearly, this is a case where, to use C. Wright Mills's words, history (in the form of the Black Power Movement) and biography (at the close of adolescence) came together to catalyze students' understanding and appropriation of what it meant to be African American in the late 1960s.[3] I asked Joseph (HU '71) what Howard University students had demanded:

> *Joseph*: Well, mostly a voice in how things were done. You know, we needed covisitation [with] girls. . . . We needed to know more about black history. Just more emphasis on Blackness—black business, black everything. 'Cause up until very, very shortly before that, it was an insult to be called black. You don't remember that.

> *Sarah Willie*: That changed while you were there?

> *Joseph*: Oh, yeah. I was on both sides. I remember when you couldn't call me black. You know, Negro was acceptable; nigger was okay. Negro was just a nicer way of saying it. But we went from that to Black, and everybody had to accept Black. And Black was cool, you know.

From Joseph's description, what it meant to be black changed over time.

Luke explains what it meant to be black at Northwestern in the late 1960s and early 1970s: "Everybody was very close. I mean, I you going down the street and someone [black] was across the street that you didn't know, you speak to them. You probably go across the street and talk to them. Introduce yourself and talk. Very close type thing. . . . Your blackness was more important than anything else. That was the key kind of thing. Black Consciousness" (Luke, NU '72). If he were making the decision today, Luke would be hard-pressed to decide between a historically black or an Ivy League college. Although he feels like he "missed something"—camaraderie and tradition—by not matriculating at an HBCU, his priorities have shifted: "Maybe I would go east. Maybe I would go to a Harvard. I was purposely avoiding something like a Harvard because of the reputation and all that, it's like, you're so stuck-up and stuff and I'm not into that. But now, I'm certainly a lot more oriented toward money and like, well, hey, if that's where you have to go to meet people and rub shoulders for contacts, I would do it" (Luke, NU '71). In today's atmosphere, Luke is convinced that he could go to Harvard and not risk his blackness. Not appearing stuck-up was important to Luke's sense of racial self. This is common: Fordham argues that black parents rather consciously teach their children to not put on airs, to not think and act as if they are better than others just because they are staying in school (1988). If part of what it means to be black for Luke is not seeming "stuck-up," then he perceives that today he could make the choice to attend an Ivy League university without sanction.

As I argued in chapter 5, fictive kinship means a great deal to most black people. They regard this family model as the ideal by which members of the group are judged

(Fordham and Ogbu 1986: 183, 185).[4] Appearing "stuck-up" might have left Luke vulnerable to ostracism or the accusation that he had "forgotten who he was."

RACE AS STATUS

Blackness is not only a conception of self influenced by experience with others; it is also a status. By telling us what she and fellow black leaders at NU thought would be fun to do to celebrate graduation, Jennifer demonstrates what is expected behavior and acceptable entertainment if one is black as well as how blackness operates as a negative status:

> William and I and three or four of the guys would get together and we planned a Black Senior Week. We were always kind of the militant wing and once we got the senior week calendar [that the Associated Student Government put out] and saw stuff like "Cubs games," we thought, "No. Who wants to go to a Cubs game? Let's plan a Black Senior Week." And so we did and that was really fun. . . . The first day we all went to Great America [Amusement Park], and one night we had a talent night. . . . Then the next night we rented a big-screen TV from [the student center] and showed a bunch of black exploitation movies and that was fun. What else did we do? Oh, we went to a nightclub on the south side. . . . We went there and saw Redd Foxx, who is so ignorant, but it was fun. (Jennifer, NU '88)[5]

This is a case in which a narrower expectation of racial identity exists at least in part because the subcommunity feels under attack or excluded (see chapter 5). Jennifer and William's decision to "plan a Black Senior Week" reflects the different kinds of activities they assume black students would want to participate in. It also implies their recognition that black, as a status, is of lesser value or importance or they would have been consulted as a constituency when NU's student leaders, who at the time were all white, designed the Senior Week program.

In her explanation of why she loves Howard, Lydia shows us three conceptualizations of race: how race operates as a status, how blacks suffer from internal colonialism, and how race is symbolically interpreted:

> I was raised in the ghetto in New Jersey. And I think you'll always hear "Niggers can't do this and niggers can't do that," and "Niggers ain't this and niggers ain't that." Looking up there and [seeing them] standing around on the corner. And it was just so uplifting to go to a black institution that has been there for over one hundred years. And it's still standing and it's operating day to day and you're turning out the *crème de la crème* of black society. So we must be doing something right. . . . [I]t's very positive

and uplifting. And that was part of the excitement in being there. And it was good to be a part of that. . . . I was excited to be a part of history, because I felt connected to everybody that had been through there. And you can take me to Howard right now and take me up on the yard and I will fall out crying. Because I can just feel them all just moving through me. It's wonderful. (Lydia, HU '79)

Lydia's testimony also provides an example of how crucial one's social context is to how one sees oneself.

STATUS CONTRADICTION

The changing social context, however, meant that not everyone could challenge expected behavior with impunity, especially not at Northwestern. Black Wildcats who had grown up in predominantly white environments and expected to spend time with white friends faced a challenge. I asked Robert, "Tell me about the ten percent of the black community who never sat at the black tables." He answered, "Everyone talked about them, *everyone*. They were snubbed. Not necessarily ostracized, because I think the ostracism was more on the part of those individuals than on the part of the community itself" (Robert, NU '80). Katrina (NU '81) was one of those black students who was snubbed. Having grown up surrounded by white people, she entered college ignorant of the fact, she says, that from the start, her blackness was in question. Trying to make sense of her marginality, she recalls her disappointment at not being invited to the prefreshman summer program that NU sponsored for many of its entering black students: "I wasn't even invited. I didn't know anything about it, which I still get a crick in my neck about because I don't know how they determine who goes to [it] exactly. So you get up here and the Black people are already cliqued off. . . . And I had made these [white] friends and so I like ate with my friends. And I guess it took me a while before I realized what a big deal some of the rules were" (Katrina, NU '85). Katrina was expecting to find a niche more easily than she did in the black community at Northwestern. Her friendships with whites from the first day, however, had negative symbolic significance for some of her black classmates. Beyond symbolic interaction, the concepts of performance and status help us to understand Katrina's position. In retrospect, she says she is now aware of the racial expectations of blacks: because she did not spend a certain amount of time with black students, she was ostracized. Although she spent the majority of her time with white friends, she was neither asked to dance at white parties nor pursued romantically by whites. Socialized in an affluent and highly educated family and surrounded by white people as a high school student, Katrina entered college to a confusing reception. As a high school student, her advanced academic placement and affluence allowed her an elevated status. As she entered adulthood at NU, she discovered that the elevated status she had enjoyed at home was not necessarily consistent with the denigrated status of being black. She eventually found another "outsider" to date, a black student who had pledged a white fraternity but soon deactivated. To a certain extent, then, Katrina faced the dilemma of status contradiction.

All college-educated African Americans, not just those like Katrina who are unique among the group, experience "a status dilemma, a contradiction of status." Hughes continues: "[T]he more [she], as an individual, acquires of those elements of American culture which bring to others the higher rewards of success, the greater is [her] dilemma" (1984: 221). For Hughes, the American Negro (usually thought of as a man) and the American woman (usually thought of as white) are marginal persons in spheres of prestige or power. To explain what makes a marginal person, Hughes gives us the example of the woman or the Negro who becomes a physician and the problem he or she poses for the white American male who must interact with the marginal person: "[T]he question arises whether to treat her or him as physician or as woman or Negro. Likewise, on their part, there is the problem whether, in a given troublesome situation, to act completely as physician or in the other role. This is their dilemma" (1984: 223).[6]

Hughes mentions two ways for the marginality of persons in such contradictory status locations to be reduced. The first way is dependent upon the actions of the individual, and the second way is dependent upon the society. The marginal individual may "give up the struggle" and live according to the status or role that the dominant society has assigned her, or the individual may attempt to "resign from" the lower status to which the society would assign her. In such a case, she defines herself only as physician, for example, and works hard to avoid playing the role of "woman." This, Hughes admits, is a "tragic theme of human drama. The temptation to resign, and even to repudiate, is put heavily upon marginal people" (1984: 224).

The second way to reduce the marginality of persons in contradictory status locations is for the larger society itself to undergo change. One of the statuses could simply "disappear," ceasing to have social meaning; "[o]ne or both of the statuses might . . . be so broadened and redefined" that formerly marginal people no longer face a dilemma; or the society might designate additional and discrete categories for people who occupy such marginal statuses (1984: 223–24).

Hughes did not carefully examine how people negotiate their statuses. Some people—even in 1945—no doubt negotiated such contradictory status positions with certain amounts of success. A close analysis of their situations would have revealed the extent to which their statuses were malleable and performative. But Hughes did admit a need for further research: "I suppose we might distinguish between that kind of protest which is merely a squirming within the harness, and that which is a questioning of the very terms and dimensions of the prevailing status definitions. . . . [T]here is still much work to be done . . . on the processes by which the human biological individual is integrated . . . into a status system" (1984: 228). Considering how Hughes uses the language of roles and status, it is striking that he did not bring us closer to a serious questioning of race and sex roles as well as discussion of their performative nature.[7]

It is also interesting that, for Hughes, the only choices that he sees as open to the so-called marginal man or woman are (1) a complete embrace of the degraded status, (2) a complete rejection of the degraded status, or (3) patience in waiting for the society to change. In Hughes's schema there is no place where the individual may negotiate status, creating new definitions of reality with colleagues, family, or friends; in short, there is no continuum of hybrid behaviors. Moreover, there is no place where Hughes expresses his horror at (or even with restraint an analysis of) the intransigence of social stratification and its accompanying roles.

OTHERS' EXPECTATIONS INFLUENCE ONE'S OWN

Like Hughes, Goffman (1963) imagined several ways to ameliorate the situation of the members of stigmatized groups, his parallel to Hughes's marginal people. First, Goffman argues, a member of a stigmatized group may accept that there are stigmatized and stigma-free groups while claiming personal exemption from the negative traits associated with the stigmatized group. Second, a member of a stigmatized group may reject the norm of inferior status and protest the ideology upon which it is founded. And finally, a member of a stigmatized group may quietly opt out of the discussion, attempting to pass as a member of the dominant accepted group, assimilating as completely as is possible.

In this scholarship of Goffman's, one can see the development of his thinking beyond Hughes's prescription. His second adaptation suggests individual agency as he notes that stigmatized group members might attempt to change the understanding of dominant-group members. No doubt, this is after Goffman observed the successes of the Civil Rights Movement of the 1950s. What strikes me about his description, and those of the men and women with whom I spoke, is that challenging others' understandings of blackness does not preclude attempting to embrace high-status roles.

The two examples below show individuals taking such direct action on their own behalf. One way to work on one's own behalf is to associate with fellow group members who are successful at one's goals. Hannah's story reveals this endeavor:

> I pledged the business [fraternity as a] sophomore. It's called Delta Sigma Pi. It's supposed to be teaching you how to be a professional businessperson. I'm glad I pledged that, too. Because my friends [and] my focus on professionalism came from there. And also the idea of getting a higher education. . . . And we would have seminars in professional dress, how to

handle yourself on the job. One of the reasons why I wanted to pledge the business fraternity is because they were all leaders on campus . . . and they all had good grades. And I was thinking to myself, I wanted to be around people who were moving forward. (Hannah, HU '88)

Another way to achieve these goals is to build such a group from the ground up, as Henry remembers doing:

Peers can help you [to study and focus]. Junior year, we got a black engineering society together. I was among the founding fathers. That created a networking and peer structure that enabled us to help ourselves. By junior year, I had blacks in my class and we studied together, and that helped me do better. Junior year I started off bad, but then we formed the black engineers society, and things just went uphill from there. (Henry, NU '77)

People can have several responses, Goffman and Hughes observed, to inhabiting a denigrated status. One response is often a conscious self-improvement program. Surrounding oneself with positive role models is one such program.

Another outside influence is the media. Many students, including the men and women with whom I spoke, arrive on campus as freshmen and have little idea just how much they have been influenced by television, movies, music videos, video games, magazines, and the like. A significant number of Howard and Northwestern alumni thought of themselves, or at least some part of themselves, as either racially or educationally inauthentic because they invariably perceived their experiences as different from the experiences of others, especially other blacks. While their experiences were often different, what is troubling is that before meeting a range of black people, they did not have the knowledge that a range of African Americans with economic and educational attainments (rarely, if ever, portrayed in America's mass media) existed. They were often surprised to learn that they were not freaks if they did not fit a stereotype of black people.

Most likely, this is as recent a phenomenon as desegregation. While desegregation is ultimately about breaking down barriers across all segments of our common cultural life, most African Americans and European Americans are caught in the world of a transition to desegregation not yet complete. Many black Americans come of age in predominantly black neighborhoods where phenotypically black professionals are no longer normative. Others come of age in mostly white neighborhoods, and do not socialize with Americans of African descent outside of their neighborhoods. Many blacks and whites learn most of what they know about blacks and whites from media portrayals that are warped, truncated—in short, one-sided fiction, especially when it comes to the portrayal of racial minorities. Is this a failure of desegregation? Yes. Does this mean that desegregation has failed? No, since few places have achieved true desegregation. It is worth studying those organizations, cities, and towns that have successfully desegregated. What is inarguable is that those late-adolescent African Americans who get to college, like their European-American counterparts, often arrive with incomplete and erroneous conceptions of African-American experiences. The implications for them, however, are even more serious than for white students, since their sense of entitlement to the resources that enable one to take advantage, confidently and "naturally," of full citizenship is at stake.

PLAYING WITH RACIAL EXPECTATIONS

conscious (adjective): aware, cognizant, able to feel and think; knowing what one is doing and why . . .

consciousness (noun): the state of being conscious; awareness of one's own feelings [and] what is happening around one . . .
—*Webster's New World Dictionary*

Several NU alumni admitted to playing with or against white people's expectations of black behavior. This was a way to accomplish several goals, including using humor to allow white people to make fools of themselves or exploiting whites' fears of black people to maintain distance and prevent interaction with whites. Using clothes and attitude as symbols of self-possession and anger, Deborah explains, "[Y]ou know, when you had a 'fro out to here and your hat on and sunglasses, I mean nobody was messin' with you!" (Debbie, NU '75).

One Northwestern Wildcat, Christine ('74), remembers using the racial expectations of most whites consciously and explicitly: by mimicking expectations, she was able to undermine the construction of blackness to which she knew some white adults she met were loyal:

Christine: I remember one of my [sorority sisters] had a [white] roommate: she was extremely rich. Her name was Sally, and Pat [my sorority sister] was her roommate. . . . Sally was flexible [and she realized that the whole time while she had been growing up] her parents told her that blacks were this and blacks were that. The whole stereotypical [thing]. So when she came [to Northwestern], it was like [she was] smart, you know. [She realized] "You're just like me." She had a car, [and] you weren't supposed to have a car freshman year, but she knew somebody [in the administration] at Northwestern so she was able to have a car. Her mom and her sister and them came up, so what we did is we gave them the stereotypical black. And Sally pretended like she had assimilated so well [to her black roommate] that now she was like us . . .

Sarah Willie: Oh my god.

Christine: Her parents ran out. [And then] she said, "Oh my gosh!" So we had to [run after them,] grab 'em, and bring 'em back. And then finally we became very good friends with her mom and dad. And we laugh about it to this day.

The ability to "play" with stereotypes or assume them for a specific purpose tells us about the malleability of race and racial stereotypes. Unlike "passing," this is less about pretending to be something one is not and more about pretending to be something one is thought to be. As Butler has observed, parody is often subversive (1995: 134). Such subversive play with race is not necessarily aimed at simply making the dominant group seem foolish or feel humiliation at having been fooled. Such play can also be consciously aimed at subverting or contradicting directly stereotypical assumptions in order to ultimately assist dominant-group members in confronting false stereotypes they've held.

According to John, simply interacting with white people demands a certain amount of pretending. Below, he characterizes living in a predominantly white world as "a game" or performance, albeit a very serious one, that does not necessarily demand twenty-four-hour attention:

[T]here's a game that gets played from nine to five. And if you realize it's a game, then you win at the game. Because then you play from nine to five and after five o'clock you don't play it anymore. And unless you realize that, and that teaching, I think, comes from being around white people and realizing that there's a certain time when you can click this shit off. 'Cause they don't want to be at your parties either, okay? (John, NU '80)

What characterizes both of the two preceding examples, even more so than the examples of Henry and Robert that opened this chapter, is the explicit awareness of manipulating one's audience through the act of performing race.

RACIAL AND GENDER IDENTITY: MUTUAL INFLUENCE

The women who pursued majors and careers in the natural or technological sciences were challenging traditional gender expectations at both universities, and they each spoke of confusion and loneliness. Lucy (HU n.d.) is an example of such a student.

Lucy: I didn't [make a big deal about dressing] and you could get away with that more so in engineering. . . . All the while I was in school I would always wear like eyeliner and lipstick, and girls in engineering would make some little comments about how I would wear eyeliner and lipstick all the time [saying], "*I* don't have time for that!" And since I didn't have the grades, they would . . . make little snide comments like, "Too much time on your physical and not enough on your grades." . . . And then outside engineering, people would come and be like, "These girls do not take care of themselves. What is their problem?!"

Sarah Willie: Sounds like you couldn't win?

Lucy: Yeah, and I usually, you know, I didn't change myself. I wasn't going to. I probably went more in the opposite direction [of what anybody said] because I felt like there was pressure to be one way or the other.

Excluded from being able to achieve European-American conceptions of beauty, African-American women have long struggled with the desire to be desirable on their own terms rather than on those of the dominant group, be it European or male. This personal and cultural struggle has made millions of dollars for the hair care and makeup industries at a painful cost of, among many things, time. The women pursuing technological or science degrees, however, were exempted (or exempted themselves) from such preoccupations because of their pursuit of male-dominated majors. Their choices fit Hughes's argument, discussed earlier, that persons with subordinate status in prestigious careers often attempt to resign from their subordinate status by minimizing the characteristics that so label them. In *Men and Women of the Corporation* (1977), Kanter argues that numerical minorities are often pressured to conform to dominant-group expectations, whether those expectations are to conform to the dominant group or fill a prescribed role acceptable to the dominant group.

Deborah (NU '75) expresses below the precollege anxiety she had around gender. She was nervous because she had gone to a private, predominantly white, all-girl high school. Hoping to date African Americans when she got to college, she was unsure how social expectations and behavioral norms might be different.

Deborah: When you're a freshman—well, I don't know what freshman girls do now—but you basically hang around other ladies, you know. And then, as you get more confidence about your sexuality and about your individuality, then you start to kind of pair off. . . . The first year, I was just trying to get comfortable with myself and get comfortable with the feeling of being black again. . . . Actually, I never worried about the scholastic end of it. I had been working pretty hard. When I was going to high school, it was like going to college basically. So that part of it wasn't a problem. The social adjustments were a problem. I worried about that a lot.

Sarah Willie: Why did you worry?

Deborah: Well, first of all, I had been around a lot of whites for a long time and . . . I was worried about interacting with other blacks and the social aspects, you know, [having been] in a girls' school and then dealing with boys [in college].

Her admission reveals her understanding that masculinity and femininity may have different meanings for different groups of people. To play the role successfully takes time, observation, and practice.

Deborah goes on to note an incident that happened before she arrived at NU that illustrates well the distinct expectations that defined what it meant to be a black man and what it meant to be a black woman on that predominantly white campus:

I knew there were some instances where some sisters got bothered and the men went and beat the shit out of the [white] people [who bothered them]. It was like, "Did you hear about [what happened to the sisters]?" "Yeah, we went and kicked their asses!" And I don't ever remember encountering any problems. [White people] were too scared! See, it's when black folks started actin' civilized that this racism came back [laughs heartily]! (Deborah, NU '75)

Luke corroborated the particular story to which Deborah alludes: several black male students sought vengeance on behalf of a black female student who had been accosted by a white male student in one of the cafeterias. These black men were even willing to face expulsion from the university to carry out what they saw to be the male responsibility of protecting or avenging the black women on campus.

CONCLUSION

Constructing any identity for anyone can pose a challenge. For the subaltern, constructing a positive identity can become the challenge of a lifetime. Although all of us live out socially constructed identities, certain groups, because of their privilege and prestige, are allowed wider boundaries and greater degrees of freedom in the ideal types to which they, too, are pressed to conform. Persons who find themselves with characteristics that exclude them, epistemologically or ontologically, from even attempting to conform to dominant-group ideals have a difficult life course. They must work harder at facing, building, interpreting, and acting out what it will mean to live with, perhaps even embrace, characteristics that the larger society may reject or may fail to even recognize. The evidence presented in this chapter begs for future research that broadly examines the construction of racial identities, including whiteness.

While my interviewees provide evidence for the argument that people together decide the meaning of race and how it will be performed, these are not individuals who can avoid being black simply by acting white. "[T]o say that race is performative," argues Moore, "is *not* to suggest that a Black person can perform and therefore *be* white. This is why [race is] not [only] political; it's deeper."[8] [In other words, race is experiential, more than group affiliation, context-dependent, occasionally malleable, performative, and the preeminent metaphor for difference in U.S. culture.[9]] No surprise, our feelings about it are strong.

The social-construction perspective challenges an understanding of race as a discrete category by showing that people's understanding of race changes over time. Our conceptions of race are "emergent and symbolic—in short, the result of a social construction process" (Hein 1994: 283).[10] How one sees oneself is not only dependent on how one's group sees itself but on two more things as well—how one sees one's group and how one's group is seen by the majority of others in the society. Eventually, Berger and Luckmann observe, "[w]hat is real 'outside' [of the individual] corresponds to what is real 'within' " (1966: 123). Since that is the case, if those with whom we identify are denigrated in the world outside of the home or neighborhood, we are likely to suffer some degree of self-loathing, even if we have received positive messages from our close relatives, significant others, ethnic enclave, or peer group. That is just one reason why it is so important that people receive accurate messages about themselves as individuals and as groups. For members of those groups who receive more than their share of negative messages, the guidance counselor, the mentoring teacher, the campus climate with high expectations, the roommate with a different life experience all become important in the construction of self, especially during the college years.

As is evidenced above, the experiences of black college students reveal that status, class, and era are all significant to understanding the contexts within which their racial identities are to be understood. In addition, they reveal that their awareness of racial expectations, coupled with the ability to maneuver within, around, and beyond these expectations, is important. Insofar as this awareness leads to behavior modification and so long as behavior continues to be associated with race, then race should be considered as a characteristic that is performed.

IMPLICATIONS

If we are to improve the situation of Black students in U.S. higher education—whether they attend black colleges and universities or white ones—we must focus our attention on social-support systems that buffer and/or solve academic difficulties and increase satisfaction with campus life.
—Walter R. Allen, Edgar G. Epps, and Nesha Z. Haniff

The conversations with black alumni from Howard and Northwestern universities have allowed us a window onto their experiences as students. Our examination of these memories reveals that experiences shared by black college students result less from the particularities of individual personality than from institutional dynamics and societal expectations. Of course, such dynamics and expectations affect the experiences of students of other racial backgrounds as well. Similar research on the experiences of different groups of students will be welcome to the literature of higher education and the social construction of race. In this chapter, I discuss the implications that *Acting Black* has for educational policy, public policy, and the practice of sociology.

IMPLICATIONS FOR EDUCATIONAL POLICY
CLASSROOM, CURRICULUM, CAMPUS

Northwestern University appears to have done an excellent job of recruiting black students compared to many other colleges and universities. That said, admission of students is not where any university's responsibility ends. Black Northwestern alumni faced a wide range of legitimate problems—from premature attrition among fellow students to having very few nonblack students as friends, club mates, and study partners. Especially on a racially polarized campus (as NU's was from the 1960s through the early 1990s), faculty and administrators must take responsibility for helping adolescent students of all colors to find arenas in which to connect. Such places of connection can include small-group work in classrooms, assigned study partners, and appropriate promotion and support of multiracial clubs and activities. Furthermore, if universities continue to endorse sorority and fraternity life, they must also be diligent in promoting nondiscriminatory organizations.

The absence of connection with white students was not just a problem for black students at Northwestern. Many Howard alumni, too, especially those who grew up in segregated settings and completed their elementary and postsecondary education in all-black schools, graduated from college without interacting with white people to any significant and sustained extent. As individuals who then joined a predominantly white graduate school or workforce, that lack of opportunity to interact with a range of people is noted by them as a difficulty in navigating this world. Unlike women's colleges, where most of the students have had previous experiences in which they interacted with boys and men in their families, neighborhoods, and schools, black students from segregated neighborhoods and schools have not necessarily had primary bonding experiences with whites.[1]

Howard appears to have done a wonderful job of offering an inspirational setting for black students to pursue higher education without the fear or actuality of racial reprisal. At the same time, Howard and all HBCUs need to pursue explicitly a healthy percentage of nonblack, especially white, students. Paradoxically, it is Edward, a Northwestern alumnus who regrets the lack of interracial involvement at NU, who eloquently states the case for more interracial involvement, even at black colleges:

> There's a richness there that can be remembered and can be given honor to, in the best way, by maintaining [historically black] institutions . . . but I don't think that they should have [only] black students in them. And I think they should not have [only] black faculty, and I think they shouldn't necessarily even have a black head of department. As a matter of fact, I think that they should develop so they do encompass more people. But I think their charter, their mission, and their intent should be to always maintain an institution where African-American people can come and get an education and can learn firsthand about the struggles of African-American people in America. It makes them richer institutions; to be exclusive really denies one of the undeniable components of African-American life in America: that we are very much a part of European Americans, and that there's no way you can really separate the two, 'cause the two cultures have grown side-by-side. There's a lot of love between those two cultures . . . a lot of individual struggles, one-on-one struggles with people; people have helped one another on both sides of the equation. For people to continue to grow . . . you have to maintain that type of thing, and particularly at the university level. The essence of the university, of college, is to nurture all different types of ideas.

And I think universities and colleges should always strive to be more open, to help to create that classic open society where everyone has an opportunity at higher education, so that they have an opportunity at developing society, really. (Edward, NU '79)

Learning to deal more effectively with white students—as Howard appears to have done with a multiracial faculty (Willie 1981)—may have translatable consequences for helping the school to deal with class difference. Both class and race heterogeneity offer those students who have grown up in homogeneous settings the opportunity to learn from and with those unlike themselves, and, ultimately, such diversity allows students to be able to interact successfully with a wider range of people.

Heterogeneity on campus can often translate into greater ease of relations with people off campus. The problems of strained relations between college and community mirror those within the campus community, and not just among students. As Sidel reminds us, "Racist behavior on college campuses is . . . not limited to students" (1994: 82), and, I would add, the problem is not just racism. Most administrators and faculty would agree that universities must educate students about each institution's relationship with and responsibility to the surrounding community. What many campus administrators do not recognize is that in order for such a relationship to be as constructive as possible, it must be preceded by the work of consensus building, where explicit discussions take place among representatives from every facet of the organization about its mission. In addition, discussions should also focus on elitism, classism, racism, and other forms of oppression. This is time consuming, uncomfortable, and yet rewarding work that is best undertaken by *all* members of the university community, including administrators and faculty.[2]

Despite claims made by conservative scholars that ethnic studies programs and social justice courses only fuel campus separatism and replace "traditional" or "valid" courses, ethnic studies programs offer both minority and majority students more holistic and accurate representations of history, literature, philosophy, religion, and politics. Complaints about rigor and intellectual relevance can be lobbed at any department or discipline, be it canonically sanctioned or not. More accurate information with more rigorous investigation and debate is always better. For those in the society with a false sense of their own inferiority (often minority students and even some minority faculty), the opportunity to take and teach courses in these areas can be part of restoring a balanced and realistic sense of self. For those in the society who have a false sense of their own superiority (often majority students and even some majority faculty), the opportunity to take and teach courses in these areas can be part of restoring a balanced and realistic sense of self and of the world.

The surprise that African-American alumni noted at discovering black history as well as the range of possibilities open to them testifies to the fact that many if not most African Americans still reach college age without an accurate sense of our past, present, or future when it comes to race. Students need to be explicitly taught about the complexities of the histories of all people and helped to understand that each of us has a claim to dignity based on past achievement and potential achievement. For those who do not have a sense of themselves or others' humanity based on religious conviction, school is likely where they will learn that "each person is somebody." For those who grow up in homogeneous neighborhoods, particularly students of color, school and television are often the only places where they see the possibilities for their lives. This puts a heavy, but crucial, burden on schools of every racial composition at every level from primary through graduate.

That said, race-specific strategies are not enough to allow students to transcend the way history and human claims for dignity have long been made. Race-specific strategies alone do not allow students to locate the sources for their dignity outside those histories. What, then, is the charge to persons who make up the communities of colleges and universities? It's a big one and there's no substitute for it: They must sit down together as departments, divisions, and groups with representative employees from throughout the organization to talk through crucial issues of how race, gender, and class stratification are played out with regard to students, staff, and faculty.

A supportive and healthy learning community, however, is not one in which students are coddled or misled by false portraits of their abilities. Howard alumna Lydia, now a college professor herself, muses,

> I think there's a place for [HBCUs], but I also think that there's a responsibility that white institutions have to black students in providing them with faculty that are going to give them the kind of role modeling and the diversity of that role modeling that's going to be of value to them, without draining that faculty and having them do outrageous . . . work . . . because they're black. . . . [T]he main thing is the education. . . . If you walk away from a white institution without a stronger sense of self . . . within the context of your own personal history and collective history, it's not serving you. If you come out as a clone, it's not serving you. It's very complex and it's something that the family cannot take [responsibility] as the sole provider for. . . . That's something that really comes through [social] interaction. (Lydia, HU '68)

Taylor confirms Lydia's point and my own suggestion: "Parents, Black faculty members and administrators, and White administrators must initiate programs and address these issues" (1986: 200). Indeed, faculty sometimes forget they are the ones "in charge," failing to model frank and civil exchange (not only in the classroom with students but with their colleagues), abdicating responsibility in the setting of boundaries and expectations, and abusing authority when they feel unduly challenged or uncomfortable.[3]

A NOTE ABOUT AFFIRMATIVE ACTION

Regardless of how the law describes affirmative action, its purpose is not only the redress of past discrimination but an acknowledgment of contemporary discrimination. When it comes to college admissions, as long as whites are represented in numbers disproportionate to their numbers in the population, the current rules of undergraduate admission at highly selective colleges and universities advantage whites. That fact is rarely articulated. Since selective colleges and universities have, for the most part, avoided interrogating their criteria for admissions, they have also avoided examining whose interests they serve and their role in the replication of society's system of privilege, and they have forgone an opportunity to challenge that system. This is not a victimless crime: by shirking this responsibility, admissions committees, and those administrators who charge them, have often laid the burden of explaining the presence of their "special admit" students at the feet of those students.

When colleges and universities refuse to change admissions criteria, there is no way to include those usually excluded by "traditional" criteria other than by making exceptions to the rules. Doing so affirms the legitimacy of the rules already in place, making them appear culturally and socially neutral, apolitical, objective, serving the interests only of an idealized meritocracy, which itself is (inappropriately) conflated with justice.[4] If the only approach that a college uses to face the challenge of admitting a racially diverse study body is the suspension of "regular" criteria for specific groups, the members of those groups are suspected and resented. A genuine reexamination of admissions criteria focuses everyone's attention on whose interests the rules of admissions serve and what aspects of inequality in the society the rules help to replicate. Faculty can play a role in helping everyone to understand this: "When students and others object to searching out and establishing special compensatory programs for those traditionally excluded from higher education, perhaps we should puncture the myth of individual achievement and 'merit' and tell our students the truth—that few of us succeed simply on the basis of individual effort" (Sidel 1994: 251).

One can visit the admissions office of any selective college or university in the country and hear admissions officers complain about the negligible number of black high school graduates who are prepared for their college's program of studies. As more universities and colleges seek students who can pay their way through college, the numbers of eligible African Americans, so the argument goes, declines. Financial complaints do not correspond to complaints about students who could do the work. But the complaints also go to the heart of what a college's or university's mission is, and that's where the admissions office is out of its element.

Selective, predominantly white colleges and universities need to rethink admissions requirements and their commitment to being part of constructing healthier and more racially and economically balanced student bodies. If one accepts the idea that colleges exist to educate, the model of selective admissions based on test scores and prior grades makes little sense. If an institution exists to educate students, its mission is to produce certain desirable changes in students or, more simply, to make a difference in each student's life. This "value-added" approach to the goals of higher education suggests that admissions procedures should be designed to select students who are likely to be influenced by the educational process, regardless of their entering performance level (Astin et al. 1982: 148). Many schools instead choose only students whose precollege aspirations and preparedness guarantee to "add value" to the reputation of the school. (Of course, this also means that faculty at the most selective colleges and universities may have a great deal to learn from faculty who teach a very wide range of students at historically black and community colleges.) The pernicious effects of rankings in *U.S. News and World Report* and the manipulation of admissions selectivity to appear more selective are just two contemporary examples of how the mission of many such schools gets lost in the marketing of them.

COLLEGE AND RACE CONNECTED

The centrality of race in American life and its "historical flexibility and immediacy in everyday experience" (Omi and Winant 1994: 2) are patently clear in the comments of these fifty-five men and women whom I interviewed. A broader understanding of race that includes agency might help educators ameliorate the pain and anxiety that many students experience, more generally students of color at predominantly white colleges and female students at coeducational colleges. Conscious, public, and repeated positive reinforcement appears to influence positively group and individual consciousness and sense of dignity.

For faculty and administrators, reaching an understanding of race as performed and malleable will encourage them to avoid treating groups of minority or majority students monolithically or stereotypically. Helping to create a black cultural house or add a course in African-American history to the catalogue are crucial steps; at the same time, very often they do not acknowledge or problematize the fact that people who identify as African American may not agree about what it means to be black. Achieving a critical mass of students who identify as black can alter the dialogue about the diversity of black experiences and change the tenor of everything from classroom discussions to the composition of the student council to senior thesis topics and community service projects.

Stereotypes of racial authenticity are held by faculty, staff, and students, all of whom find themselves at some time or another wondering about the class and race backgrounds of others and their loyalties and affiliations. These ideals of authenticity informed the judgments that the alumni in this study confess to making against one another when they met blacks who made different decisions than they did. By demonstrating that blackness has multiple meanings for the people in this study, I hope that racial authenticity has also been revealed as fictional.

IMPLICATIONS OF TREATING RACE AS PERFORMED

Unlike gender, race has been given much more careful consideration as a determinant, discrete, and intractable characteristic that either helps one or hurts one. The probability that one will live to a certain age or the chances that one will complete high school are life situations we have come to think of as determined by race. As such, however, race has figured prominently in analyses of educational success rates, crime, deviance, and stratification.

Although these statistics are crucial in monitoring the society's progress away from institutionalized racism, the tendency to focus on race as a variable with a fixed meaning that determines a person's social place, quality of life, or life chances runs the risk of obscuring how individuals and groups are also proactive agents. People are not only acted upon by the racial circumstances of their situations; they also act and are often aware of and negotiate racial meanings and expectations. What I was seeing in the ways in which black alumni described their behavior during and after college, their sense of themselves as racial actors, was the presence of consciousness, control, and manipulation—in short, agency. Their stories both affirmed the arguments of postmodernist scholars that identity is neither unitary nor unchanging and at the same time provided ample evidence that scholars must take seriously how individuals understand identity and value representation. Although many African Americans and European Americans are committed to seeing blacks in a positive way, the society's racial pathology is regularly replicated, supporting the misguided belief that blacks are "the root of the problem" (Woodson 1933, DuBois [1903] 1965, Williams 1991). All people in the United States need to learn about the heterogeneity of the African-American public. This has special ramifications for identity development so that young people learn early on that no one is racially inauthentic.[5]

Sociologists who analyze large data sets that include race as a significant variable must be newly wary of how they conceptualize race and how they interpret "racial" findings. The significance and meanings of race and racial identities are conceptualized differently not only among groups but, as this study reveals, among individuals, from setting to setting, and across generations. Sociological statements about race must, therefore, be made carefully and with acknowledgment of the inadequacies of treating race as a binary or static variable. Researchers who do ethnographic and qualitative work, too, must be wary of using references to race as a way to make their arguments stronger without having talked to people about race. Race has a shifting and slippery nature. If the concept is going to be treated in the complicated way in which it deserves to be treated, first-person narratives and accounts are one way to appreciate accurately how people define themselves and are defined by others.

Despite its shifting and slippery nature, race is also a malleable characteristic and a powerful structural predictor of life quality. Race can undermine and inflate identities in psychological ways; it can limit and privilege the social structural realities of individuals and groups, and it does this by infiltrating all aspects of life in the United States and in most countries where imperialism and colonialism have brought people of different origins together.[6]

Expectations around race create paradoxical situations for us, and the temptations to essentialize and reify race are tremendous in a society that on the one hand systematically counts race through elaborate quantitative studies and on the other denigrates specific racial categories and identities. Both positive and negative racial stereotypes are constraining and often inaccurate. Indeed, racial categories themselves can be reductive and can have destructive implications for our lives. At the same time, since racial stereotypes and categories are so embedded in our understanding and ordering of life, they offer us a crucial stability. Treating race differently theoretically and conceptually will mean that we will have to start thinking about others, and ourselves, differently. This effort will no doubt prove unsettling.

The way that race has been treated, especially by the media and more implicitly in the sociological literature, is as a braided *personal* and *structural* variable at which one succeeds or fails. One is dealt first the structural reality of being born one color in a highly color-conscious and racially stratified society. And then, one succeeds or fails at being black, white, red, yellow, or brown, according to too many criteria to list. If we all attempted to challenge our own ideals of racial authenticity and began appreciating the performative aspect of race, I think we would find ourselves further along the road to justice, racial and otherwise.

CONCLUSION

Although "college is not the place to start if we desire to achieve mutual racial acceptance" (Fleming 1984: 158–59), the reality is that college will be for many the first place where they will have the opportunity to encounter racial difference. For this reason, the university setting has a burdensome but crucial responsibility to provide the space in which students, faculty, and staff learn to participate as citizens, argue with each other, resolve conflicts, learn about and come to value a range of histories and experiences, and celebrate our differences as well as our similarities.

APPENDIX: METHOD AND SAMPLE

MORE ABOUT THE METHOD

As with any technique, attention to one thing usually means inattention to another. In the case of interviewing, this can lead to a reliability-validity trade-off. In the open-ended format there is more informality and the opportunity for the interviewer to ask for clarification and for discussion. This leads to greater validity of answers. But such informality also means that another researcher may interview people with similar characteristics using similar questions and the results may differ. This leads to lower reliability—that is, greater difficulty repeating the study.

Finally, there are drawbacks to asking people about a time in the past. The most obvious problem is that we all remember selectively. Disagreement exists as to whether pleasant or unpleasant memories are more likely to stay with us. Those who argue that we are more likely to forget unpleasant memories are also highly suspicious of relying on memory at all as a site or resource in research. On the other hand, while only certain things are committed to memory, it is not clear that we experience any less selectively than we remember. In short, while salient memory is not necessarily synonymous with accurate memory, memories that stand out for people can serve as useful places to begin any investigation. Memories are too often the only data extant. "The emergence of the 'projective past' introduces into the narratives of identity and community a necessary split between the time of utterance and the space of memory. This 'lagged' temporality is not some endless slippage; it is a mode of breaking the complicity of past and present in order to open up a space of revision and initiation" (Bhabha 1995: 59). It was with this attitude of exploration, then, and an attempt to "open up a space of revision and initiation," that I approached the study. Having spoken with people who were also experiencing college while I was in college for my undergraduate thesis, my interests had shifted and I became interested in the retrospective sense African Americans made of their college experiences. And, although I was willing to live with the limitations of this approach, the whole picture demands photographs from multiple angles. No one piece of research should be taken as the whole truth.

All research projects require the researcher to become familiar with the topic before diving in. This took four forms for me: interviewing black people who had gone to college, reading the published research on black college students, noting when and where black students showed up in the popular media, and critically examining my own college experience.

I located respondents three ways. Primarily I found people by snowball sampling (McCall and Simmons 1969). Snowball sampling consists of relying on an informant either to pass the researcher's name on to other potential respondents or to refer the researcher to potential respondents directly. Each respondent similarly passes names on in this fashion. As I said above, interviewing can pose challenges to reliability, but so too can snowball sampling: when interviews are elicited from people who know each other or are associated with each other, their similar jobs, interests, or college experiences may not reflect the experiences of other clusters of people with slightly different interests and experiences. Carefully analyzing the content of what people say, however, can capture the complexity of an issue in a way that other forms of analysis obscure (Babbie 1983: 275).

At the beginning of the project, I did not have enough leads. Secondarily, I received the jump-start I needed from one Howard alumnus who lent me his alumni directory. And finally from Northwestern's alumni relations office, I was given the names of two black Northwestern alumni who were active in the alumni association. As it turned out, many black Northwestern and Howard alumni knew each other. I was quick to learn that Chicago's professional black population is the proverbial "small world." Several people who had been undergraduates at Northwestern had also attended Howard for professional school, and several graduates of Howard's undergraduate college had attended one of Northwestern's graduate or professional schools.

All of the respondents identified as African American. In addition, however, one respondent identified as both African American and West Indian, and three identified as African American and biracial.

One should be aware that African Americans have a history of being misrepresented (and subsequently mistreated) by social scientists. Psychologists Gurin and Epps explain the suspicion with which they were received when they attempted their study *Black Consciousness, Identity, and Achievement* (1975): "[L]egitimate suspicion [among respondents] also resulted from the publication of a few uninformed, insensitive, and invidious accounts of the historically Black colleges that nonetheless received unusual attention in educational circles" (1975: ix). Indeed, the few potential interviewees to whom I placed "cold calls" without some prior contact manifested suspicion concerning my intentions. I therefore attempted to contact as many people as I could first by a letter in which I thoroughly introduced myself. The letter allowed me to establish who I was, my own experience with the topic, and the ultimate purposes of the research. In the letter, I introduced myself as an African American who had attended both a historically black as well as a predominantly white school. I explained that I felt the stories of black alumni were underrepresented in the literature on the college experience and I wanted the chance "to hear [their] story." Every potential respondent whom I called without having sent a letter of introduction asked me pointedly if I were black. It is clear to me that their willingness to proceed with the interview and their candor during the interview were in very large part based on whether they believed I was trustworthy and empathetic, and those characteristics were connected to the knowledge that we shared a similar racial experience.

Interviewing people who had had similar experiences to my own had both positive and negative ramifications for the outcome of the interviews. Zweigenhaft and Domhoff argue that "earlier studies [have shown] that black subjects are more forthcoming with black interviewers in survey studies" (1991: 12).[1] Though sharing a racial identity with respondents was important to what I heard, it also presented complications. In attempting to trust each other, there were occasions when I did not understand a response and failed to probe further or when respondents did not understand what I was getting at with a question and did not press me for further explanation. Some of this is the natural by-product of one-on-one interviews between strangers. But some of it, I believe, is the added difficulty of interviewing people with whom one is *supposed* to share cultural meanings.

As a racial minority in the same country, African Americans have a great deal in common. We are, however, often assumed (by others and ourselves) to have more knowledge and understanding of one another, because of our shared racial background, than we do. Even more assumptions are made about the similarities among the relatively small number of college-educated African Americans. Despite my own knowledge, and the shared knowledge of some of my respondents, of the breadth and diversity of African America, we were all guilty of assuming, I believe, that our shared status as college-educated black people gave us more of a shared language than it did. The racial constraints and social expectations imposed on us, then, contributed to our own idealization and homogenization of "the black experience." I believe this tendency to see only commonality occasionally discouraged respondents and me from probing questions and/or answers that left us confused. This was another complication of being an African-American researcher interviewing African-American subjects.

While the stories of respondents were varied and included humor and hope, they also included memories of disappointment, exclusion, confusion, betrayal, and anger. Since I asked respondents not only about their college experiences but also about their precollege and postgraduate lives insofar as these related to college, many of them took the opportunity of a sympathetic ear to confide experiences that had been deeply troubling to them. Several alumni described the deaths and/or divorces of their parents before, during, or after college. Others told how they had suffered explicit racial and sexual harassment and discrimination in and out of the classroom, how they had watched roommates or friends suffer nervous breakdowns, or how they had dealt with the suicides of friends or roommates. Men and women told me about surviving robberies, muggings, and long-term depression.

The incidents that respondents shared with me included disclosures that were clearly difficult for them to reveal and difficult for me to hear. One interviewee told me what it was like to visit home the day after Christmas and find her mother had died alone in her armchair. Another told of the financial straits in which his parents' sudden divorce left him: only by living in his car and getting a night-shift job was he was able to avoid dropping out of college. Alumni with whom I spoke seemed relieved to unburden themselves. As one brother confided,

> You see, most people feel that my life has just been easy. Most people don't even know about these experiences that I've had in my life. They just think that I was [an] only child and that I was born with a silver spoon. I don't know what it is about me, why I come across that way to people. But they get the impression that I've lived a very sheltered life until somebody will sit down and talk with me. But most people think that I've had it easy all my life. (Mark, HU '76)

While traumatic events were not the central focus of the interviews, the powerful presence of such events gave the project a heaviness that I had not anticipated. A number of interviewees thanked me for what they referred to as an impromptu therapy session. Yet many others told their difficult stories with lack of affect disproportionate to the drama of what they were conveying and the pain they most certainly had experienced. These latter interviews were often the most draining, for the force of their experiences did not impress me until I later reviewed the interview and was then alone with the unacknowledged emotion of the memory of the incident.

Unlike individuals who participate in studies of victim/survivors, the African Americans who had attended Howard or Northwestern generally understood themselves to have been privileged. In short, the interviews were usually weighty as the contradictions of very difficult, often exhausting and painful experiences unfurled in tandem with a celebration of an experience that had allowed or was allowing them entrée to tremendously increased opportunities.

MORE ABOUT THE SAMPLE

Although those students who came to college from working-class backgrounds almost always talked about feeling dislocated or unaware of how to take advantage of resources, many of the alumni in my sample came from backgrounds that included a history of education. Like previous studies of blacks in college, this one suggests a relationship between children's levels of educational attainment and those of their parents. Since, with one exception, I only interviewed alumni who had completed college, it is impossible for me to add to the larger argument that the educational level of one's parents is primary to black students' college completion in general.

The educational attainment of mothers is higher than what one would expect from the mothers of comparable white students. I have educational data on both parents for forty-nine of the fifty-five respondents. Of those forty-nine, mothers had more education than students' fathers in 40 percent (twenty of forty-nine) of the households. Mothers had equal education to their partners in almost 30 percent (sixteen of forty-nine) situations. And mothers had less education than respondents' fathers in fewer than one-quarter (twelve of forty-nine) of their homes. *Fully 25 percent of respondents' mothers had master's degrees or Ph.D.s.* And only 6 percent of mothers (three women) had not completed high school. Fathers' educational attainment was much more varied. While more than 25 percent of all respondents' fathers had not completed high school, another 25 percent had advanced degrees, including master's, J.D.s and Ph.D.s.

Of the Howard men, four out of thirteen of their mothers have more education than their husbands. Of the Howard women, five out of eight of their mothers have more education than their husbands. In other words, almost half (nine of twenty-one) of the mothers of Howard respondents had more education than respondents' fathers.

Of the Northwestern men, five out of thirteen of their mothers have more education than their fathers. Of the Northwestern women, five out of fourteen mothers have more education than their partners. In other words, like their Howard counterparts, more than a third of the mothers of Northwestern respondents had more education than respondents' fathers.

In short, whether a respondent attended Northwestern University or Howard University, chances were very high that the respondent's mother had as much if not more education than the respondent's father. Altogether, then, more than 75 percent of respondents come from homes in which the mother had as much if not more education as the father of their children.

JOBS RESPONDENTS HELD AT TIME OF INTERVIEW

Howard

1. public school teacher
2. just graduated, not yet working
3. private practice lawyer

4. corporate finance associate
5. engineer for public schools

Northwestern

1. senior business consultant
2. partner in own law firm
3. graduate student in electrical engineering
4. field test engineer
5. financial services advisor

6. program coordinator, private mental health facility
7. corporate banking officer

8. manager for top oil company

9. architect for city
10. playwright

11. corporate banking officer
12. marketing, consulting for own business
13. real estate agent, house renovator

14. college humanities professor
15. features editor, major black magazine

16. division engineer

17. lawyer for private firm
18. sales representative, credit card processor
19. clergy
20. attorney
21. real estate broker

22. assistant district manager, financial firm
23. physician
24. civil engineer
25. corporate banking officer
26. graduate student and secretary

6. grad student in sociology mental health facility
7. project manager for consulting engineering work

8. vice president and director for new business development, banking

9. lawyer for private firm
10. account manager, sales representative for major corporation

11. marketing consultant
12. administrative associate for small company business
13. meeting planner for large Greek-letter organization

14. underwriter
15. planning engineer for major company magazine

16. assistant director, nonprofit health organization

17. engineer for local power company
18. vice president of commercial lending, bank processor
19. sales trainer consultant
20. newspaper reporter
21. accounts manager, pharmaceutical company

22. senior editor, major black magazine

23. library administrator
24. attorney
25. account systems engineer
26. product manager, state utility company

27. account executive, black public relations firm

28. attorney and judicial law clerk
29. human resources director

QUESTIONNAIRE

[First, I reintroduced myself, having already done so by letter, in most cases, or over the phone.]

Just so you know a little bit about what I'm doing, I'm interviewing black alumni who completed their undergraduate work at Northwestern and Howard about their college experiences for my Ph.D. project. I'm hoping to interview about thirty people from each school. In the end, I'll look for themes and salient issues. I will never use your name and I will keep any identifying characteristics to a minimum in my dissertation. Mostly, I'll be drawing a composite from what several people tell me. Everything you tell me will remain absolutely confidential. With this in mind, may I tape record you?

I'd like to begin with a few questions about your background. Then we'll spend most of the interview on questions about your college experience. And then I'll ask you a few questions about your current situation and finally I'll ask you to get wise and reflective at the close of the interview. This should take about an hour, a little longer or shorter depending on how much you want to tell me. Feel free to interrupt me or ask me to go back to an earlier question if something comes to mind as we're going along.

1. Where are you from?
2. Do you have sisters and brothers? If so, how far have they gone in school?
3. How far did your parents go in school?
4. What were your parents' jobs while you were growing up?
5. What was your high school like? (Probe: size, public/private, racial composition?)
6. What kind of a student were you in high school? How would people have known that? (Probe: What were your grades like? Did you participate in any clubs or sports? If so, which ones?)
7. Do you remember how you did on the standardized tests at the end of high school? If so, what were your scores?
8. What colleges did you apply to? Which of those did you get into? (Probe: How did you find out about Northwestern/Howard? Did you have help from a guidance counselor?)
9. Did your parents participate in your decision of where to go to college?
10. Did you apply for financial aid from Northwestern/Howard? If yes, was it a good package? Even considering the financial aid, would you say it was difficult to pay for college?
11. I'd like you to think back to how you were feeling and what you were thinking before you went to college. What did you expect it to be like?

12. What years were you at Northwestern/Howard?

13. Northwestern only: Were you invited to participate in a prefreshman summer program at Northwestern, either MEOP or SAW? If so, would you say that was a good thing? If not, was that a problem coming onto campus having not participated?

14. What was your first year in college like? (Probe: classes taken, grades received, live on/off campus, roommate, friends, clubs, sports?)

15. What did you do the summer after freshman year? (If they worked, How did you get that job?)

16. Tell me about your sophomore year. What was it like? (Probe: classes taken, grades received, live on/off campus, roommate friends, clubs, sports?)

17. What did you do the summer after your sophomore year? (How did you get that job?)

18. How 'bout junior year? How did that go? (Probe: major, grades received, live on/off campus, roommate, friends, clubs, sports?)

19. What did you do the summer after junior year? (How did you get that job?)

20. And tell me about senior year. What was that like? (Probe: major, grades received, live on/off campus, roommate, friends, clubs, sports, decisions about after college?)

21. If applicable, ask about fifth year.

22. What did you do after you graduated? (Probe: What was your first job out of college? How did you get that job? Or how did you decide to go to graduate school?)

23. If they did not already answer this question: Did you join a fraternity or sorority while you were an undergrad? If not, did you ever consider joining?

24. Did you ever feel pressure to rush or to pledge? Do you think others felt pressure to join?

25. There's been a lot of negative publicity about Greek-letter organizations criticizing everything from hazing to their exclusiveness. Do you have any comment on that?

26. For Northwestern only, if they haven't already answered this: Tell me about the black community when you were on campus. (Probe: Would you have called it cohesive? Were there ever any protests or campaigns that you can remember? Were you involved in those at all?) How would you characterize the racial climate while you were on campus?

27. For Howard only: Were there any white undergraduate students while you were there? If yes: How did they fit in? Were you friends with any of them? Did white graduate students participate in the undergraduate campus life at all? How would you describe the racial climate on campus—considering there were some white teachers and some white students?

28. Was your social life what you had hoped it would be in college? Did you date at all? (If yes, men or women?)

29. For Northwestern only: Was there any visible black gay community while you were in school? Would you say it was easy or difficult to be black and gay while you were in school?

30. For Howard only: Was there any visible gay community while you were in school? Were gay people an accepted part of the campus community?

31. How would you characterize the relationship between black men and women on campus? (Probe: Would you have considered it healthy, unhealthy, positive, negative . . . ?)

32. For Northwestern only: Was there any interracial dating or were there many interracial friendships while you were there? If so, how was that looked upon?

33. Were there any experiences that stand out for you as extraordinary during college? (Good or bad. If so, what were they and why?)

34. Along the same lines, were there any faculty who stand out in your mind as people who helped get you through, who acted as mentors or were just more supportive than average?

35. Were there any faculty who stand out who were the opposite of that?

Now on to the current questions:

36. If not already answered: Did you go on to graduate school? If so, which one, what kind?

37. What is your job title now?

38. How did you get this job?

39. What is your current address?

40. How old are you?

We're almost finished. These are the final reflective questions:

41. Are there any ways that you think Northwestern/Howard helped or hurt you either personally or professionally, especially ways that might not be obvious to others?

42. If you could choose one word to describe your college experience, what would it be?

43. Would you make the same choice again to attend Howard/Northwestern knowing what you know now?

44. For Northwestern only: Do you think there's still a place for historically black colleges in the education of black students today?

45. For Howard only: Do you think there's still a place for predominantly white colleges in the education of black students today?

46. What advice about education or college or life would you give to a seventeen-year-old today who comes from a background similar to your own?
47. That's really it. Is there anything else that you'd like to add that you think I missed or that you always wanted to say about college?

Thank you so much for your time . . .

BIBLIOGRAPHY

Abel, Elizabeth, Barbara Christian, and Helene Moglen, editors. 1997. *Female Subjects in Black and White: Race, Psychoanalysis, Feminism.* Berkeley: University of California Press.

Alexander, Suzanne. 1990. "Freshmen Flood Black Colleges, Defying Trend." *Wall Street Journal*, July 9, B1.

Allen, Walter R., Edgar G. Epps, and Nesha Z. Haniff, editors. 1991. *College in Black and White: African American Students in Predominantly White and in Historically Black Public Universities.* Albany: State University of New York Press.

———. 1988. "Black Students in U.S. Higher Education: Toward Improved Access, Adjustment, and Achievement." *The Urban Review* 20(3): 165–88.

———. 1987. "Blacks in Michigan Higher Education." Pp. 53–68 in *The State of Black Michigan: 1987*, edited by Michigan State University Urban Affairs Program and the Council of Michigan Urban League Executives, East Lansing.

———. 1985. "Black Student, White Campus: Structural, Interpersonal, and Psychological Correlates of Success." *Journal of Negro Success* 54(2): 134–47:

———. 1982. "Black and Blue: Black Students at the University of Michigan." *LSA Magazine* 6(1): 13–17.

Altbach, Philip G., and Kofi Lomotey. 1991. *The Racial Crisis in American Higher Education.* Albany: State University of New York Press.

Altbach, Philip G., Kofi Lomotey, and Shariba Rivers. 2002. "Race in Higher Education: The Continuing Crisis." Pp. 23–42 in *The Racial Crisis in American Higher Education, Revised Edition*, edited by William Smith, Philip Altbach, and Kofi Lomotey. Albany: State University of New York Press.

Andersen, Margaret. 1988. *Thinking About Women: Sociological Perspectives on Sex and Gender.* New York: Macmillan.

Andersen, Margaret, and Howard Taylor. 1999. *Sociology: Understanding a Diverse Society.* New York: Wadsworth.

Anderson, James D. 2002. "Race in American Higher Education: Historical Perspectives on Current Conditions." Pp. 3–22 in *The Racial Crisis in American Higher Education: Continuing Challenges for the Twenty-first Century, Revised Edition*, edited by William A. Smith, Philip G. Altbach, and Kofi Lomotey. Albany: State University of New York Press.

Appiah, Anthony. 1992. *In My Father's House: Africa in the Philosophy of Culture.* New York: Oxford.

Aronowitz, Stanley. 1995. "Reflections on Identity." Pp. 111–146 in *The Identity in Question*, edited by John Rajchman. New York: Routledge.

Asamen, Joy K., and Gordon LaVern Berry. 1989. *Black Students: Psycho-social Issues and Academic Achievement.* Newbury Park, CA: Sage.

Asante, Molefi Kete, and Hana S. Noor Al-Deen. 1984. "Social Interaction of Black and White College Students: A Research Report." *Journal of Black Studies* 14(4): 507–16.

Astin, Alexander W., Helen S. Astin, Kenneth C. Green, Laura Kent, Patricia McNamara, and Melanie Reeves Williams. 1982. *Minorities in American Higher Education.* San Francisco: Jossey-Bass.

Astin, Alexander W., and Robert J. Panos. 1969. *The Educational and Vocational Development of College Students.* Washington, D.C.: American Council on Education.

Babbie, Earl. 1983. *The Practice of Social Research, Third Edition.* Belmont, CA: Wadsworth.

Baldwin, James. 1961. *Nobody Knows My Name: More Notes of a Native Son.* New York: Vintage.

Banks, James A., and Jean D. Grambs. 1972. *Black Self-Concept: Implications for Education and Social Science.* New York: McGraw-Hill.

Barker, Kim. 1990. "Black Greek Nationals to End Pledging." *Daily Northwestern*, February 21, 1, 8.

Barnes, Denise. 1992. "Stars Come out for Howard's 125th Year," *Washington Times*, April 4, C1, C2.

Beckham, Barry. 1984. *The Black Students Guide to Colleges.* Providence, RI: Beckham House.

Beem, Edgar Allen. 1994. "Color on Campus: Confronting Racial Ignorance." *Maine Times*, May 6, 1–5.

Berger, Peter L., and Thomas Luckmann. 1966. *The Social Construction of Reality: a Treatise in the Sociology of Knowledge.* Garden City, NY: Doubleday.

Bhabha, Homi. 1995. "Freedom's Basis in the Indeterminate." Pp. 47–62 in *The Identity in Question*, edited by John Rajchman. New York: Routledge.

Birnbach, Lisa. 1984. *Lisa Birnbach's College Book.* New York: Ballantine.

Blackwell, James Edward. 1981. *Mainstreaming Outsiders: The Production of Black Professionals.* Bayside, NY: General Hall.

Blalock, M. 1967. *Toward a Theory of Minority Group Relations.* New York: Capricorn.

Blauner, Robert. 1989. *Black Lives, White Lives: Three Decades of Race Relations in America.* Berkeley: University of California Press.

———. 1969. "Internal Colonialism and Ghetto Revolt." *Social Problems* 16: 393–406.

Bloom, Allen. 1987. *The Closing of the American Mind.* New York: Simon and Schuster.

Blumer, Herbert. 1998. "Race Prejudice as a Sense of Group Position." Pp. 31–40 in *New Tribalisms: The Resurgence of Race and Ethnicity*, edited by Michael W. Hughey. New York: New York University Press.

Bonacich, Edna. 1994. [1972]. "A Theory of Ethnic Antagonism: The Split Labor Market." Pp. 474–486 in *Social Stratification: class, race, and gender in sociological perspective*, edited by David B. Grusky. Boulder, CO: Westview.

Bowen, William G., and Derek Bok. 1998. *The Shape of the River: Long-Term Consequences of Considering Race in College and University Admissions.* Princeton, NJ: Princeton University Press.

Bowles, Frank, and Frank A. De Costa. 1971. *Between Two Worlds: A Profile of Negro Higher Education.* New York: McGraw-Hill.

Bowman, Phillip J. and William A. Smith. 2002. "Racial Ideology in the campus community. Pp. 103–120 in *The Racial Crisis in American higher education*, edited by Willilam A. Smith, Philip G. Altbach, and Kofi Lomotey. Albany: State University of New York Press.

Boyd, Blanche McCrary. 1993. "Dorothy Allison, Crossover Blues." *A Queer Nation* 257(1): 20, 22.

Boyd, William M., II. 1974. *Desegregating America's College: A Nationwide Survey of Black Students, 1972–1973.* New York: Praeger.

Brodie, James Michael. 1991. "The Best and the Brightest: Black College Honors Programs Seek to Challenge and Keep Gifted Students." *Black Issues in Higher Education.* March 14, 6–8.

Brown, Lyn Mikel and Carol Gilligan. 1992. *Meeting at the Crossroads: Women's Psychology and Girls' Development.* Cambridge, MA: Harvard University Press.

Butler, Judith. 1995. "Debate: Discussion." Pp. 129–144 in *The Identity in Question*, edited by John Rajchman. New York: Routledge.

Butler, Judith. 1991. "Imitation and Gender Insubordination." in *Inside/Out: Lesbian Theories, Gay Theories*, edited by Diana Fuss. New York: Routledge.

———. 1990. *Gender Trouble: Feminism and the Subversion of Identity.* New York: Routledge.

Calhoun, Cheshire. 1997. "Separating Lesbian Theory from Feminist Theory: The Case of the Lesbian Not-Woman." Pp. 199–218 in *Feminist Social Thought: a reader*, edited by Diana Tietjens Meyers. New York: Routledge.

Camper, John. 1990. "Colleges Want Blacks, but Racism Persists." *Chicago Tribune*, February 4, 2:1–2.

Cannon, Lynn Weber, Elizabeth Higginbotham, and Maeianne L. A. Leung. 1998. "Race and Class Bias in Qualitative Research on Women." *Gender and Society* 2(4): 449–62.

Cary, Lorene. 1991. *Black Ice.* New York: Knopf.

Césaire, Aimé. 1972. *Discourse on Colonialism.* New York: MR.

Chickering, Arthur W. 1981. *The Modern American College: Responding to the New Realities of Diverse Students and a Changing Society.* San Francisco: Jossey-Bass.

Chodorow, Nancy. 1989. *Feminism and Psychoanalytic Theory.* New Haven, CT: Yale University Press.

Cohen, Marshall, Thomas Nagel, and Thomas Scanlon. 1977. *Equality and Preferential Treatment.* Princeton, NJ: Princeton University Press.

Collins, Patricia Hill. 1989. *Toward a New Vision: Race, Class, and Gender as Categories of Analysis and Connection.* Memphis, TN: Memphis State University Center for Research on Women.

———. 1990. *Black Feminist Thought.* New York: Routledge.

Collins, Randall. 1979. *The Credential Society: An Historical Sociology of Education and Stratification.* New York: Academic.

Collison, Michele N.-K. 1991. "As Black Colleges Grow More Selective, Some Worry They Are Becoming Elitist." *Chronicle of Higher Education,* July 3, A1, A23.

Committee on Race Relations, Harvard College. 1980. *A Study of Race Relations at Harvard College.* Cambridge, MA: Office of the Dean of Students, Harvard College.

Cone, James. 1991. *Martin and Malcolm and America: A Dream or a Nightmare.* Maryknoll, NY: Orbis.

Cone, James. 1975. *God of the Oppressed.* New York: Seabury.

Connell, R. W. 1987. *Gender and Power: Society, the Person, and Sexual Politics.* Stanford, CA: Stanford University Press.

Cook, Samuel DuBois. 1978. "The Socio-Ethical Role and Responsibility of the Black College Graduate." Pp. 51–67 in *Black Colleges in America,* edited by Charles Willie and Ronald Edmonds. New York: Teacher's College Press.

Coughlin, Ellen K. 1991. "In Multiculturalism Debate, Scholarly Book on Ancient Greece Plays Controversial Part." *Chronicle of Higher Education,* July 31, A4, A6.

Crenshaw, Kimberlé. 1995. *Critical Race Theory: The Key Writings that Formed the Movement.* New York: New Press.

Crenshaw, Kimberlé. 1990. "A Black Feminist Critique of AntiDiscrimination Law and Politics." Pp. 195–218 in *The Politics of Law: A Progressive Critique,* edited by David Kairys. New York: Pantheon.

Cross, William E., Jr. 1991. *Shades of Black: Diversity in African-American Identity.* Philadelphia: Temple University Press.

Crowley, Dana Jack. 1991. *Silencing the Self: Women and Depression.* Cambridge, MA: Harvard University Press.

Curry, George E. 1989. "Howard Protesters Follow in Parents' Steps." *Chicago Tribune,* March 19, 1, 18.

Davis, DeWitt, Jr. 1980. "Location Preferences of Black University Students." *Phylon* 41(3): 247–56.

Davis, F. James. 1991. *Who Is Black? One Nation's Definition.* University Park: Pennsylvania State University Press.

De Beauvoir, Simone. [1952] 1989. *The Second Sex,* translated by H. M. Parshley. New York: Knopf.

Deskins, Donald R. 1991. "Winners and Losers: A Regional Assessment of Minority Enrollment and Earned Degrees in U.S. colleges and universities, 1974–1984." Pp. 17–40 in *College in Black and White,* edited by Walter R. Allen and Edgar E. Epps. Albany: State University of New York Press.

Donald, James, and Ali Rattansi, editors. 1992. *"Race," Culture, and Difference.* Newbury Park, CA: Sage.

Drake, St. Claire, and Horace R. Cayton. 1945. *Black Metropolis: A Study of Negro Life in a Northern City.* New York: Harcourt, Brace.

Drewry, Henry N., and Humphrey Doermann. 2001. *Stand and Prosper: Private Black Colleges and Their Students.* Princeton, NJ: Princeton University Press.

D'Souza, Dinesh. 1991. *Illiberal Education: The Politics of Race and Sex on Campus.* New York: The Free Press.

DuBois, W. E. B. [1903] 1965. *The Souls of Black Folk.* In *Three Negro Classics.* New York: Avon.

Dugger, Karen. 1990. "Social Location and Gender-Role Attitudes: A Comparison of Black and White Women." *Gender and Society* 2(4): 425–48.

Durkheim, Emile. [1938] 1982. *The Rules of Sociological Method.* New York: The Free Press.

Early, Gerald. 1994. *Lure and Loathing: Essays on Race, Identity, and the Ambivalence of Assimilation.* New York: Penguin.

———. 1992. "Their Malcolm, My Problem." Pp. 62–69 in *Harper's Magazine* December.

———. 1992. *Tuxedo Junction: Essays on American Culture.* New York: Ecco.

———. 1989. "The American Mysticism of Remembrance." *Hungry Mind Review* (Spring): 53–57.

Edwards, Harry. 1970. *Black Students.* New York: The Free Press.

Edwards, John J., III. 1989. "Black Profs Call Student Protest Encouraging." *Daily Northwestern*, April 24, 3.

Erikson, Erik. 1968. *Identity, Youth, and Crisis.* New York: Norton.

Evans, Grace. 1988. "Those Loud Black Girls." *Learning to Lose: Sexism and Education.* London: Women's Press.

Exum, William. 1985. *Paradoxes of Protest: Black Student Activism in a White University.* Philadelphia: Temple University Press.

Fanon, Franz. [1961] 1968. *The Wretched of the Earth.* New York: Grove.

Feagin, Joe R., Hernàn Vera, and Nikitah Imani. 1996. *The Agony of Education: Black Students at White Colleges and Universities.* New York: Routledge.

Feiner, Susan F., and Bruce R. Roberts. 1990. "Hidden by the Invisible Hand: Neoclassical Economic Theory and the Textbook Treatment of Race and Gender." *Gender and Society* 4(2): 159–81.

Fish, Stanley. 1993–94. "Affirmative Action and the SAT." *Journal of Blacks in Higher Education.* (Winter): 83.

Fleming, Jacqueline. 1984. *Blacks in College: A Comparative Study of Students' Success in Black and in White Institutions.* San Francisco: Jossey-Bass.

Foucault, Michel. 1980. *Power/Knowledge: Selected Interviews and Other Writings, 1972–1977.* New York: Pantheon.

Fordham, Signithia. 1993. " 'Those Loud Black Girls': (Black) Women, Silence, and Gender 'Passing' in the Academy." *Anthropology and Education Quarterly* 24(1): 3–32.

———. 1988. "Racelessness as a Factor in Black Students' School Success: Pragmatic Strategy or Pyrrhic Victory." *Harvard Educational Review* 58(1): 58–84.

Fordham, Signithia, and John U. Ogbu. 1986. "Black Students' School Success: Coping with the Burden of 'Acting White.' " *Urban Review* 18(3): 176–206.

Frankenberg, Ruth. 1993. *White Women, Race Matters: The Social Construction of Whiteness.* Minneapolis: University of Minnesota Press.

Franklin, John Hope, and Alfred A. Moss, Jr. 1988. *From Slavery to Freedom: A History of Negro Americans, Sixth Edition.* New York: Knopf.

Frazier, E. Franklin. 1957. *Black Bourgeoisie.* New York: The Free Press.

Fuss, Diana, editor. 1991. *Inside/Out: Lesbian Theories, Gay Theories.* New York: Routledge.

Gilkes, Cheryl Townsend. 1998. " 'Plenty Good Room': Adaptation in a Changing Black Church. " Pp. 101–21 in *The Annals of the American Academy of Political and Social Science* 558 (July).

Gilroy, Paul. 1993. *The Black Atlantic: Modernity and Double Consciousness.* Cambridge, MA: Harvard University Press.

Giroux, Henry A. 1993. *Border Crossings: Cultural Workers and the Politics of Education.* New York: Routledge.

Glanton, Dahleen. 1991. "Blacks on Campus: You Discover Which Battles Need Fighting." *Chicago Tribune,* May 19, 4: 1, 4.

Goffman, Erving. 1963. *Stigma: Notes on the Management of Spoiled Identity.* Englewood Cliffs, NJ: Prentice-Hall.

Goffman, Erving. 1959. *The Presentation of Self in Everyday Life.* Garden City, NY: Doubleday.

Gossett, Thomas F. 1965. *Race: The History of an Idea in America.* New York: Schocken.

Grant, Joanne. 1969. *Confrontation on Campus: The Columbia Pattern for the New Protest.* New York: Signet.

Grossman, Ron. 1989. "Debate Heating up on Campus Moves to Curb Free Speech." *Chicago Tribune,* May 14: 1, 8.

Grusky, David B. 1994. *Social stratification: class, race, and gender in Sociological Perspective.* Boulder, CO: Westview.

Guinier, Lani. 2001. "Colleges Should Take 'Confirmative Action' in Admissions." *Chronicle of Higher Education,* December 14, B10, B12.

Guinier, Lani, and Susan Sturm. 2001. *Who's Qualified?* Boston: Beacon.

Guinier, Lani. 1998. *Lift Every Voice: Turning a civil rights setback into a Strong New Vision of Social Justice.* New York: Simon and Schuster.

Gurin, Patricia, and Edgar Epps. 1975. *Black Consciousness, Identity, and Achievement: A Study of Students in Historically Black Colleges.* New York: John Wiley and Sons.

Hamilton, Robert S. 1949. *Present Status of the Philosophy of Society.* NY: Wescott.

Hall, Stuart. 1994. "Cultural Identity and Diaspora." in *Colonial Discourse and Post Colonial Theory,* edited by Patrick Williams and Laura Chrisman. New York: Columbia University Press.

Harvard Committee on Race Relations. 1980. *A Study of Race Relations at Harvard College.* Cambridge: Office of the Harvard College Dean of Students.

Haverford College. 1999. *Haverford College Self-Study.* Haverford, PA: Haverford College.

Haverford College. 2000. *Haverford College Factbook.* Haverford, PA: Haverford College. December.

Hein, Jeremy. 1994. "From Migrant to Minority: Hmong Refugees and the Social Construction of Identity in the United States." *Sociological Inquiry* 64(3): 281–306.

Helms, Janet, editor. 1993. *Black and White Racial Identity: Theory, Research, and Practice.* Westport, CT: Praeger.

Hemmons, Willa Mae. 1982. "From the Halls of Hough and Halsted: A Comparison of Black Students on Predominantly White and Predominantly Black Campuses." *Journal of Black Studies* 12(4): 383–402.

Higginbotham, Evelyn Brooks. 1992. "African-American Women's History and the Metalanguage of Race." *Signs* 17(2): 252–74.

Holland, Dorothy C., and Margaret Eisenhart. 1990. *Educated in Romance: Woman, Achievement, and College Culture.* Chicago: University of Chicago Press.

Homans, Margaret. " 'Racial Composition': Metaphor and the Body in the Writing of Race." Pp. 77–101 in *Female Subjects in Black and White: Race, Psychoanalysis, and Feminism*, edited by Elizabeth Abel, Barbara Christian, and Helene Moglen. Berkeley: University of California.

Howard, Jeff, and Ray Hammond. 1985. "Rumors of Inferiority: The Hidden Obstacles to Black Success." *New Republic*, September 9, 17–21.

Howells, William W. 1971. "The Meaning of Race." Pp. 3–10 in *The Biological and Social Meaning of Race*, edited by Richard H. Osborne. San Francisco: W. H. Freeman.

Hughes, Everett C. [1971] 1984. *The Sociological Eye: Selected Papers.* New Brunswick, NJ: Transaction.

Hughey, Michael W., editor. 1998. *New Tribalisms: The Resurgence of Race and Ethnicity.* New York: New York University Press.

Hunter, Allan. 1993. "Same Door, Different Closet: A Heterosexual Sissy's Coming-out Party." Pp. 150–168 in *Heterosexuality: A Feminism and Psychology Reader*, edited by Sue Wilkinson and Cecelia Kitzinger, Newbury Park, CA: Sage.

Hyllegard, David, and David E. Lavin. 1992. "Higher Education and Challenging Work: Open Admissions and Ethnic and Gender Differences in Job Complexity." *Sociological Forum* 7(2): 239–60.

Jack, Dana Crowley. 1991. *Silencing the Self: Women and Depression.* Cambridge: Harvard.

Jackson, Derrick Z. 1994. "Trapped below 'The Bell Curve.' " *Boston Globe*, November 18, 23.

Jackson, Kenneth W., and L. Alex Swan. 1991. "Institutional and Individual Factors Affecting Black Undergraduate Student Performance: Campus Race and Student Gender." Pp. 127–41 in *College in Black and White: African American Students in Predominantly White and Historically Black Public Universities*, edited by Walter R. Allen, Edgar G. Epps, and Nesha Z. Haniff. Albany: State University of New York Press.

Jackson, P. 1968. *Life in Classrooms.* New York: Holt, Rinehart, and Winston.

Jacobs, Jerry A., David Karen, and Katherine McClelland. 1991. "The Dynamics of Young Men's Career Aspirations." *Sociological Forum* 6(4): 609–39.

Jaschik, Scott. 1992. "Black College Presidents Plan a 'Summit' amid Displeasure with Lobbying Group." *Chronicle of Higher Education*, January 15, A1, A29.

Jencks, Christopher. 1985. "Affirmative Action for Blacks." *American Behavioral Scientist* 28(6): 731–60.

Jencks, Christopher, and David Riesman. 1968. *The Academic Revolution.* New York: Doubleday.

Jenifer, Franklyn G. 1991. "Point of View: The Supreme Court Must Act to Preserve and Strengthen Historically Black Colleges." *Chronicle of Higher Education*, October 16, A60.

Jewell, K. Sue. 1985. "Will the Real Black, Afro-American, Mixed, Colored, Negro Please Stand Up? Impact of the Black Social Movement Twenty Years Later." *Journal of Black Studies* 16(1): 57–75.

Jones, Ann. 1973. *Uncle Tom's Campus*. New York: Praeger.

Kairys, David, editor. 1990. *The Politics of Law: A Progressive Critique*. New York: Pantheon.

Kanter, Rosabeth Moss. 1977. *Men and Women of the Corporation*. New York: Basic.

——. 1972. *Commitment and Community: Commune and Utopias in Sociological Perspective*. Cambridge, MA: Harvard University Press.

Kaplan, David, and Karen Springen. 1990. "The NCAA Tries Again: What Rules for Colleges and Their Student Athletes?" *Newsweek*, January 8, 59.

Karen, David. 1991. " 'Achievement' and 'Ascription' in Admission to an Elite College: A Political-Organizational Analysis." *Sociological Forum* 6(2): 349–80.

Keller, Evelyn Fox. 1985. *Reflections on Gender and Science*. New Haven, CT: Yale University Press.

King, Deborah. 1988. "Multiple Jeopardy, Multiple Consciousness: The Context of a Black Feminist Ideology." *Signs* (Autumn): 42–72.

Kochman, Thomas. 1981. *Black and White Styles in Conflict*. Chicago: University of Chicago Press.

Laclau, Ernesto. 1995. "Universalism, Particularism and the Question of Identity." Pp. 193–110 in *The Identity in Question*, edited by John Rajchman. New York: Routledge.

Ladner, Joyce. 1973. *The Death of White Sociology*. New York: Random House.

LaMar, Jake. 1991. *Bourgeois Blues: An American Memoir*. New York: Summit.

Leatherman, Courtney. 1990. "D.C. University Closed after Students Take over 2 Buildings." *Chronicle of Higher Education*, October 3, A2.

Lederman, Douglas. 1992. "Black Athletes Graduate at a Higher Rate Than Other Blacks, NCAA Reports." *Chronicle of Higher Education*, July 8, Section A: 32–42.

LeGates, Richard T., and Frederic Scott, editors. 1996. *The City Reader*. New York: Routledge.

Lenski, Gerhard Emmanuel. 1966. *Power and Privilege*. New York: McGraw-Hill.

Lerner, Gerda. 1973. *Black Women in White America: A Documentary History*. New York: Vintage.

Levine, Judith. 1994. "White like Me: When Privilege Is Written on Your Skin." *Ms.*, March–April, 22–24.

Levine, Lawrence W. 1977. *Black Culture and Black Consciousness*. New York: Oxford University Press.

Lieberson, Stanley. 1985. *Making It Count: The Improvement of Social Research and Theory*. Berkeley: University of California Press.

——. 1961. "A Societal Theory of Race and Ethnic Relations." *American Sociological Review* 26: 902–10.

Lieberson, Stanley, and Marcy C. Waters. 1988. *From Many Strands: Ethnic and Racial Groups in Contemporary America*. New York: Russell Sage Foundation.

Logan, Rayford W. 1969. *Howard University: The First Hundred Years, 1867–1967*. New York: New York University Press.

Loo, Chalsa M., and Gary Rolison. 1986. "Alienation of Ethnic Minority Students at a Predominantly White University." *Journal of Higher Education* 57(1) Pp. 58–77.

Lorde, Audre. 1984. *Sister Outsider: Essays and Speeches.* Trumansburg, NY: The Crossing Press.

Lukacs, Georg. [1968] 1971. *History and Consciousness: Studies in Marxist Dialectics.* Cambridge, MA: MIT Press.

Mannheim, Karl. 1936. *Ideology and Utopia.* New York: Harvest-HBJ.

Manuel, Diane. 1994a. " 'Family Feeling' Gives Black Colleges and Universities Their Appeal." *Boston Globe,* July 31, B7.

Manuel, Diane. 1994b. "Future's Uncertain for Black Colleges." *Boston Globe,* July 31, B1, B6.

Marable, Manning. 1984. *Race, Reform, and Rebellion: The Second Reconstruction in Black America, 1945–1982.* Jackson: University Press of Mississippi.

Martin, Michelle. 1990. "Days of Rage: In 1970, NU Students Took a Stand." *Daily Northwestern's Midweek,* February 7, 1, 4, 5.

Marx, Karl. 1981. *Capital: Volume Three.* New York: Vintage.

———. 1978. "The Eighteenth Brumaire of Louis Bonaparte." In *The Marx-Engels Reader,* edited by Robert C. Tucker. New York: Norton.

———. 1977. *Capital: Volume One.* New York: Vintage.

Marx, Karl, and Frederick Engels. 1948. *The Communist Manifesto.* New York: International Publishers.

Mason, Alpheus T., and D. Grier Stephenson, Jr. 1987. *American Constitutional Law: Introductory Essays and Selected Cases, Eighth Edition.* Englewood Cliffs, NJ: Prentice-Hall.

Mayhew, Lewis. 1973. *The Carnigie Commission on Higher Education Report.* San Francisco: Jossey-Bass.

McCall, George J., and Simmons, J. L., editors. 1969. *Issues in Participant Observation.* Reading, MA: Addison-Wesley.

McCarthy, J. D., and W. L. Yancey. 1971. "Uncle Tom and Mr. Charlie: Metaphysical Pathos in the Study of Racism and Personal Disorganization." *American Journal of Sociology* 76: 648–72.

McIntosh, Peggy. 1997. "White Privilege, Male Privilege." Pp. 120–28 in *Race: An Anthology in the First Person,* edited by Bart Schneider. New York: Crown.

Mead, George Herbert. 1934. *Mind, Self, and Society: From the Standpoint of a Social Behaviorist,* edited by Charles W. Morris. Chicago: University of Chicago Press.

Memmi, Albert. [1957] 1967. *The Colonizer and the Colonized.* Boston: Beacon.

Meyers, Diana Tietjens. 1997. *Feminist Social Thought: a reader.* New York: Routledge.

Meyers, Samuel L. 1987. "Blacks in College: NAFEO Trend Analysis." *American Visions,* October: 44–46.

Mills, C. Wright. [1959] 1967. *The Sociological Imagination.* New York: Oxford University Press.

Monro, John U. 1978. "Teaching and Learning English." Pp. 235–262 in *Black Colleges in America,* edited by Charles Willie and Ronald Edmonds. New York: Teacher's College Press.

Moore, Darrell. 1993. "Now You Can See It: The Liberal Aesthetic and Racial Representation in 'The Crying Game.' " *Cineaction* 32: 63–66.

Morrison, Toni. 1992. *Playing in the Dark: Whiteness and the Literary Imagination.* Cambridge, MA: Harvard University Press.

Muhammad, Erika. 1990. "Study Shows White Schools a Fast Trade for Minority Students." *Chicago Maroon,* November 27, 1, 4.

Mullane, Dierdre. 1993. *Crossing the Danger Water: Three Hundred Years of African-American Writing.* New York: Doubleday.

Myers, Samuel L. 1987. "Blacks in College." *American Visions,* October, 44–46.

Nabrit, James, Jr. 1969. Forward to Rayford W. Logan, *Howard University: The First Hundred Years, 1867–1967.* New York: New York University Press.

Napper, George. 1973. *Blacker than Thou: the struggle for campus unity.* Grand Rapids: Eerdmans.

Nettles, Michael T. 1991. "Racial Similarities and Differences in the Predictors of College Student Achievement." Pp. 75–94 in *College in Black and White: African-American Students in Predominantly White and Historically Black Public Universities,* edited by Walter R. Allen, Edgar G. Epps, and Nesha Z. Haniff. Albany: State University of New York Press.

Nicholson, David. 1992. "My Generation: Worlds Apart or "Notes of Another Native Son." *Washington Post Magazine,* August 23, Pp. 6–27.

Nicklin, Julie L. 1992. "Black College Fund Will Close 6 Offices, Lay Off 25 People." *Chronicle of Higher Education,* April 8, A1, A33–34.

Nisnoff, Laurie, Susan J. Tracy, and Stanley Warner. N.d. "Stories out of School: Poor and Working-Class Students at a Small Liberal Arts College." *Radical Teacher* 41.

Northwestern University Office of Administration and Planning. 1991–1992. *Northwestern University Data Book, Twenty-fourth Edition.* Evanston: Northwestern University.

Omi, Michael, and Howard Winant. 1994. *Racial Formation in the United States: From the 1960s to the 1990s, Second Edition.* New York: Routledge.

Osborne, Richard Hazelet. 1971. *The Biological and Social Meaning of Race.* San Francisco: W. H. Freeman.

O'Sullivan, Katherine, and William J. Wilson. 1988. "Race and Ethnicity." *Handbook of Sociology,* edited by Neil J. Smelser. Newbury Park, CA: Sage.

Page, Clarence. 1989. "Atwater, Horton, and Student Ideals." *Chicago Tribune,* March 12, 4:3.

Park, Robert Ezra. 1950. *Race and Culture.* Glencoe, IL: The Free Press.

Park, Robert Ezra, Ernest W. Burgess, and Roderick D. McKenzie. 1928. *The City.* Chicago: University of Chicago Press.

Parrillo, Vincent N. 1994. *Strangers to These Shores: Race and Ethnic Relations in the United States, Fourth Edition.* New York: Macmillan.

Parsons, Talcott. 1954. "A Revised Analytical Approach to the Theory of Social Stratification." Pp. 386–439 in *Essays in Sociological Theory, Revised Edition.* New York: The Free Press.

———. 1954. "An Analytical Approach to the Theory of Social Stratification." Pp. 69–88 in *Essays in Sociological Theory, Revised Edition.* New York: The Free Press.

Payne, Charles M. 1995. *I've Got the Light of Freedom: The Organizing Tradition and Freedom Struggle.* Berkeley: University of California Press.

Persell, Caroline Hodges, Sophia Catsambis, and Peter W. Cookson, Jr. 1992. "Differential Asset Conversion: Class and Gendered Pathways to Selective Colleges." *Sociology of Education* 65(July): 208–25.

Peterson's Guides, Inc. 1989. *Peterson's Guide to Four Year Colleges*. Princeton: Peterson's Guides, Inc.

Peterson, M. W., 1979. *Black Students on White Campuses: The Impacts of Increased Black Enrollments*. Ann Arbor, MI: Institute for Survey Research.

Phelan, Peggy. 1993. *Unmarked: The Politics of Performance*. New York: Routlege.

Pickney, Alphonso. [1969] 1993. *Black Americans, Fourth Edition*. Upper Saddle River, NJ: Prentice-Hall.

Pifer, Alan. 1973. *The Higher Education of Blacks in the United States* [reprint of The Alfred and Winifred Hoernlé Memorial Lecture, Johannesburg, South Africa]. New York: Carnegie Corporation.

Pitts, James. 1975. "The Politicization of Black Students: Northwestern University." *Journal of Black Studies* 5(3): 277–319.

Pounds, Augustine W. 1987. "Black Students' Needs on Predominantly White Campuses," Pp. 23–38 in *Responding to the Needs of Today's Minority Students*, edited by Doris J. Wright. San Francisco: Jossey-Bass.

Rajchman, John, 1995. *The Identity in Question*. New York: Routledge.

Ransby, Barbara. 1988. "The Politics of Exclusion: Black Students Fight Back." *The Nation*, March 26, 410–413.

Reinharz, Shulamit. 1992. *Feminist Methods in Social Research*. New York: Oxford University Press.

Reynolds, Larry T., and Leonard Lieberman. 1993. "The Rise and Fall of 'Race.' " *Race, Sex, and Class* 1(1): 109–28.

Rhoden, William C. 1990. "Black Student-Athletes Find Life of Privilege and Isolation." *New York Times*, January 8, 1, 37.

Rich, Adrienne. 1980. *Compulsory Heterosexuality and Lesbian Existence*. Denver: Antelope.

———. 1979. *On Lies, Secrets, and Silence: Selected Prose, 1966–1978*. New York: Norton.

Robinson, Randall. 2000. *The Debt: What America Owes Blacks*. New York: Dutton.

Rowland, Debran. 1990. "Black Colleges Put out the Welcome Mat." *Chicago Tribune*, November 12, 2:2.

Schlesinger, Arthur Meier. 1998. *The Disuniting of America: Reflections on a Multicultural Society*. New York: Norton.

Schneider, Bart, editor. 1997. *Race: An Anthology in the First Person*. New York: Crown.

Scott, James C. 1985. *Weapons of the Weak: Everyday Forms of Peasant Resistance*. New Haven, CT: Yale University Press.

Scott, J. F. 1965. "The American College Sorority: Its Role in Class and Ethnic Endogamy." *American Sociological Review* 30:514–27.

Scott, Joan W. 1995. "Multiculturalism and the Politics of Identity.," Pp. 3–12 in *The Identity in Question*, edited by John Rajchman. New York: Routledge.

Scott, Lisa, and Elaine Walker. 1989. "Protest Calls for More Blacks." *Daily Northwestern*, April 21, 1, 4.

Sedlacek, William E., and Dennis W. Webster. 1978. "Admission and Retention of Minority Students in Large Universities." *Journal of College Student Personnel* 19(3): 242–48.

Sennett, Richard, and Jonathan Cobb. 1973. *The Hidden Injuries of Class*. New York: Vintage.

Shange, Ntozake. 1975. *For Colored Girls Who Have Considered Suicide when the Rainbow Is Enuf.* New York: Bantam.

Sidel, Ruth. 1994. *Battling Bias: The Struggle for Identity and Community on College Campuses.* New York: Viking.

Sizemore, Barbara. 1972. "Social Science and Education for a Black Identity." Pp. 141–70 in *Black Self-Concept: Implications for Education and Social Science,* edited by James A. Banks and Jean D. Grambs. New York: McGraw-Hill.

Smelser, Neil J. 1988. *Handbook of Sociology.* Newbury Park, CA: Sage.

Smith, A. Wade. 1991. "Personal Traits, Institutional Prestige, Racial Attitudes, and Black Student Academic Performance in College." Pp. 111–126 in *College in Black and White: African American Students at Predominantly White and Historically Black Public Universities,* edited by Walter R. Allen et al. Albany: State University of New York Press.

Smith, A. Wade, and Walter R. Allen. 1984. "Modeling Black Student Academic Performance in Higher Education." *Research in Higher Education* 21(2): 210–24.

Smith, William A., Philip G. Altbach, and Kofi Lomotey. 2002. *The Racial Crisis in American Higher Education: Continuing Challenges for the Twenty-first Century, Revised Edition.* Albany: State University of New York Press.

Solomon, Lewis C., and Paul Taubman, editors. 1973. *Does College Matter?* New York: Academic.

Sowell, Thomas. 1972. *Black Education: Myths and Tragedies.* New York: David McKay.

Stangor, Charles, editor. 2000. *Stereotypes and Prejudice: Essential Readings.* Philadelphia: Psychology Press.

Steele, Claude. 2001. "Understanding the Performance Gap." Pp. 60–68 in *Who's Qualified?* edited by Lani Guinier and Susan Sturm. Boston: Beacon.

Steele, Claude, and Joshua Aronson. 2000. "Stereotype Threat and the Intellectual Test Performance of African Americans." Pp. 369–390 in *Stereotypes and Prejudice: Essential Readings,* edited by Charles Stangor. Philadelphia: Psychology Press.

Steele, Shelby. 1990. *The Content of Our Character: A New Vision of Race in America.* New York: St. Martin's.

———. 1989. "The Recoloring of Campus Life: Student Racism, Academic Pluralism, and the End of a Dream." *Harper's Magazine,* February, 47–55.

Stoltenberg, John. 1989. *Refusing to be a Man: Essays on Sex and Justice.* Portland, OR: Breitenbush.

Suen, H. K. 1983. "Alienation and Attrition of Black College Students on a Predominantly White Campus." *Journal of College Student Personnel* 24: 117–21.

Tatum, Beverly Daniel. 1997. *"Why Are All the Black Kids Sitting Together in the Cafeteria?" And Other Conversations about Race.* New York: Basic.

Taylor, Charles A. 1986. "Black Students on Predominantly White College Campuses in the 1980s." *Journal of College Student Personnel,* May, 196–202.

Teddlie, Charles, and John A. Freeman. 2002. "Twentieth Century Desegregation in U.S. Higher Education: A review of five distinct Historical Eras." Pp.   in *The Racial Crisis in American Higher Education, Revised Edition,* edited by William A. Smith, Philip G. Altbach, and Kofi Lomotey.

Tescher, Jennifer. 1989. "Panelist: Low Black Enrollment Widespread." *Daily Northwestern,* April 27, 4.

Thio, Alex: *Sociology: An Introduction.* New York: HarperCollins.

Thomas, Gail E. 1991. "Assessing the College Major Selection Process for Black Students." Pp. 61–74 in *College in Black and White: African American Students in Predominantly White and Historically Black Public Universities,* edited by Walter R. Allen, Edgar G. Epps, and Nesha Z. Haniff. Albany: State University of New York Press.

————. 1981. *Black Students in Higher Education: Conditions and Experiences.* Westport, CT: Greenwood.

Thomas, W. I., and Dorothy Swaine Thomas. 1928. *The Child in America.* New York: Knopf.

Thompson, Daniel C. 1978. "Black College Faculty and Students: The Nature of Their Interaction." Pp. 180–194 in *Black Colleges in America: Challenge, Development, Survival,* edited by Charles Vert Willie and Ronald R. Edmonds. New York: Teachers College Press.

Tierney, William G. and Jack K. Chung. 2002. "Affirmative Action in a post-Hopewood era." Pp. 271–284 in *The Racial Crisis in American Higher Education Revised Edition,* edited by William A. Smith, Philip G. Altbach, and Kofi Lomotey.

Tifft, Susan. 1990. "Education: Diamonds in the Rough: An Unusual Program Propels Young Blacks Toward College." *Time Magazine,* August 6, 58.

Tinto, V. 1975. "Dropout from Higher Education: A Theoretical Synthesis of Recent Research." *Review of Educational Research* 45: 89–125.

Tracey, Terence J., and William E. Sedlacek. 1987. "A Comparison of White and Black Student Success Using Noncognitive Variables: A Lisrel Analysis." *Research in Higher Education* 27(4). Pp. 333–345.

Trice, Dawn. 1989. "Blacks on Campus: Some Things Don't Change, But You Must." *Chicago Tribune,* May 19, 4:1, 4.

Tuggle, Denise. "People of Color at White Elitist Colleges." *Heresies* 7(1): 62–65.

Turner, Castelano B., and Barbara F. Turner. 1982. "Gender, Race, Social Class, and Self-Evaluations among College Students." *Sociological Quarterly* 23(Autumn): 491–507.

Udell, Jonathan. 1979. *Toward Conceptual Codification in Race and Ethnic Relations.* Roslyn Heights, NY: Libra.

U.S. Census Bureau. 2001. *Statistical Abstract of the United States.* Washington, D.C.: U.S. Government Printing Office.

U.S. Department of Education. 1991. *Historically Black Colleges and Universities, 1976–1990.* Office of Educational Research and Improvement, NCES 92–640, National Center for Education Statistics.

Ware, Vron and Les Back. 2002. Out of Whiteness: Color, Politics, and Culture. Chicago: University of Chicago Press.

Waters, Mary C. 1990. *Ethnic Options: Choosing Identities in America.* Berkeley: University of California Press.

Wattleworth, Bonnie. 1989. "Norington Lends Voice at Protest." *Daily Northwestern,* April 21, 3.

Watts, Jerry. 1989. "Dilemmas of Black Intellectuals: What Role Should We Play?" *Dissent* (Fall): 501–07.

Weber, Lynn. 2001. *Understanding Race, Class, Gender, and Sexuality: A Conceptual Framework*. Boston: McGraw-Hill.

Weber, Max. 1948. *The Protestant Ethic and the Spirit of Capitalism*, translated by Talcott Parsons. New York: Scribner.

Weizel, Richard. 1994. "Unable to Find Books for Their Children, They Start Black Books Galore." *Boston Globe*, July 31, B8.

West, Cornell. 1993–94. "The Dilemma of the Black Intellectual." *Journal of Blacks in Higher Education* 2 Winter:59–67.

———. *Race Matters*. 1993. Boston: Beacon.

Wilkerson, Isabel. 1989. "Black Fraternities Thrive, Some on Adversity." *New York Times*, October 2, 1, 9.

Wilkinson, Sue, and Celia Kitzinger, editors. 1993. *Heterosexuality: A Feminism and Psychology Reader*. Newbury Park, CA: Sage.

Williams, Patricia J. 1991. *The Alchemy of Race and Rights: Diary of a Law Professor*. Cambridge, MA: Harvard University Press.

Williamson, Harold F. and Payson S. Wild. 1976. *Northwestern University: A History, 1850–1975*. Evanston, IL: Northwestern University Press.

Willie, Charles Vert. 1987. *Effective Education: A Minority Perspective*. New York: Greenwood.

———. 1981. *The Ivory and Ebony Towers*. Lexington, MA: Lexington Books.

———. 1973. "Perspectives on Black Education and the Education of Blacks." Pp. 231–235 in *Does College Matter?* edited by L.C. Solomon, and P. Taubman, New York: Academic.

Willie, Charles Vert, and Ronald R. Edmonds, editors. 1978. *Black Colleges in America: Challenge, Development, Survival*. New York: Teachers College Press.

Willie, Charles Vert, Antoine M. Garibaldi, and Wornie L. Reed, editors. 1991. *The Education of African-Americans*. New York: Auburn House.

Willie, Charles Vert, and Marlene Y. Mac Leish. 1978. "The Priorities of Presidents of Black Colleges." Pp. 132–148 in *Black Colleges in America: Challenge, Development, Survival*, edited by Charles Vert Willie and Ronald R. Edmonds. New York: Teachers College Press.

Willie, Charles Vert, and Arline Sakuma McCord. 1972. *Black Students at White Colleges*. New York: Praeger.

Willie, Sarah Susannah. 1986. *The Best Years of Our Lives? The Perseverance Experience of Black Students at White Colleges*. Unpublished senior thesis in partial completion for the B.A. at Haverford College.

Wilson, Robin. 2002. "Stacking the Deck for Minority Candidates?" *Chronicle of Higher Education*, July 12, A10–11.

———. 1990. "Many Institutions Report Sharp Drops in Freshman Rolls." *Chronicle of Higher Education*, October 3, A1, A35–36.

Wilson, William Julius. 1978. *The Declining Significance of Race: Blacks and Changing American Institutions.* Chicago: University of Chicago Press.

——. 1973. *Power, Racism, and Privilege.* New York: Free Press.

Winant, Howard. 2001. *The World Is a Ghetto: Race and Democracy since World War II.* New York: Basic.

——. 1994. *Racial Conditions: Politics, Theory, Comparisons.* Minneapolis: University of Minnesota Press.

Wirth, Louis. [1938] 1996. "Urbanism as a Way of Life." Pp. 189–97 in *The City Reader*, edited by Richard T. LeGates and Frederic Scott. New York: Routledge.

Wittig, Monique. 1992. *"The Straight Mind" and Other Essays.* Boston: Beacon.

Woodson, Carter G. [1933] 1990. *The Mis-Education of the Negro.* Trenton, NJ: Africa World.

Wright, D. J., editor. 1987. *New Directions for Student Services: Responding to the Needs of Today's Minority Students.* San Francisco: Jossey-Bass.

Wright, Erik Olin. 1985. *Classes.* New York: Verso.

Wright, Lawrence. 1994. "Annals of Politics: One Drop of Blood." *New Yorker*, June, 46–55.

Young, Iris Marion. 1990. *Justice and the Politics of Difference.* Princeton, NJ: Princeton University Press.

Zweigenhaft, Richard L., and G. William Domhoff. 1991. *Blacks in the White Establishment: A Study of Race and Class in America.* New Haven, CT: Yale University Press.

NOTES

Chapter 1

1. Every interviewee represented has been given a pseudonym. There may be black alumniae at each institution that have the some of the names I've chosen, but that is purely coincidental. I refer to the two institutions attended, however, by their actual names. This is not a study about Howard and Northwestern *per se,* but about student experience at two similar schools with different racial compositions. The experiences that students had at each place are, of course, representative of the time they were there, just as memories of my own college experiences at Haverford and Spelman are limited to the time I was there. Since these four institutions have undergone important changes in recent years, I'd recommend that students interested in attending these schools look to contemporary research.

2. Snowball sampling consists of relying on an informant either to pass the researcher's name on to other potential respondents or to refer the researcher to potential respondents directly. See the appendix for further discussion of my method. All but one respondent graduated from college.

3. The names and some identifying characteristics of all respondents and the names of teachers and administrative staff to whom they refer have been changed to protect their anonymity.

4. See the appendix for an outline of the interview schedules and deeper discussion of interviewing challenges.

5. Sociologists Margaret Andersen and Howard Taylor (1999) offer this definition:

Racism is the perception and treatment of a racial or ethnic group, or member of that group, as intellectually, socially, and culturally inferior to one's own group. . . . Racism is not only in individual overt behavior, but also in society's institutions. Institutional racism is negative treatment and oppression of one racial or ethnic group by society's existing institutions based on the presumed inferiority of the oppressed group. Key to understanding institutional racism is seeing that dominant groups have the economic and political power to subjugate the minority group, even if they do not have the explicit intent of being prejudiced or discriminating against others. Power, or lack thereof, accrues to groups because of their position in social institutions, not just because of individual attitudes or behavior. (288–89)

6. Although I argue that Peggy McIntosh's (1997) metaphor for white privilege is incomplete, it is also tremendously useful.

7. This study does not enter the debate about which kinds of colleges are best for which students. Many kinds of colleges are necessary to meet the educational and social needs of a diverse nation. Nor does the study offer narratives of the lives of the men and women who were interviewed. This is for two reasons. First, the focus of the study was the college experience only, and second, more information would have jeopardized the anonymity of respondents. Some additional information about respondents, such as their parents' level of education and the jobs that they held at the time of the interview, is available in the appendix.

Chapter 2

1. Pifer elaborates on the racial composition of the nation before the Civil War:

> By 1790, when the United States had its first census, there were some 628,000 black slaves in the country. In addition, there were some 60,000 free blacks, making a total of 688,000 or nearly one black to four whites in the total population of just under four million. By 1860, on the eve of the Civil War, there were about four million black slaves and half a million free blacks in a total population of about 31 million, a ratio of about one black to six whites in the population. (Pifer 1973: 7)

2. Although only one-quarter of whites in the South owned slaves, both Southern and Northern whites who did not own slaves benefited from the economic fruits of having a huge unpaid workforce. Many white people, especially in the South, accepted the legitimacy of slavery as an institution, even if though the majority did not own slaves. Abolitionism, though it had its greatest following in the North, was a distinctly minority view.

3. Gilkes made this point about the rising tide of black Civil War–era literacy in a discussion following a paper entitled " 'Plenty Good Room': Adaptation in a Changing Black Church" given at the Eastern Sociological Society in Philadelphia, Pennsylvania, in 1998. The paper was subsequently published (1998).

4. See the work of James Cone, particularly *God of the Oppressed* (1975).

5. Blacks who lived in states where slavery was legal, even if no white owner could show papers of ownership, were considered slaves by whichever white man could claim them. There were also pockets of resistance where blacks joined up with Seminole Native Americans and defended themselves, traveling from as far southeast as Florida to as far west and north as Oklahoma.

6. The Morrill Act of 1862 provided "federally owned land to endow a system of public colleges in all of the states" (Pifer 1973: 12).

7. Bowles and DeCosta (1971: 30, 32). Today there are about 100 *historically* black colleges and universities, though in total there are more than 120 *predominantly* black colleges and universities, and some of these are two-year and non–degree granting or unaccredited institutions (Fleming 1984: 1).

8. These are among the largest and most well known, but hundreds, perhaps thousands, of benefit societies among blacks were established after Reconstruction ended. People would

contribute a portion of their incomes for burial costs, life insurance, and sickness insurance since white insurance agencies did not usually take their business or make good on their claims when they did.

9. Alphens T. Mason and D. Grier Stephenson explain the situation of the high court regarding *Brown:*

> After hearing argument in a group of public school segregation cases presented at the 1952 term, the justices were unable to reach a decision. In setting the cases for reargument during the 1953 term, the Court took the unusual step of requesting counsel to provide answers to a long list of questions. . . . The Court's caution . . . was understandable. Its decision would affect the school systems of 17 states and the District of Columbia where segregation was required by law, and four states where segregation was permitted by local option. . . . Even greater issues were involved: if segregation in public schools were deemed a denial of equal protection of the laws, it would be difficult, if not impossible, to defend segregation in other sectors of public life. (1987: 541)

10. "During the first two decades of the twentieth century," Anderson writes,

> [99] percent of African Americans enrolled in college were in private schools. This pattern of postsecondary enrollment stood in marked contrast to the national pattern in which significant proportions of students were enrolled in publicly supported colleges. . . . African Americans were forced to rely heavily on the private sector for support of Black colleges and universities. The founding of the United Negro College Fund (UNCF) in 1944 underscored the need for an organized effort to secure funds from private sources. (2002: 9)

11. Drewry and Doermann explain the evolution of Title III:

> The Higher Education Act of 1965 not only launched a large need-based student-aid program for low-income postsecondary students, it also began direct-support institutional grants to historically black private and public colleges. In its first eleven years, Title III lacked any race-specific language, referring to the eligible colleges only as "developing institutions.". . . By the mid-1980s, however, more than half the grant funds were being awarded to predominantly white institutions that also served large numbers of low-income students and that declared that they too were "developing." In 1986, Title III was amended to contain separate sections providing support not only for historically black colleges, but also for Hispanic-serving institutions and tribally controlled colleges. . . . Title III allocations in the federal budget for 2000 included a targeted institutional subsidy of $179 million for historically black colleges, $42 million for Hispanic-serving institutions, and $6 million for aid to tribally controlled Native American colleges. In contrast, the federal student aid budget (for all undergraduate colleges and universities) for 2000 is more than a hundred times larger than the Title III budget for minority-serving institutions: $50.6 billion, the largest part of which is for new student loans. (2001: 256)

12. Positive publicity came in the form of Bill Cosby's situation comedy *A Different World*, about life on the fictional campus of historically black Hillman College. The show aired during the 1980s.

13. From the National Center for Education Statistics: Historically Black Colleges and Universities: 1976–1994. Available at: http://nces.ed.gov/pubs/96902.html.

14. Anderson offers current numbers on students of color in the academy:

Students of color have made steady increases in college enrollment—by 61.3 percent from 1986 to 1996, including an increase of 22.2 percent since 1991. From 1986 to 1996, the college enrollment of African Americans has increased by 38.6 percent, Asian Americans by 83.8 percent and Latina/os by 86.4 percent. In 1996, African Americans made up 12.5 percent of the U.S. general population and 11 percent of all college students. Latina/os constituted 11 percent of the total population and 8.7 percent of all undergraduate students. Asian Americans comprised 3.7 percent of the U.S. total population and 5.8 percent of the undergraduate student population. These levels of college participation by students of color represent significant increases over the past ten years. (2002: 13)

15. Beverly Daniel Tatum explains,

The term *affirmative action* was introduced into our language and legal system by Executive Order 11246, signed by President Lyndon Johnson in 1965. This order obligated federal contractors to "take affirmative action to ensure that applicants are employed, and that employees are treated during employment without regard to their race, color, religion, sex, or national origin." As set forth by this order, contractors were to commit themselves to "apply every good faith effort" to use procedures that would result in equal employment opportunity for historically disadvantaged groups. The groups targeted for this "affirmative action" were White women, and men and women of color (specifically defined by the federal government as American Indian/Alaska Natives, Asian or Pacific Islanders, Blacks and Hispanics). In the the 1970s, legislation broadened the protected groups to include persons with disabilities and Vietnam veterans. . . . Executive Order 11246 . . . did not specify exactly what affirmative action programs should look like. (1997: 116–17).

16. This statistic is from the *Black Collegian* (September–October 1989).

17. According to the *2001 Edition of the Statistical Abstract of the United States* (see table 215), 43.2 percent of white Americans had completed four or more years of high school compared to 20.1 percent of black Americans in 1960. The increase in school completion rates over the last thirty years has been dramatic: by 2000, 84.9 percent of whites had completed high school and 78.5 percent of blacks had completed high school. While there are no figures available for Asians and Hispanics in 1960, in 2000, their group high school completion rates were 85.7 and 57.0, respectively.

18. In 1965, 9.9 percent of whites compared to 4.7 percent of blacks had completed four or more years of college. By 2000, the percentages had risen to 26.1 and 16.5, respectively (*2001 Edition of the Statistical Abstract of the United States*: table 215).

19. For an excellent discussion of affirmative action and the illusion of merit, see Iris Marion Young's *Justice and the Politics of Difference* (1990).

20. For discussion of Bill Clinton's stance on affirmative action, see *Lift Every Voice: Turning a Civil Rights Setback into a New Vision of Social Justice*, by Lani Guinere (1998).

21. The expressions of racism that Feagin and colleagues (1996) note include the following:

- [At] Michigan's Olivet College [d]uring the spring of 1992 trouble began brewing when some white students openly objected to black male students dating white females. . . . [A]n interracial fight ensued. . . . [S]omeone distributed Ku Klux Klan literature on campus (5).

- [E]arly in 1995 at Iowa's Grinnell College more than sixty students of color, most of them African American, organized a protest over racist incidents on campus, including the use of racial slurs by disc jockeys on the campus radio and by white spectators at a basketball game (6).

- In reply to the question, "Since you have been on this campus, how often have you had experiences with whites that you thought were racially discriminatory or hostile?" sixty-nine percent said occasionally, and another fourteen percent said fairly often. Only seventeen percent replied that they never had such experiences. Asked, "How often have you been mistreated by white students at this campus because of your race?" about half said once or twice, while thirty-one percent said several times or many times. Only nineteen percent said that they had not been mistreated by white students on racial grounds. . . . [T]hese estimates of discrimination are probably on the low side. Past studies have shown that one way for African Americans to cope with everyday racism is not to "see" as much of it as possible, just to be able to survive in traditionally white spaces (59).

- [A] 1989 survey of black students at a mid-Atlantic university found most had heard negative comments about African Americans by others on campus, with about half noting they heard such comments often. Most reported being victims of racial harassment, and over half feared for their safety on campus. One-third had changed their activities in some way to avoid racial harassment (60).

- A 1993 study at the predominantly white University of San Diego found that not only had eighty percent of the black students heard derogatory racial comments or jokes in the last year, but seventy-five percent of the white students reported hearing similar comments or joking (60).

- Between 1993 and 1996 racist graffiti were reportedly scrawled on dorm doors, on bulletin boards, and in other public places at a number of colleges and universities across the nation [including undergraduate colleges, large universities, law schools, schools in the North, South, East, and West, Ivy League, and colleges and universities with reputations for being progressive] (61).

- For the most part the black students we interviewed more or less felt unwelcome. They were asked on an exit questionnaire to assess this statement: "Today State University is a college campus where black students are generally welcomed and nurtured." Eighty-nine percent of the students *disagreed* with the statement (55–56).

22. Anderson also offers figures for other groups: "In 1996, Asian Americans graduated from college at a rate of 64 percent, Whites 59 percent, Latina/os 45 percent, African Americans 38 percent, and American Indians 37 percent" (2002: 14).

Chapter 3

1. Each of my parents grew up in a working-class home: my paternal grandparents were African American and worked as a Pullman porter and a homemaker; my maternal grandparents were European American and worked as a minister and a homemaker. Both of my parents had moved into the middle class with the help of college and advanced degrees.

2. It is still an unlikely trajectory, since less than 3 percent of faculty at predominantly white colleges and universities are African American (Wilson 2002: A1).

3. METCO is the acronym for the Metropolitan Council for Educational Opportunity. The program was established in 1966 under Massachusetts's Racial Imbalance Law, passed by the state's General Court in 1965. Its purpose was to provide an opportunity for an integrated public school education for urban black children and other children of color who found themselves in racially unbalanced schools, to provide a more racially diverse learning experience for suburban students, and to facilitate suburban-urban cooperation. Thirty-four suburban communities have participated in the program.

4. In the preencounter stage of racial development that Cross describes (1991), my racial identity was not salient for me in high school. Clearly METCO students were other black students who could have been friends. Although I was friendly with several METCO students, since few if any of them shared my classes or participated in the same clubs, I did not feel drawn to them because of shared interests. Indeed, their presence made me anxious, for it highlighted the fact that social difference existed at all. Unused to discussing and negotiating my own difference, I was uncomfortable with my racial difference from Concordians and my socioeconomic difference from Bostonians.

5. According to the college, 29 students of color graduated from my class, the class of 1986, which had a total of 262 students. Thus, Asian and Asian-American, black, and Latino and Latina students made up 9 percent of my class at graduation (Haverford 2000: 24). During my senior year, I interviewed twenty-two black students on campus about their college experiences. I had interviewed 50 percent of the black students currently enrolled in all four classes at the college.

6. See Derrick Z. Jackson's "Trapped below 'The Bell Curve' " (1994). See the bibliography for Steele's works. Steele's conclusions ring truer than those reached by Jeff Howard and Ray Hammond in their essay "Rumors of Inferiority" (1985). They argue, somewhat tautologically, that black students do poorly in school because they fear failing. Black students, they continue, avoid situations of intellectual challenge because they have internalized the stereotype of black intellectual inferiority. Steele's research reveals a more complicated interpretation. In-

deed, what Steele calls "stereotype threat" has been confirmed as a phenomenon among white students as well.

7. For Cross, the five stages of racial identity development for African Americans, which he calls *Nigrescence,* are preencounter, encounter, immersion/emersion, internalization, and internalization-commitment. For a complete discussion of each stage, see chapter 6, "Rethinking Nigrescence," in *Shades of Black: Diversity in African American Identity* (1991).

8. Although absolute numbers have remained low at Haverford since it began recruiting faculty and students of color in the 1970s, it has continually ranked similarly to or better than its peer institution with regard to percentages of such individuals (Haverford 1999:11).

9. Helms's typology fails to acknowledge the multiple racial configurations in which even a person who appears black or white might find themselves.

10. Advising students is no easy task, and I know that many white advisors are hesitant to encourage students of African descent to pursue courses that relate to the history and culture of African America. It is, rather, a hindsight observation that the black professors on campus had outstanding reputations in areas in which I had expressed interest—political science, philosophy, and English. Neither my upper-class advisor nor the faculty advisor assigned to me before I declared a major encouraged me to take their courses, and, before my junior year, I did not pursue courses without encouragement.

11. I had spent time with other African Americans at family reunions and at celebrations for my father's alma mater, Morehouse, a historically black men's college in Atlanta, Georgia. And, due to the efforts of then dean of the college Freddye Hill, a black woman sociologist, I also spent four weeks as an intern for the Caribbean Conferences of Churches in Barbados, West Indies. While it was enlightening to be in a majority-black country, it did not change how I felt as an African American.

12. The unpublished thesis is titled "The Best Years of Our Lives? The Perseverance Experience of Black Students at White Colleges." The texts with which I offer comparisons are *Black Students at White Colleges* (1972) by Willie and McCord; *Desegregating America's Colleges* (1974), by William M. Boyd; *A Study of Race Relations at Harvard College* (1980), by the Harvard Committee on Race Relations; and *Blacks in College* (1984), by Fleming. I have learned from white friends and acquaintances that while most would repeat their Haverford experience, a number would not. Their reasons, however, do not include racial homogeneity or racial hostility.

Chapter 4

1. For more complete descriptions, I suggest *Northwestern University, a History: 1850–1975* (1976), by Williamson and Wild, and *Howard University: The First Hundred Years, 1867–1967* (1969), by Rayford W. Logan.

2. Under Howard president Mordecai Johnson's administration (1926–60), Congress was convinced to enact a law on December 13, 1928, guaranteeing that Howard would always be the beneficiary of federal funds. "Annual appropriations are hereby authorized to aid in the construction, development, improvement, and maintenance of the university, no part of which shall be used for religious instruction. The university shall at all times be open to inspection by the Bureau of Education and shall be inspected by the said bureau at least once each year"

(quoted in Logan 1969: 258). Howard's board, under the leadership and moral suasion of the university's president, Johnson, won this privilege with the argument that Howard was *the* national university for African Americans, and that the amount the federal government was donating was really only a fraction of what Negro students should be receiving in their home states from public funds but were not (Logan 1969: 260–61).

3. Beckham (1984) and Birnbach (1984), respectively.

4. "Between 1965 and 1967 the number of black freshmen registered at Northwestern had risen from 5 to 70. In all, by the spring of 1968 there were about 160 black students on the Evanston campus, out of a total undergraduate population of 6,500 and a [*sic*] total graduate registrations of 2,500 part-time and full-time students" (Williamson and Wild 1976: 329).

5. Logan elaborates: The post-Reconstruction backlash led to "the spread of segregation [specifically] in the Nation's Capital [which] did contribute to the evolution of Howard University as a predominantly Negro institution as far as students were concerned" (Logan 1969: 110).

Chapter 5

1. Although affirmative action was conceived as a program to redress past practices of race and sex discrimination (see Anderson 2002), its proponents see it as a policy with contemporary goals to ensure a modicum of racial and sexual representation in the workplace and educational settings. It is inaccurate, however, to refer to affirmative action as a policy. It has only ever been an ideal toward which the federal government required those organizations receiving federal funding to aspire and show a good faith effort toward achieving. That said, government-funded institutions at the state level and below have sometimes codified the policy in setting goals for admission, employment, and bidding for contracts. White women have been the primary beneficiaries of affirmative action policies instituted since the mid-1960s. Since the 1980s, with the nation's turn toward the right, the policy has been associated almost exclusively with race rather than sex representation.

2. See Williamson and Wild, *Northwestern University: a History*, in Bibliography. In 1965, there were 5 black students in the freshman class at NU. By 1973, there were a total of 650 black undergraduates out of 6,500 students (1976: 329, 338). The *Northwestern Data Book* (44, and table 39) indicates that in 1988—the last graduation year for the youngest of my respondents—African-American students made up about 6 percent of the student body.

3. This picture is confirmed by William E. Sedlacek and Dennis W. Webster, who found "that private schools have not only performed better than public schools in enrolling minority students, but they have done a better job of retaining them" (1978: 246).

4. For a fuller discussion, see Williamson and Wild, *Northwestern University: a History* (1976).

5. The 1987 *U.S. Statistical Abstract*, published by the U.S. Department of Commerce, records a figure of 39.8 percent black for the city of Chicago from the 1980 census (Table 36).

6. The kinship metaphor has been observed by Willie and McCord (1972), Fleming (1984), Exum (1985), and Manuel (1994a, 1994b).

7. Laurie Nisnoff, Susan J. Tracy, and Stanley Warner (n.d.) buttress this observation in their discussion of poor and working-class students who felt left out at Hampshire College.

8. The phenomenon of choosing sides also revealed itself in Exum's study of the black student movement at New York University. Black student leaders often ridiculed black students who did not conform to their expectations of what it meant to be black. Especially vulnerable were those students who came from middle-class families. Black solidarity was occasionally coerced through severe peer pressure when it did not happen on its own. Exum argues that black student leaders became autocratic, drawing few connections between the demands for greater representation within the university and the importance of representation within their group. Feeling threatened by disloyalty, student leaders often refused to recognize the rights of fellow black students to have a contrary opinion or to abstain from participating in discussions altogether. These contradictions, Exum argues, severely strained the movement (1985).

9. Those supportive people—both white and black—who were mentioned over several interviews included one white administrator from the Technological Institute, a white male administrative assistant from the School of Journalism, and two Medill professors, everyone who was ever on the staff of the Black House, and five African-American professors.

10. Willie and McCord (1972), Charles Vert Willie and Ronald R. Edmonds (1978), Charles A. Taylor (1986), and Augustine W. Pounds (1987) all note the special case of black faculty and staff for black students on predominantly white campuses.

11. Sources are the U.S. Department of Education, National Center for Education Statistics, Higher Education General Information Survey, September 1996 (5), and the U.S. Census Bureau's *Statistical Abstract of the United States* (2001: 139).

12. "Harry Edwards has stated that small black student populations foster tightly knit cohesive black communities on white college campuses. . . . Our findings indicate that very small black populations on white college campuses merely give the appearance of a tightly knit cohesive community . . . such relationships [can be] supportive at times, but also stultifying and confining" (Willie and McCord 1972: 23).

13. Kanter defines a skewed group as one where the minority group makes up 0 to 15 percent of the total group. A tilted group is one where the minority group makes up 15 to 39 percent of the total group (1977: 209).

14. Charles Willie describes the goal for racial representation in campus populations:

Ideally, any group . . . that is the majority of the students should not be more than two-thirds of the total student body; and any group that is the minority should not be less than one-fifth of the total student body. . . . [O]ne-fifth seems to be the critical mass of a minority population that is necessary for the minority to have an educational impact upon the system and for the minorities to feel that they are not an oddity engaged in an experiment. (1981: 61)

15. Willie and McCord remind us of the dynamic tendencies of communities:

Louis Wirth pointed out in his famous essay on "Urbanism as a Way of Life" that the relationships between people in a community are directly affected by the number of inhabitants . . . that if the number of inhabitants of a community was increased beyond a few hundred, this phenomenon was sure to limit the possibility of each member of the community knowing all the others personally. In terms of our study, an increase in the black student population from 75 to 200 or so seemed to be associated with an increase in freedom, flexibility, and some degree of anonymity. . . . Harvey Cox, influenced by Wirth, called anonymity a liberating phenomenon, which ". . . helps preserve the privacy which is essential to human life." (1972: 22)

Chapter 6

1. Many theories of personality development stress individual achievement and equate such achievement with psychological health. Such theories are based on studies of white Americans. Gurin and Epps (1975) recognize that individual success has not always been of primary importance to persons who strongly identify with a group and yet who see themselves as achieving on behalf of the group. African Americans are regular examples of such persons but were typically excluded from portraits of psychologically healthy individuals. In their research, Gurin and Epps discovered that individuals were indeed able to achieve healthy personalities by a route that included collective success as equally important to—or even more important than—individual success. This finding had eluded many European American scholars because they had not studied the personality portraits of members of subaltern groups in general or African-American college students in particular. The naturalness of rational self-interested behavior, which economists have taken for granted, had seeped into assumptions of healthy personality development as well. Many majority scholars, Gurin and Epps note further, ignored the "naturalness" of collective or group-oriented behavior (not necessarily mutually exclusive with self-interest) for minorities. Moreover, they observed that minority status was often positively understood among black students, providing a characteristic around which to develop both personal and group identity. Fordham's work affirms that of Gurin and Epps: "Achieving human status means perceiving oneself as being intimately connected to other people. Consequently, the most highly valued group strategies are those that enable the individual to be seen as embodying those qualities and characteristics that will enhance the status of the group" (1993: 12).

2. Seventeen respondents reported being good or very good students in high school as demonstrated by high grade point averages combined with multiple extracurricular activities; six said they were average; two said they were below average; data are missing for two cases.

3. Perhaps because the university was so expensive, for an even greater proportion of Northwestern alumni—twenty-one out of twenty-eight—the financial aid package was very important, sometimes the sole determinant, in their decision to attend NU. When explaining how her parents helped her in the decision of what college to attend, Lynn remarks, "We're not talking about people who are sophisticated about college. . . . [My parents] just wanted me to be where I [was] happy and where I got the most financial aid" (Lynn, NU '83).

4. Likewise, many assume that those African Americans who choose a predominantly white college identify with white Americans. Neither was this the case. While many of the black alumni I interviewed expected less racist behavior and more reaching out from white classmates and professors alike, many of them assumed that racism and fear were adolescent attributes that all people would outgrow.

5. The ideas in this section benefited from discussion with Adam Weisberger while we were both faculty at Colby College.

6. Trust of one's teachers and opportunities to connect with teachers are cited in Willie and McCord (1972), Fleming (1984), and Terence J. Tracey and William E. Sedlacek (1987) as important variables in the success experiences of black students at any kind of college.

7. The rates of eating disorders and binge drinking, among other mental health problems, on most predominantly white college campuses belies the image of four years of idyllic life. Still, many of the problems that white students face are different from the problems *most* black students face. And what students go to college to find is neither the sum of what their professors would hope for them nor what many of them get.

8. Spelman, a historically black women's college, has a large proportion and number of black women who major in the natural sciences and sends a large fraction of graduates on to medical school and graduate school in the sciences.

9. N=27; missing for two cases.

10. Those African Americans who have been able to "make it" by the narrow definition of high income and occupational prestige have done so in an era of expanding—albeit still limited—opportunities in the United States for racial minorities and women.

Chapter 7

1. *The Statistical Abstract of the United States* (U.S. Census Bureau 2001: table 604) .

Chapter 8

1. I would add white.

2. Helms (1993) paraphrases the literature on racial identity theory, a post–Civil Rights Era approach to appreciating the psychological signficance of race as it is experienced by the individual. Distinguishing between racial identity and racial categorization, racial identity and ethnic identity (see chapter 6), Helms identifies two umbrella approaches to racial identity with implications for therapy: the black client-as-problem (or CAP) perspective and the Nigrescence or racial identity development (or NRID) perspective (1993: 9).

What defines perspectives in client-as-problem models is their virtually exclusive focus on Black identity development as a consequence of societal pressures and their linking of clients' other-directed negative reactions (e.g., anger, hostility, rage) and behaviors to Black rather than assimilated identities or personality types. . . . [T]he primary goal of such models seems to have been to diffuse counselor anxiety by making the occurrence of aversive Black behaviors more predictable. Nevertheless, the perspective did recognize that Black identity comes in many forms and it challenged the a priori assumption that cultural assimilation was necessarily the most healthy form of adjustment for the Black person. . . . Nigrescence can be defined as the developmental process by which a person "becomes Black" where Black is defined in terms of one's manner of thinking about and evaluating oneself and one's reference groups rather than in terms of skin color per se. The NRID models attempted to separate those aspects of Black identity development that occurred primarily in response to racial oppression (e.g., some forms of ascribed identities and reference-group orientations) from those aspects (e.g., personal identity) that occurred as a normal part of the human self-actualization process. (16–17)

3. "To address the theoretical issue of whether racial identity does proceed according to a relatively stable linear process, longitudinal studies of racial identity development, in which people's levels of identity are measured at more than one point in time, are needed" (Helms 1993: 41).

4. These ideas conform to the three assumptions implicit in most racial identity developmental models (see Helms 1993: 37).

5. Psychologists, unlike most sociologists, have wrestled with the meaning of the self in relation to the larger society in far greater depth than I have presented here. Stanley Aronowitz is one social scientist who takes both disciplines seriously in his examination of identity:

It remained for George Herbert Mead to break from the spiritual positings of Locke and James. For Mead, the social contradiction between the "I" individual ego that remains the ideological *a priori* of all liberal thought—and the "me"—the social self—is resolved outside the ethical appeal to a higher authority. There is, for Mead, only a biological self that is mediated by a social self formed by the interaction between the individual and "significant" others—family members, civil authorities, peers—all of whom underdetermine what we mean by the individual. Like Freud's superego, these together constitute a generalized other—the totality of values, beliefs and, even more important, rules of conduct—by which individuals live. And, like Freud's concept of introjection, Mead's notion of internalization describes how society and its constitutive institutions, including Locke's "club," *determine* individuality: "The environment of living organisms is constantly changing, is constantly invaded with other and different things. The assimilation of what occurs and that which recurs with what is elapsing and what has elapsed is called 'experience.' ". . . Experience, then, is a process of "assimilation" of the environment, but one which is understood to be inescapably part of the self. Mead's notion of the social self entails two moments: the continually changing environment, and its assimilation by a living organism. The two terms are constantly in motion, and their relation is always indeterminate from the point of view of the subject. (1995: 114)

Chapter 9

1. Portions of this chapter appeared in *Race Odyssey 2001*, edited by Bruce Hare (Syracuse, NY: Syracuse University Press, 2002).

2. An African-American student whom Fordham interviewed provides a similar lens through which to understand Henry:

[A]t some level, [this smart and rebellious girl] believes that American society is truly democratic and that the individual makes it or fails based solely on ability. In the school context she is committed to the meritocratic ideals promulgated there and does not want to have any information around her that might suggest that what she has learned, and perhaps is learning, in school is misleading or even untrue. She is definitely a child of the post-civil rights era, in that, like many nonblack persons, she wants to believe that African-Americans have achieved socioeconomic parity with the dominant group: white Americans. (Fordham 1993: 17)

3. "Neither the life of an individual nor the history of a society can be understood without understanding both" (C.Wright Mills, *The Sociological Imagination*, 1959: 3).

4. The following work is cited in their footnote: M. D. Williams, *On the Street Where I Lived* New York: Holt, Rinehart, and Winston, 1981.

5. Feagin, Vera, and Imani find that this problem of racially separate activities continues at a predominantly white campus on the East Coast a decade after I spoke with Jennifer, who had graduated from NU in the 1980s:

To be recognized as valued members of the campus community is important to all groups of students, but especially to those who are underrepresented on a large campus like State University. The omission of African American students [in our study] from the yearbook suggests a general lack of recognition of the black presence and achievements on campus and hints at the low status the whites who prepared the yearbook apparently granted to black students. This kind of neglect encourages black students to congregate in their own groups and plan their own activities and publications, a reaction that may bring white condemnation of this black "segregation." (1996: 54)

6. Hughes calls acting as a Negro or a woman "the other role." This is one of the places where, as I mentioned in chapter 8, a thoughtful scholar walks up to the idea of race (or sex) as a role rather than an essence, but then fails to develop the idea.

7. At the same time, Hughes appears to have assumed that the status system itself was beyond question. He, therefore, focuses on how individuals are integrated into such systems, and even how they protest assigned status, rather than questioning the validity of the systems themselves.

8. From a private conversation with Darrell Moore, December 1992.

9. For a wonderful discussion of race and sex as real or unreal categories and the literary debates that surrounded the topic, see " 'Racial Composition': Metaphor and the Body in the Writing of Race," by Margaret Homans (1997).

10. Jeremy Hein's description is meant for ethnicity. Since race could be similarly described, I took sociological license.

Chapter 10

1. Of course, some women who attend women's colleges do not have opportunities to interact with boys and men before college. Together with the advantage of learning to take oneself seriously as a thinker and a citizen in a culture still wrestling with institutionally and individually expressed sexism, the disadvantage of not learning to be in community with men during this developmental stage is also real.

2. There are many ways to accomplish these goals. They can include workshops, retreats, or reading groups, for example, and they usually are most successful with help from trained facilitators.

3. It should be noted, however, that the presence of female faculty and faculty of color—together with the challenge to the authority of the professorate embedded in the client/consumer model of higher education—have complicated the dynamic between faculty and students. Students who see themselves as consumers are not immune to the prejudices of the larger society, and they often challenge the authority of minority and women professors in ways they never challenge white male professors.

4. Young has a particularly articulate and cogent argument that interrogates U.S. concepts of merit and qualifications in her book *Justice and the Politics of Difference* (1990). Lani Guinier also has an excellent article on this topic, "Colleges Should Take 'Confirmative Action' in Admissions," in the December 14, 2002, issue of *The Chronicle of Higher Education* (B10).

5. Indeed, all students need to learn about the experiences of all racial and ethnic groups in the United States and in relation to white supremacy. Learning about the black experience and learning about other experiences are not mutually exclusive.

6. In fact, Winant argues that the whole world is a racial ghetto (2001).

Appendix

1. In footnote 13 to chapter 1 of their book (1991), Zweigenhaft and Domhoff suggest several sources for those interested interviewing within and across racial difference.

INDEX